Get the eBook FREE!

(PDF, ePub, Kindle, and liveBook all included)

We believe that once you buy a book from us, you should be able to read it in any format we have available. To get electronic versions of this book at no additional cost to you, purchase and then register this book at the Manning website.

Go to https://www.manning.com/freebook and follow the instructions to complete your pBook registration.

That's it!
Thanks from Manning!

Data Mesh in Action

Data Mesh in Action

JACEK MAJCHRZAK, SVEN BALNOJAN,
AND MARIAN SIWIAK, WITH MARIUSZ SIERACZKIEWICZ
FOREWORD BY JEAN-GEORGES PERRIN

MANNING
SHELTER ISLAND

For online information and ordering of this and other Manning books, please visit
www.manning.com. The publisher offers discounts on this book when ordered in quantity.
For more information, please contact

Special Sales Department
Manning Publications Co.
20 Baldwin Road
PO Box 761
Shelter Island, NY 11964
Email: orders@manning.com

Manning Publications Co.
20 Baldwin Road
PO Box 761
Shelter Island, NY 11964

Development editor:	Ian Hough
Technical development editor:	Michael Jensen
Review editor:	Adriana Sabo
Production editor:	Andy Marinkovich
Copy editor:	Sharon Wilkey
Proofreader:	Keri Hales
Technical proofreader:	Al Krinker
Typesetter:	Gordan Salinovic
Cover designer:	Marija Tudor

ISBN 9781633439979
Printed in the United States of America

brief contents

contents

foreword

The data mesh is to data as agile is to software engineering, or as microservices are to architecture patterns. It will be an essential component of your future data strategy. *Data Mesh in Action* addresses both the technology of the data mesh and the methodology your organization can follow to implement it.

This book teleports you into the seat of the chief architect on a data mesh project. The authors will coach you through the chaotic process of your first data product. As you gain more and more of those components, your mesh will build itself. The authors' collective experience drives this transformation. Your responsibility will be to pick, choose, and adapt this framework to your needs and organization.

The data mesh is based on four key principles: domain ownership, data as a product, federated computational governance, and self-serve data platform. The book details organizational impact of these principles, as well as their technology, in great length. Individually, all those principles are well-known to engineers and architects; the real (r)evolution of the data mesh is its ability to combine them and deliver a global approach to building modern data platforms.

In my more than 15 years of building hybrid data platforms, I have always been missing something. Whether it was due to the strict approach of ingesting data in a warehouse or the lack of governance of a lake, to name two popular patterns, there was always this feeling of "it ain't gonna work." The mesh is different. It does not focus solely on technology; it puts governance and quality at the center and allocates ownership to the real owner, not some central commanding and demanding group. As a result, with adequate self-service tools, the data mesh will liberate the forces of innovation in your organization. And that is what this book will help you achieve.

—Jean-Georges Perrin,
Intelligence platform lead at PayPal,
president and cofounder of AIDAUG,
and Lifetime IBM Champion

preface

Each one of us authors has experienced—at length and at different companies—the old way of "doing data," usually through centralized data lakes and data warehouses in combination with a set of central teams organized inside an analytics function. The old way basically looked like this:

1. Multiple decentralized development teams have data that is accessible through storage systems like a shared drive, a decentralized database, a Representational State Transfer (REST) API, or any other interface.
2. One or more centralized data teams are tasked with collecting this data into one monolithic pot. This is either a data lake or a data warehouse.
3. The same set of teams is tasked with transforming this data into something useful.
4. Multiple decentralized analysts, development teams, or machine learning (ML) teams pick up that transformed data and convert it into value in the form of reports, recommendation systems, or anything else they can think of.

We learned the hard way that this concept has its limits, producing a bottleneck in terms of both technology and team capacities. We all saw companies struggling to get the flow from data to value to be as productive as the companies needed it to be. Then the data mesh and the ideas behind it appeared on the horizon.

The *data mesh* is a decentralization paradigm. It decentralizes the ownership of data, its transformation into information, and its serving. It aims to increase the value extraction from data by removing bottlenecks in the data value stream by these means.

The concept of the data mesh appeared on the stage in 2019 and has since lit not just the data world, but the whole technology world, on fire. The data mesh concept breaks with the current world of data, which usually treats data as a by-product of software components. This new approach turns the spotlight on data producers and gives them the responsibility to handle the data just as they would handle their software.

With this, the data mesh takes the same journey software components have taken, with microservices architectures and with the DevOps movement. It takes the same journey frontends are currently taking with *microfrontends*. And just as in these examples, we believe that the data mesh is the right approach to finally gain the *flexibility to extract value from our data at scale*, be that in business intelligence (BI), ML learning, or any other use case you can think of.

The data mesh concept is often referred to as a *socio-technical* paradigm shift: its core is not about technology but about the alignment of people, processes, and organizations. This significant complexity is why we wrote this book. However, we don't just present the available theoretical knowledge that is out there; we focus on parts of the data mesh that are, in our experience, critical for successful implementation. We have organized those parts into a digestible resource to help you put a data mesh *in action!*

To guide you through the process, we've prepared hands-on examples with a lot of architecture sketches, describing various technologies, workshop techniques, team organization forms, and the like. After reading this book, you should be able to do the following:

- Evaluate whether a data mesh will suit your organization's business needs
- Lay the groundwork for data mesh development
- Develop a minimal data mesh to start your journey
- Keep iteratively developing and expanding your data mesh

Don't expect to find a lot of code in this book, other than a little JavaScript Object Notation (JSON) here and there. That's because we truly believe *the magic is not in the technology, but in the people, processes, and organizations*. But, of course, you can expect to find a lot of technology inside this book in the form of deep architecture sketches with reference to various technologies and cloud providers, explanations, and blueprints inspired by multiple real-world examples.

That said, we don't believe in a black-and-white implementation of the data mesh idea. This book will help you adjust the data mesh idea to your company by offering a lot of degrees of freedom, shortcuts, and a healthy level of pragmatism.

To tie together our experience, we will use an imaginary company called Messflix LLC, which resembles a lot of what we've seen out there in the data world. This company will be our go-to example as we go through the "mess-to-mesh" journey; however, since we also focus on making the data mesh adaptable to many types of companies, not just one, this is not the only example we utilize throughout the book. Later in this front matter, we provide a brief introduction to Messflix by taking a look at the data mess the company has gotten itself into.

acknowledgments

First, we would like to express our gratitude to the community engaged with data mesh development. Their discussions and openness about problems and challenges helped us broaden our perspectives and put our particular experiences into the generalized framework you'll find in this book.

We owe our thanks to the wonderful people at Manning who made this book possible: Publisher Marjan Bace, Development Editor Ian Hough, and last but not least, Acquisitions Editor Andrew Waldron. Without their patience with our ever-evolving view on the data mesh, and their ability to make us synthesize it into a coherent view, we wouldn't be able to finish *Data Mesh in Action* in a form we could so proudly present to you. We would like also to thank the marketing, editorial, and production teams, without whom this book would gather dust in a Manning drawer.

A heartfelt thanks also to Michael Jensen and Al Krinker for technical reviews, which allowed us to further condense and clarify data mesh concepts.

We would also like to thank all our reviewers, who trusted us and invested their time in reading this book, even when no one was sure it would make it to publication. To Alain Couniot, Arnaud Castelltort, Arnaud Estève, Jean-Georges Perrin, Juan Gabriel Guzmán Guerra, Mary Anne Thygesen, Massimo dr, Matthias Busch, Mike Fowler, Milan Sarenac, Nathan B. Crocker, Pradeep Bhattiprolu, Rahul Jain, Richard Vaughan, Salil Athalye, Sampath Chaparala, Shiroshica Kulatilake, Simon Tschöke, Stefano Ongarello, Sumih Damodaran, Suriyanto Bongso, and Yi Wei, your suggestions helped make this a better book.

about this book

This book serves two purposes. First, it organizes and presents knowledge about the new socio-technological paradigm of the data mesh. Second, it will help you implement a data mesh. From considering whether the data mesh is a suitable solution for your organization, to laying the groundwork, to developing a minimum viable product (MVP), to implementing data mesh principles, this book provides the tools needed to get you well on your way on your data mesh journey.

Who should read this book?

The most general description of our reader is someone who is involved in extracting value from data. However, because that describes almost everyone in our modern economy, we'll outline the benefits this book will bring to various audiences.

The first group is people involved in creating, managing, and utilizing data within companies that have the following:

- High socio-technological complexity (e.g., big corporations)
- Complex data use cases
- Many and diverse data sources

This encompasses, but is not limited to, roles including data architects, data engineers, software architects, tech leads, and senior developers.

The more you feel like these quantifiers apply to your business, the more likely it is that a data mesh could be a good solution. This book will help you understand data mesh concepts, including whose cooperation you need to secure, and what steps to take in both your organization and technical environment to move from a data mess to data mesh.

Beyond that, as the data mesh is a company-wide transformation process, the book's content will be directly useful to executive-level personnel, including the technical C-suite, engineering directors and managers, enterprise architects, chief and lead architects, and solution/program owners. This book will help you decide to what extent and level of priority you should shift your company's data environment into a data mesh direction, and help you plan the change management.

How this book is organized: A road map

While the book is meant to be read linearly, it is broken into three main parts and allows you to skip sections. The first part is a quick and hands-on introduction, the second explains the four principles of the data mesh in detail, and the third tackles the technical side of things in detail as well as the complete enterprise journey.

Part 1: Foundations

The goal of the first part of the book is to familiarize you with the data mesh paradigm as quickly as possible. To do so, we first go through the basics of the data mesh and then get our hands dirty by building our first data mesh within a month.

CHAPTER 1: THE WHAT AND WHY OF THE DATA MESH

This chapter gives the overview needed to put the rest of the book into the proper context, including why you might want to consider following the data mesh mindset shift as well as a short explanation of the four key principles detailed in part 2.

CHAPTER 2: IS A DATA MESH RIGHT FOR YOU?

This chapter provides you with the context of the data mesh implementation and the drivers to consider when deciding on the transformation. It helps you decide whether you want to start the journey now and to identify your place on the data maturity scale. This helps you to match your data mesh journey to your particular situation.

CHAPTER 3: KICKSTART YOUR DATA MESH MVP IN A MONTH

This chapter is a hands-on example of how to go about building an MVP. The Messflix MVP focuses a lot on the organizational challenges and stays light on the technology side of things, which an MVP should. The technology details will be picked up later. The chapter provides you with tools like stakeholder mappings and FAIR principles (findable, accessible, interoperable, reusable) to get you started.

Part 2: The four principles in practice

The goal of the second part of the book is to provide you with the tools to tackle the four principles of the data mesh so you can advance your data mesh beyond the first month.

CHAPTER 4: DOMAIN OWNERSHIP

This chapter is all about domains and business capabilities and how you can identify suitable owners for data inside a company. It provides you with a lot of workshop techniques, including domain storytelling.

CHAPTER 5: DOMAIN DATA AS A PRODUCT

Data is often treated as a by-product. This chapter is about changing to a product perspective called *data as a product*. The chapter provides examples of data products from Messflix and explains in detail concepts like the data product canvas and data ports.

CHAPTER 6: FEDERATED COMPUTATIONAL GOVERNANCE

This chapter tackles data governance in the data mesh context. Inside data meshes, this is called federated computational governance, because of the balance of central and distributed governance aspects as well as an automated execution needed to unfold the data mesh. This chapter contains a discussion of centralized versus decentralized aspects, hands-on examples from Messflix, and a guide for setting up a governance team.

CHAPTER 7: THE SELF-SERVE DATA PLATFORM

The last chapter on data mesh principles covers the platform, the enabling technology that makes the data mesh work. The chapter works through three iterations on our data platform for Messflix and explains important concepts like *platform thinking* along with these examples.

Part 3: Infrastructure and technical architecture

The third part focuses on all things technical. We break out of the Messflix example to highlight various architectures and discuss multiple options for moving from your existing structure to a data mesh.

CHAPTER 8: COMPARING SELF-SERVE DATA PLATFORMS

This chapter explains blueprints for data mesh platforms that fit various cloud providers as well as different sizes of companies.

CHAPTER 9: SOLUTION ARCHITECTURE DESIGN

In this chapter, we focus on the migration from your existing system to various kinds of architectures step by step and component by component. We talk about data lakes, data warehouses, REST APIs, and more.

How to use this book

We don't want to present just another theory of the data mesh. This book is more of a structured, collective diary of actions leading to data mesh development in various environments. The emphasis is on *actions leading to*. We arrived at the data mesh after a long and often painful journey through multiple other solutions. Over the years, we've been testing, researching, discussing, and, last but not least, failing a lot in the process. In this book, we share with you the summary of "I wish someone had told me earlier" insights. We hope you will be able to immediately put the information you'll get out of it, well, *in action*.

Depending on your goal, there are a few focal points you could set while reading this book to dive deeper into. If your interest is purely *informational*, and your goal is to be able to explain the concepts to your team, your management, or your company, we recommend you put a lot of focus on chapters 1 and 2, which provide a quick overview, as well as the MVP presented in chapter 4. In addition, by reading through chapter 9 for a deeper dive into the reasons for this paradigm shift and a lighter look into part 2, you will be well equipped to explain the data mesh paradigm to someone else.

If you want to launch a *larger initiative inside your company*, you'll need to be convincing. In that case, we recommend you take a deep dive into the entirety of chapter 9 and pay close attention to chapter 3, which offers insight into the question of whether you should start this journey at all. Chapter 4, presenting the full-scale data mesh MVP development, and chapter 2, offering a quick glance into a lightweight application of data mesh principles, will allow you to balance the big-picture view with notes on requirements of quick implementation and getting results fast. All together, this material should equip you with enough convincing material to get top-level buy-in.

If you're interested in the *technical side of things*, like automated governance and the self-serve platform, chapters 5 to 8 will provide you with a lot of interesting content to dig through.

If you work inside a *development team*, we particularly recommend that you turn your attention to chapter 4. This chapter explains exactly what is broken in the current mode of thinking and should also help you advance your ways of working without ever touching the data mesh concept. Additionally, we recommend chapter 8, as it explains possible architecture alternatives for serving data from a development team's point of view.

If you want to advance the way you work inside your *data team*, you could focus on chapters 3 and 4 to deeply understand the source of your current troubles. You could also focus on chapter 6 to understand what *platform thinking* in a data context means. Both could help you advance your ways of working without actually adopting a full data mesh approach inside the company.

We're sure there are many more reasons for you to open up this book; these are simply a few possible ways you could go about putting this book into use.

The Messflix case study

To help you conceptualize the practical aspects of putting a data mesh in action, we combined our experiences and merged them into a single data mesh journey of Messflix LLC.

Messflix, a movie- and TV-show streaming platform, just hit a wall. A *data* wall. The company has all the data in the world but complains about not even being able to build a proper recommendation system for its movies and shows. The competition seems to be able to get it done; in fact, the competition is famous for being the first movers in a lot of technology sectors.

Other companies in equally complex industries seem to be able to put their data to work. Messflix does work with data, and analysts are able to get some insights from it, but the organization's leaders don't feel like they can call themselves *data driven*.

The data science trial runs seem to all end in "pretty prototypes" with no clear business value. The data scientists tell their managers that it's because the "product team just doesn't want to put these great prototypes on the roadmap," or, in another instance, "because the data from the source is way too messy and inconsistent."

In short, Messflix hopefully sounds like your average business, which for some reason doesn't feel like it's able to *let the right data flow to the right use cases*. The data landscape, just like the technology landscape, has grown organically over time and has become quite complex.

The two key technology components of Messflix are its Messflix Streaming Platform and Hitchcock Movie Maker. The streaming platform does just what it says: enable subscribers to watch shows and movies. The movie maker is a set of tools helping the movie production teams choose good movie topics, themes, and content.

Additionally, Messflix has a data lake with an analytics platform on top of it taking data from everywhere. A few teams manage these components. The teams Orange and White together operate a few of the Hitchcock Movie Maker tools. Team Green is all about the subscriptions, the log-in processes, etc., and team Yellow is responsible for getting things on the screen inside the streaming platform. Figure 1 depicts a rough architecture sketch of a few of these components before we briefly discuss how data is currently handled at Messflix.

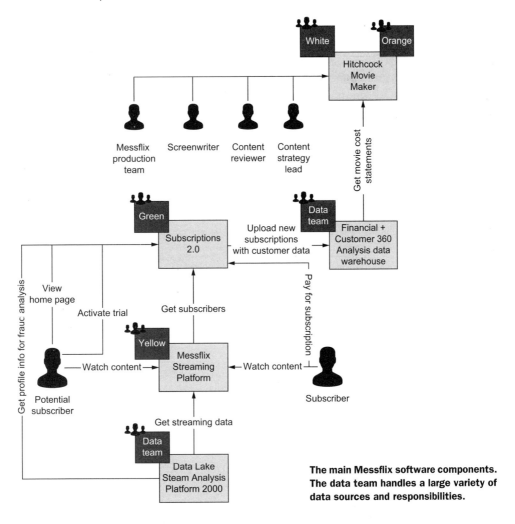

The main Messflix software components. The data team handles a large variety of data sources and responsibilities.

The Data team gets data into the data warehouse from a few different places—for example, cost statements from the Hitchcock Movie Maker and subscriptions from the subscriptions service. The team also gets streaming data and subscription profiles from the data lake.

Then the Data team does some number crunching to transform this data into information for fraud analysis and business decisions.

Finally, this information is used by decentralized units to make those business decisions and for other use cases. This currently is a centralized workflow. The data team "sits in the middle."

No matter where you're coming from and where you want to go, you will find yourself somewhere along the Messflix journey. So let's take one final look at the complete journey Messflix is going through.

No data journey is a simple straight line. Likewise, we don't pretend that the Messflix journey is a simple linear progression of a series of steps. You'll see different approaches in the chapters and ways to make the data mesh fit your company, even though the Messflix example illustrates one main thread to guide you.

You can follow that main thread used by Messflix throughout chapters 2 through 6 and chapter 9. Table 1 gives you an overview of the stages of the company, as we highlight two dimensions alongside the journey to a data mesh. The first is the number of organizational units and teams affected. The second is the types of company responsibilities that are decentralized.

The core of the data mesh paradigm shift is the decentralization of the responsibility for data. But *responsibility for data* today is practically split into multiple parts, all of which need to be decentralized. Thus we highlight all four kinds of responsibility for data in table 1; each corresponds to one of the principles presented in part 2.

Table 1 The Messflix journey

	Chapter 4	Chapter 5	Chapter 6	Chapter 7	Chapter 8
Affected teams	2 (Two data-producing teams) Few collaborators across the company	2+	2+	2+	3–10 (A dedicated platform team and more producing and consuming teams)
Types of data responsibility	A small bit of everything	True ownership through knowing the actual (data) domains	Responsibility for serving data customers	Responsibility for security, governance, etc.; in short, the needs of the whole company	Responsibility for infrastructure, technical components

liveBook discussion forum

Purchase of *Data Mesh in Action* includes free access to liveBook, Manning's online reading platform. Using liveBook's exclusive discussion features, you can attach comments to the book globally or to specific sections or paragraphs. It's a snap to make notes for yourself, ask and answer technical questions, and receive help from the author and other users. To access the forum, go to https://livebook.manning.com/book/data-mesh-in-action/discussion. You can also learn more about Manning's forums and the rules of conduct at https://livebook.manning.com/discussion.

Manning's commitment to our readers is to provide a venue where a meaningful dialogue between individual readers and between readers and the author can take place. It is not a commitment to any specific amount of participation on the part of the author, whose contribution to the forum remains voluntary (and unpaid). We suggest you try asking the authors some challenging questions lest their interest stray! The forum and the archives of previous discussions will be accessible from the publisher's website as long as the book is in print.

about the authors

JACEK MAJCHRZAK is a lead architect who implements the data mesh approach in the area of drug discovery. Jacek is a workshop facilitator with experience in moderating many techniques including event storming, domain storytelling, business capability modeling, and bounded context canvas. He also designed his own technique that helps discover and define data products in a domain-oriented way, which he calls a *data bazaar*. Jacek uses all these techniques to help people make the best possible decisions about their technology and strategy. His areas of expertise are domain-driven design, event-driven architecture, solution architecture, socio-technical system design, and architecture governance and strategy. He thinks that understanding business domains and needs is the key to a successful architecture. He blogs at https://jacekmajchrzak.com. Jacek is a husband and father of two, and a motorcyclist who is addicted to sports, especially aquatic ones.

DR. SVEN BALNOJAN is a data technologist and product person focused on helping the world extract more value from the exponentially growing amount of data. He's passionate about all things data, machine learning, AI, business intelligence, and many related fields. His endeavors include managing internal data teams and the transitions from being a service-oriented team to a platform-oriented team, as well as getting his hands dirty as a data developer in the fields of machine learning, data engineering, and Data DevOps. Sven holds a PhD in mathematics with a thesis in the field of singularity theory. He is the author of an opinionated newsletter, "Three Data Point Thursday." Additionally, he blogs at https://datacisions.com and appears in talks here and there over the internet.

Dr. Marian Siwiak is a jack of all data-related trades and a master of their integration with business operations. As a chief data science officer of Cognition Shared Solutions, he's a strategic-level data use consultant and the designer of the Trilayer Business Process Analysis framework, connecting process execution, data environments, and risk management. He has a track record of delivering multimillion-dollar IT, scientific, and technical projects covering various areas, from life sciences to robotics. He has lectured about data management at various business universities. His team was the first to publish a global spread model of COVID-19. Marian is also a husband, father of three, skier, sailor, and sci-fi writer.

about the cover illustration

The figure on the cover of *Data Mesh in Action* is captioned "Homme de Brabant," or "Man from Brabant (northern Belgium)," taken from a collection by Jacques Grasset de Saint-Sauveur, published in 1797. Each illustration is finely drawn and colored by hand.

In those days, it was easy to identify where people lived and what their trade or station in life was just by their dress. Manning celebrates the inventiveness and initiative of the computer business with book covers based on the rich diversity of regional culture centuries ago, brought back to life by pictures from collections such as this one.

Part 1

Foundations

The first part of the book will familiarize you with the data mesh paradigm. We quickly go through the theory of the data mesh and its principles and present drivers to consider when deciding on the data mesh implementation.

You will be able to evaluate at which point you are on the data maturity scale and consciously decide whether you want to start the journey.

We follow with a hands-on example of how to go about building a minimal data mesh within a month. This exercise focuses on the organizational challenges and follows the minimum viable product (MVP) philosophy on the technology side of things.

The what and why of the data mesh

1

This chapter covers

- Defining data mesh
- Introducing the key concepts of the data mesh paradigm
- Understanding why the data mesh is a socio-technical paradigm shift
- Seeing the advantages of the data mesh
- Identifying possible data mesh implementation challenges

The *data mesh* is a decentralization paradigm. It decentralizes the ownership of data, its transformation into information, as well as its serving. It aims to increase the value extraction from data by removing bottlenecks in the data value stream by these means.

The data mesh paradigm is disrupting the data space. Large and small companies are racing to showcase *their data mesh–like journey* all over the internet. It's becoming the new *thing* to try out for any company that wants to extract more value from its data. This book describes the data mesh paradigm as a socio-technical architecture, with an emphasis on the *socio*. The main focus is on people, processes, and organizations, not technology. Data meshes can, but don't have to, be implemented using the same technologies most current data systems run on.

But because the data mesh is a topic of ongoing debate, with only slowly emerging best practices and standards, we found the need for an in-depth book that covers both the key principles that make data meshes work and examples and variations needed to adapt this to any company. This book is designed to do just that: help you begin your own data mesh journey.

We will provide you with conceptual tools, including, but not limited to, the key data mesh principles and boots-on-the-ground insights and examples. This book is not meant to be a comprehensive theoretical study but offers you the practical guidance necessary to get set up.

To start off, we will look at the core ideas of the data mesh, as well as the benefits and challenges associated with it. We'll also give you our definition of a data mesh, focused on outcomes and practicality.

1.1 *Data mesh 101*

The data mesh paradigm in this book is all about decentralizing responsibility. For instance, say the development team for the customer registration component of a company also creates a dataset to analyze registered customers. The team ensures that this dataset is in an easy-to-digest format by transforming the data (e.g., to a CSV file) and serving it the way the consumers would like it (e.g., on a central file-sharing system).

But this deceptively simple definition has a lot of implications because, in most companies, data is handled as a *by-product*. It is usually turned into value only after being put as a by-product into storage, then pulled into a central technology by a centralized data team, and then picked up again by decentralized actors. This actor may be an analyst in the marketing department, a recommendation system used in a marketing campaign, or a frontend display. Figure 1.1 depicts a common form of data architecture, both organizational and technical. We have also done our best to show its pitfalls.

We can see here two levels of centralization:

- The centralized technology in the form of storage and the usual data engineering/data science machinery
- The organizational centralization of the data team

Since the development team considers the data a by-product, the ownership is implicitly assigned to the data team. But such central teams usually cannot keep up with the business knowledge specific to multiple areas of operations. The developer responsible for customer registrations would need to know only the language and the updates inside that component and the associated business. But the central data team will need the same understanding of a domain multiplied by the number of domains.

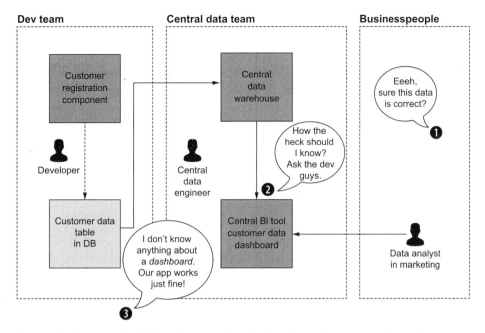

Figure 1.1   Decentralized data emission and central transformation cause problems for users because of, for example, unclear ownership and responsibility for data and its quality.

Such overload makes it unlikely that the central team will understand even a single domain to the degree that the responsible development team does. As a result, the data team cannot tell whether the data is correct, what it actually means, or what specific metrics might mean.

The data mesh paradigm shift calls for decentralization of the responsibility for data—to consider it an actual product. The situation depicted in figure 1.1 can turn into a data mesh if, for example, the development team provides the data product straight to the analysts through a standardized data port. This product could be something as simple as a plain CSV file hosted in the appropriate cloud storage spot, easy for the analyst to access. Take a look at figure 1.2 to see this shift in action.

A *platform team* could help provide a simple technology as a service to be used by development teams to quickly deploy such data products, including the data ports. Data producers focus on developing *data products*, which, together with *data consumers*, start to form connections and compose a network. We call such a network the *mesh*, where the individual *nodes* are data products and consumers.

Even in our small example, we observe a significant operational paradigm change. It encompasses both a shift in the ownership responsibility (from a central data team to the development teams) and the technical challenge of making the new setup work.

Introducing changes in the operational paradigm will result in ripples affecting many areas of your business. To stop these ripples from becoming chaos, we need

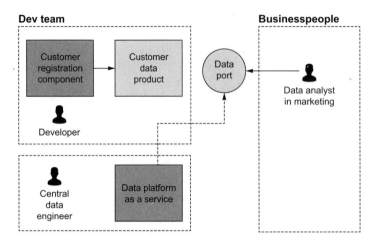

Figure 1.2 Decentralized data transformation makes data consumers happy by offering simple access to well-described data.

guiding principles. We briefly introduce them later in this chapter and examine them in detail in chapters 4 to 7. Before that, you must understand our definition of *data mesh* and its nontechnical aspects. Zhamak Dehghani made an incredible effort in curating the idea of the data mesh in 2019 (see "How to Move Beyond a Monolithic Data Lake to a Distributed Data Mesh," http://mng.bz/nNaK). She provided us with all its critical elements and introduced a structured approach to the previously discussed paradigm shift.

Since Dehghani's introduction of the data mesh approach, many data mesh–inspired business-derived and theoretical examples have appeared. A lot of this content might not perfectly fit into the initial description of the data mesh framework. A lot of businesses have seemed somewhat unsure about what exactly conforms to the definition of a data mesh and what doesn't.

In our work, as well as in this book, we opt for solutions that are first and foremost practical (hence the title, *Data Mesh in Action*). Therefore, the data mesh definition we coined aims to be broad and functional and emphasizes *decentralized* efforts to maximize the *value* derived from data.

DEFINITION *Data mesh* is a decentralization paradigm. It decentralizes the ownership of data, the transformation of data into information, and data serving. It aims to increase the value extraction from data by removing bottlenecks in the data value stream. The data mesh paradigm is guided by four principles (described in section 1.4 and in chapters 4 to 7), helping to make data operations efficient at scale: domain ownership, domain data as a product, federated computational governance, and self-serve data platform. Data mesh implementations may differ in scope and in the degree to which they use each principle.

The goal of implementing a data mesh is to extract more value from the company's data assets. That is also the reason we keep this definition so lightweight and inclusive in relation to the level at which each principle is followed. The following nontechnical use case of a data mesh will hopefully explain what we mean by that.

1.2 *Why the data mesh?*

We see three main reasons that the data world is in need of decentralization in the form of the data mesh:

- With the proliferation of data sources and data consumers, a central team in between creates an organizational bottleneck.
- With multiple data-emitting and -consuming technologies, a central monolithic data storage in between creates a technological bottleneck, which loses a lot of the information in this step in the middle.
- Both data quality and data ownership are only implicitly assigned, which causes confusion and a lack of control over both.

Over the past 30 years, most data architectures were designed to integrate multiple data sources; that is, central data teams merged data from all kinds of source systems and provided harmonized sets to users, who in turn tried to use them to drive business value. Yet, for over a decade now, the problem of big-data hangovers has plagued companies of all sizes. These data environments struggle with the scalability of the solutions, incompleteness of the data, accessibility problems, and the like. We bet that your company is also fighting to extract value from data, right?

Some approaches simply seem to not work out. Dozens of reports and dashboards seem to be of no use compared to the costs of creating and maintaining them. A bunch of data science projects seem to stay stuck in the *prototype* phase, and data-intensive applications that are running are probably facing a bunch of data-related problems. At least it seems that way, considering the effort it takes to get a software component to run.

One of the reasons for the scalability problem is the proliferation of data sources and data consumers. An obvious bottleneck emerges when one central team manages and owns data along its whole journey: from ingestion through transformation and harmonization to serving it to all potential users. Splitting the team along the data pipe does not help much either. When engineers working on data ingestion change anything, they need to inform the group responsible for transformation. Otherwise, the upstream systems may fail, or worse, will process the data incorrectly. Required close collaboration among the engineers leads to the tight coupling of all data-related systems.

The other problem arises from the monolithic nature of data platforms, such as warehouses and lakes. They often lack the diversity to reflect the reality encoded in data derived from sources and domain-specific structures. Moreover, enforced flattening of data structures reduces the ability to generate valuable insights from the collected data, as crucial domain-specific knowledge gets lost in these centralized platforms.

We could observe this problem in one of the projects we worked on. A car parts manufacturing company was buying data related to failures of various parts. Even though the provider had information on the part provenance (the model the part was installed in), the buyer had no data models allowing it to store this information. As a result, components were analyzed separately, hampering R&D's attempts to understand the big picture better.

Two more interwoven factors exacerbate the problems described earlier. One is unclear data ownership structure; the other is the responsibility for data quality. Data traveling through specialized teams loses its connection to its business meaning. Developers of centralized data processing systems and applications can't and won't fully understand the data content. In contrast, data quality cannot be assessed apart from its meaning.

Similar problems were recognized in other areas of software engineering and resulted in the emergence (and success!) of domain-driven design and microservices. Application of similar thinking (a focus on data ownership and shared tooling) to data engineering led to the development of the data mesh approach.

1.2.1 Alternatives

There are two main alternative models to the data mesh's decentralization of responsibility for data. We discuss their setups in more detail in chapter 6, but provide a quick overview here.

The first option is the centralization of both people and technology. This is the default setup for any startup. And it's a decent default option, just as the monolith is a decent default option for any software component. In the beginning, the costs of decentralization outweigh its benefits. The benefits brought in by working closely together inside one data team, having just one technology to use, make things a lot easier.

> **KEY POINT** Centralization is a sensible default option for both organizational and technical data work. Decentralization does carry costs, and centralization can mitigate those. That option does imply, though, that the value derived from centralized and decentralized data is roughly equal.

The second option splits up the work not by business domains, as data mesh suggests, but by technology. This usually results in one core data engineering team being responsible mostly for ingesting data and provisioning a data storage infrastructure. Multiple other teams (analytics teams, data science teams, analysts, you name it) pick up the raw data and turn it into something meaningful down the road. You might first centralize your data system and then layer up with this option to increase the flow.

There is nothing wrong with these two approaches. They might be reasonable default options, but both fail to align with value creation, which is deeply tied to business domains. Neither option is able to address sudden changes in just one business domain. As with microservices, which enable you to quickly extract value from one specific service by scaling it up all by itself, the data mesh is able to scale up value extraction in just one domain. All other options need to scale up everything in order to scale up value extraction in just one domain.

So, one way or another, both of these alternatives will hit a wall at some point: adding the next data source or data science project will feel extremely complex and costly compared to earlier ones. That's the point where you want to switch to a data mesh.

1.2.2   Data warehouses and data lakes inside the data mesh

There is a misconception about the data mesh. It is sometimes perceived as an exclusive alternative to the central data lake or the central data warehouse. But that does not take into account what the data mesh is: a combination of two things, technology and organization. The data mesh is an alternative to having one centralized data unit taking care of the data inside central data storage.

That still leaves the option to have central data storage and decentralized units working and owning the data. Indeed, that is a common implementation in companies that don't need complete flexibility on the data producers' side. It also is a common approach to keep data lakes and data warehouses inside a business intelligence (BI) or data science team. The data lakes and data warehouses then become a node inside the data mesh. See figure 1.3.

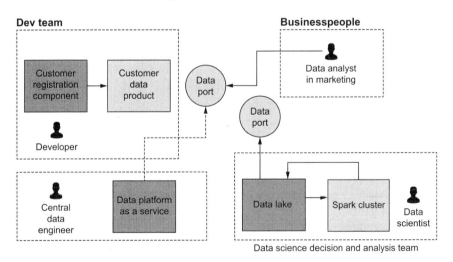

Figure 1.3   Data meshes can still use data lakes: for example, a data science team building data products may use data lakes as nodes within the data mesh.

Data meshes make heavy use of both data lakes and data warehouses in various formats. Data meshes, in general, do not try to focus on any specific technology. We discuss this dichotomy a bit deeper in section 1.6. For now, let's try to keep spirits high and focus on the benefits of the data mesh.

1.2.3   *Data mesh benefits*

Let's analyze the potential of a data mesh implementation from two perspectives: through the eyes of the business decision-makers and the technologist.

THE BUSINESS PERSPECTIVE

From a business perspective, data itself is of little value. Worse, it means incurred costs! Does this sound like heresy? To understand that statement and, if needed, convey it to your business partners, you need to understand the levels at which people can understand reality.

A good approximation of this phenomenon is the DIKW pyramid, derived from *The Rock*, a play written by T.S. Eliot in 1934. This model represents data, information, knowledge, and wisdom as a hierarchical structure, in which each next element can be derived from the former. (See "Data Demystified: DIKW Model" by Anthony Figueroa, http://mng.bz/v60M.)

The data in this context is just a set of values (the storing of which costs money!). To derive value from this data, we need to build up the context, allowing for informed decision-making. The data mesh improves the robustness of the whole pyramid.

As we mentioned, having raw data is of no use to decision-makers. We could argue that they can download it to their laptops and analyze it themselves. This is true! This option has, however, two underlying assumptions:

- To download the data, it needs to be accessible.
- To ensure the value of any performed analysis, data needs to be as complete as possible.

To address the first assumption: we mentioned already and will say repeatedly, the data mesh is very much focused on making data accessible. And not only accessible, but findable, interoperable, and reusable as well! This accessibility is embedded in one of the four data mesh principles: *data as a product* is all about making sure data is there for the taking.

Completeness of the data is another concern where data mesh shines. Unlike most data warehouse or data lake architectures, data products and their data models are not developed by IT specialists apart from the business. Instead, the development is a joint effort, ensuring the data presented outside the domain is sufficient to derive meaningful conclusions.

The data mesh also helps add value to elements higher in the hierarchy. The teams transforming data into information, knowledge, and wisdom (which businesses like to call *insight*) gain instant access to multiple interoperable data sources.

Of course, in theory, it's possible to make this instant access happen from a data lake as well. However, the reality of a single team managing technical aspects of the environment, as well as data access and transfer rights, in our experience, always makes that infeasible. And if required bits of data are stored in two different data lakes (or four, which is not that unusual), getting them all to work together is next to impossible. In short, having access to read-optimized data products enables quick prototyping of new analytical methods and opens a path for the rapid development of new business capabilities.

THE TECHNOLOGY PERSPECTIVE

The main benefit from the technological perspective is maintaining the speed of development with the organization's growth, as we mentioned previously, which is required to keep generating business benefits from the data. The data mesh is meant to address the shortcomings of other data architectures, like data warehouses or data lakes, by decentralizing data production and governance. Those other architectures introduce a bottleneck—a central team responsible for harmonizing all the data for the whole of your company and making it ready for consumption. A single team cannot scale to accommodate the varied data needs of a growing organization. Both the technology and the team knowledge quickly become scale problems. Eventually, more time is spent on maintenance, and new projects become more and more delayed.

The other benefit of data mesh is the clarity of data ownership right from the point of its creation. This approach flattens the data management structure, leaving just a thin layer of a federated governance team. And even that team's activities are limited to agreeing on standards within autonomous domains.

The speedup of development also comes from empowering the implementation teams. Since producing and maintaining the data products rests on their shoulders, the speed of change is not limited by a single central integrations team's backlog of tasks. Therefore, both the evolution of and fixes to the data product happen more quickly—especially any bug fixing and downtime. Furthermore, the team that owns the data product is better equipped to react faster because no context switching is needed, as in the case with one central team.

The other factor worth mentioning is data environment stability. With data products offering access to contracted versions of their datasets, pipelines built on them are much more robust and require much less maintenance.

1.3 Use case: A snow-shoveling business

Candace operates a snow-shoveling business. She is a proud businesswoman who started the business shoveling snow herself every winter. After a couple of years, she scaled up her operations. She focused on logistics, billing, and setting the prices across the business, and she hired three employees: Adam, who shovels the houses at Pine Road; Eve, who does the houses on Oak Street; and Bob, who is responsible for ordering new shovels, because they seem to break all the time.

Adam and Eve are responsible for both shoveling snow and bringing in new clients on their respective streets. After all, they spend quite some time around people there while shoveling snow each winter! But Candace isn't happy. Figure 1.4 depicts the initial state of Candace's operations.

Figure 1.4 In Candace's snow-shoveling business, Adam and Eve do their work, while Bob creates a stack of inventory, freezing the capital.

The previous year, Candace asked Adam and Eve to write down their working times and the number of houses cleared. She put that data in a fancy Microsoft Excel file in order to do some calculations and set prices. Figure 1.5 displays that data flow.

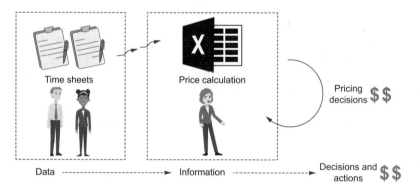

Figure 1.5 Centralized data flow from Adam and Eve to Candace for decisions

This way, we could say, Candace turned the data received from Adam and Eve into *information* in her Excel file, and then she further turned it into *decisions*, yielding the business value. Additionally, she asked Adam and Eve to provide a rough guesstimation of the number of shovels they will need. Figure 1.6 shows the data flow to Bob.

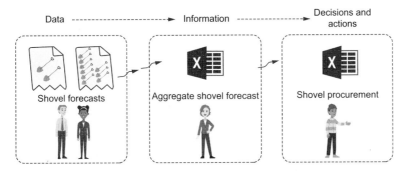

Figure 1.6 Centralized data flow from Adam and Eve, through Candace, to Bob

We could say that Adam and Eve provided raw data to Candace. She then aggregated it into information and handed it over to Bob to turn the data into decisions and business value. Notice how you again can see a *pipeline*: a sequence of steps that turns the data into value. The pipeline has two steps for setting prices (Adam and Eve collect the data in their time sheets, and Candace does her magic by aggregating the data and making decisions based on it), and three steps for the shovel procurement with Bob (Adam and Eve produce data with their shovel forecasts, Candace aggregates the data, and Bob makes decisions based on it).

But, as we said previously, Candace is not happy with the situation. Profits are not very good. The shovel procurement seems to always be off: sometimes inventory seems to stack up, and other times Adam and Eve need to delay their work because they run out of shovels.

This year, after reading a book called *Data Mesh in Action*, Candace decides to experiment. She decides to *build the foundation for a data mesh*, as described in chapter 3 of the book. She uses knowledge from chapter 4 to define domain boundaries and give the ownership of data to her main shoveling domain owners—namely, Adam and Eve. That means the following:

- Candace stops collecting the times and instead asks Adam and Eve to record their times themselves in any way they see fit.
- Adam and Eve will set the pricing for their streets.

Then something interesting happens when Eve decides to increase prices on Oak Street and Adam decreases the prices on Pine Road. It turns out they simply know more about their neighborhoods than Candace does. On Oak Street the houses have long driveways, so Eve needs to charge more for shoveling snow. On Pine Road a local kid is shoveling snow cheaper, so to be competitive Adam needs to lower his prices. Figure 1.7 shows the decentralized data flow now taking place.

If we look at the flow of data now, we could say it stays completely with Adam and Eve, from data to information, and finally into the decision—the pricing model. As profits increase, Candace decides to take it a step further. In the second year of the experiment, Candace resolves to tackle the procurement problem. To do that, she

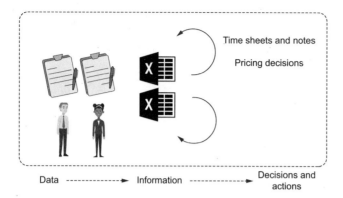

Figure 1.7   Decentralized data flow inside Adam's and Eve's domains

asks Adam and Eve to directly inform Bob about the number of shovels they will likely need.

To avoid confusion and to-and-fro emails, Adam and Eve create a spreadsheet. They update it regularly, so if current conditions or weather forecasts change their estimations, their information is timely. Figure 1.8 depicts the data flow, serving data to Bob.

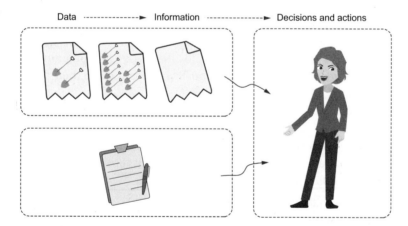

Figure 1.8   Decentralized data provisioning in Adam's and Eve's domains served to Bob for decision-making

In our data flow, Adam and Eve now keep both data and information in their domains. They try to supply Bob with a proper set of *information,* not just the raw data they were asked to collect, so he can make the procurement decisions. Bob seems much happier. When asked by Candace why this is so, he tells her that Eve realized that he also needs to know how often shovels break. Eve breaks them more often because of the longer driveways.

An unexpected business benefit of shortening the data flow emerges. In the past, Adam and Eve usually presented Candace with pessimistic approximations because they did not want to be left without shovels. Sometimes they were afraid of her reaction to too many broken shovels, so hoping for the best, they presented her with optimistic estimates. Candace usually added an extra *safety margin* before sending the order to Bob, but sometimes she got worried about spending and took a risk of lowering the received estimation.

Bob, knowing that the numbers he received were unreliable, often tried to adjust the order based on his gut feeling (and telling Candace, that, e.g., the required numbers of shovels was not available on the market). To keep the company running, he had to create a buffer of shovels, and this decreased the company's financial liquidity by freezing the capital and increasing warehousing costs. Now that he can access Adam's and Eve's direct forecasts, he is able to procure just enough shovels. He ends the year with barely any inventory left and without running out of shovels in the meantime.

For Candace, this results in a nice profit, thanks to reduced costs in year two, and she also has three happy employees. You should notice that it's the *pipeline* (the flow of data from one unit, in this case, Adam and Eve, to Candace and further to Bob) that has been the source of all problems. All that Candace has done is to break up that pipeline and *package it into one,* or at most two, pieces. That is decentralization at work.

That's really all there is to it. By breaking up this pipeline in certain situations, you will end up with better outcomes, because the decentralized parts (Adam and Eve, in our case) simply can turn that data into value better (whereas the whole pipeline could not).

Probably next year, Candace will want to introduce some form of governance. For example, she could introduce rules on the frequency of updates; or she might ensure the security of her spreadsheets so the kid from Pine Street doesn't mess with their data. Maybe she'll hire someone to create a website so people can book their services online—to do that, she'd have to develop data products with Adam's and Eve's working times and connect them with the new system by using some part of the platform. Isn't the future full of potential when you have operational profit?

Next, we will show you the four principles of the data mesh. We consider them the cornerstones of its implementation. But as we mentioned previously, our data mesh definition is inclusive and business-value oriented. Therefore, you need to prioritize these principles for yourself and determine the degree to which you should follow them to achieve your business goals. Just as Candace did, you will need to use the following principles as *guides* to successfully implement a data mesh.

1.4 *Data mesh principles*

Dehghani first described the current incarnation of the data mesh concept as a set of four principles. Throughout this book, we focus on their implementation details. Following is a summary of these four data mesh cornerstones.

1.4.1   *Domain-oriented decentralized data ownership and architecture*

The first principle is that *data and its relevant components should be owned, maintained, and developed by the people closest to it*; this means the people inside the data's domain. This calls for applying the concepts of domains and bounded contexts to the data world. This also means applying decentralization to ownership and architecture.

The idea is that, just as in the previous example, the domain-internal engineers are responsible for developing data interfaces that allow other users (data scientists, self-service BI users, data engineers, or system developers) to use that domain data. The data product engineers are expected to be experts within a single domain, which minimizes communication problems and misinterpretations of data.

Data should have clear ownership, and it should not be on the centralized level of an organization. We should put that responsibility into the hands of the people closest to it. That might be the domain team in the case of a source-oriented dataset; or it might be a data engineering team, an analytics engineering team, or a data science team for new datasets created out of multiple datasets. It could also be the organizational unit using the data if our dataset is very consumer-oriented.

The *domain* is an area or part of our business. It is a way of slicing and decomposing the company. Quite often our organizational structure resembles business domains. At Messflix, we can, for instance, find domains that distribute content, produce content, and develop a market and brand. See figure 1.9.

Messflix content streaming and production

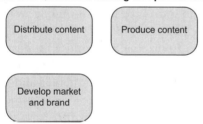

Figure 1.9   **Simplified Messflix business domain sketch**

The domain ownership principle says that each team or unit owning a domain should also own the data that has been created inside that domain. So, the team developing software to support content production is also responsible for content production data. But what does it mean to be *responsible* for data?

Being responsible for data means hosting and serving datasets to other parts of the organization (to other domains). The team is the owner of the data, and it also should be responsible for pipelines, software, cleansing, deduplicating, or enriching the data.

As with Agile principles and Agile teams, ownership on its own would not make much sense without having autonomy at the same time. This is why teams should be able to release and deploy their operational and analytical data systems autonomously.

As you can see in the example of Messflix, every business consists of many domains. Each domain can usually be further split into subdomains. By applying this principle, we will end up with a mesh of interconnected domain data nodes. Nodes of the mesh can, and even should be, connected. Data can be moved and duplicated, and the shape can be changed between the domains when needed. For example, data will usually move from source-oriented data domains (output of the operational systems) to more consumer-oriented data domains. Here, the raw data will be customarily aggregated and transformed into a more consumer-friendly shape and format.

In such a mesh of interconnected domains and subdomains, only the people close to the data know it well enough to actually work with it. Take an example from earlier: does the word *content* mean the same in all three domains? Hopefully not, because in the Produce Content domain we will have both *draft versions and ideas* for unproduced content. We will also have content that will then become truly productionized. However, in the Distribute Content domain, people will always mean productionized final content when they say *content*.

Just imagine a developer from the Distribute Content domain who is supposed to compile a list of *content pieces* from the Produce Content domain. They will likely produce a list of produced content pieces; however, that will miss the point. The requirement likely asks for a list of all content pieces, including ideas, things that are still in production, and canceled pieces. Additionally, the status of these content pieces should be included.

However, people outside this domain will not even know that these are important pieces of data. This will make the people inside the domain the only people truly able to work with this kind of data.

Source data domains usually serve data and information that represent facts about the business. Data should be exposed to other domains to serve operational purposes (like the REST API) and analytical purposes. Source data domains should expose domain events and historical snapshots aggregated over time. With the latter, we should make sure that underlying storage is optimized for big-data analytical consumption (like a data lake). In the previous example, the Produce Content domain becomes a source data domain when it exposes lists of produced content pieces. This is an original piece of data created by the business process of creating content.

Consumer data domains are aligned closely with consumption. An excellent example of such a domain could be Provide Management Reporting and Predictions. In the case of Messflix, it could be the Recommend Content domain, which might be a subdomain of Distribute Content. If the marketing team takes the list of produced content pieces and enriches it with relevant marketing materials now (the tweets the marketing team uses to promote the list, etc.), then the new list slips into a consumer data domain.

Parts of the data between data domains can be duplicated. Still, because that data is serving a different purpose, it will also be modeled differently. So usually domain boundaries will, at the same time, also be data model boundaries. Because we want to give teams as much autonomy as possible, we are not trying to achieve a single canonical model for the whole organization. We are giving them the freedom to model the data in the way they need it. Besides the source- and consumer-aligned domains, we could also encounter core data domains used across the organization. These usually represent key entities or objects.

When we share the responsibility for data across the organization, we gain tremendous scalability and maintainability. For example, when we want to add new datasets to the mesh, we will be adding a new autonomous node. At the same time, teams that own datasets will be in a comfortable situation. They will own only data that they truly understand.

1.4.2   *Data as a product*

The second principle is that *data must be viewed as a product*. This calls for an introduction of product thinking (integrated into data management).

Usually, when we talk about data, the first thing that comes to mind is either a file or a table in a database. We often envision a spreadsheet or a series of rows in a file with named columns. Taking this perspective, it is easy to reduce data to technical details. But instead, the more important question is, what gives value to the data from the organization's point of view? Or reversing this question, what is stopping our data from being turned into valuable decisions?

Without a proper set of descriptions, even the best prepared set of data will not be found and thus no value extracted from it. If it is unknown how current or complete the data might be, this could render it completely useless. That's why it's worthwhile to think of data as a product—a larger whole that ultimately makes up the experience of the users who use it.

In our experience, data offered by a data team should follow typical product features like these:

- *Viable quality*—This quality can be ensured by specialized domain experts.
- *Anticipation of user needs*—The team offering the data to the outside world should understand the enterprise's business environment. For example, present the data in a format easily digested by existing data pipelines to ensure its availability and effortless usefulness.
- *Secured availability*—The team should ensure availability of the product whenever users need it.
- *Focus on user goals*—The data team's focus on its own domain should not mean a lack of communication with other users; on the contrary, the search for synergies and shared toolsets should create an opportunity to understand each other's needs better.
- *Findable*—Any data product should be discoverable by a simple means, something a random table in a database lacks.
- *Interoperable*—Different data products should be combinable in a way that increases their value.

WHEN CAN WE CALL DATA A PRODUCT?

In everyday life, we deal with many products. A *product* might be defined as, in general, *the result of a conscious action.* If we take a pair of jeans as an example, we know that it meets certain predetermined conditions. For a product to be called a pair of jeans, it must have a suitable form and shape. In addition, it should have a unique name (especially if the manufacturer provides many products of a given type), because we buy a specific model and not a pair of jeans in general.

It should also meet some standards to ensure that a pair of jeans will not break down after a few hours of use and is made of a safe material. In addition, there should be someone responsible for this product: for example, its quality and the consequences of its use within the accepted terms of use. We can use this kind of reasoning to think about data.

Treating data as a product will mean that someone has consciously designed the product, created and released it, is responsible for it, and is mainly responsible for its quality. In the context of a data mesh, this will be the responsibility of the data product owner—who designs the data product—and the data product developers—who implement it. Just like a product on a shelf in a store, a data product has its unique name, and it has established characteristics, including the following:

- Level of quality
- Level of availability
- Security rules
- Frequency of updates
- Specific content

When we think about products, it's not enough to just expose data. We also need to make sure that we maximize its usability for the end users. In this context, the role of the data product owner is critical, because they are responsible for the final user experience of the data.

Referring to our Messflix example, we can imagine a few exemplary data products in the Produce Content domain:

- Cost statement
- Scripts
- Cast
- Movie popularity
- Movie trends

Treating data as a product brings us straight to the product thinking approach—start with the problems your customers want solved, which should drive the data product design process. Then, as a data product owner, you should deliver a data product addressing these problems based on predefined success criteria.

Data as a product also implies a degree of standardization that allows a single element to be incorporated into a larger data mesh ecosystem. To call a given set of data a data product, it should have the following characteristics:

- *Self-described and discoverable*—Data should be described, and this description should be an integral part of the data product. The data product should be able to register itself in the data mesh ecosystem, and, as a result, should be discoverable.
- *Addressable*—It should have a unique address (e.g., in the form of a URI address), so that it can be referred to and relationships between data products can be created.
- *Interoperable*—A data product should be made according to predefined standards, concerned with the form of data sharing, standardized formats, vocabularies, terminology or identifiers, security, and trustworthiness. A data product should meet the established and declared service-level agreement (SLA), and should enable controlled access, thus ensuring data security from both perspectives—intellectual property and regulations such as the European Union's General Data Protection Regulation (GDPR).

DATA PRODUCT AS AN AUTONOMOUS COMPONENT

While fulfilling the previously established conditions, a data product should at the same time constitute an autonomous component, so that it can be independently developed by the team responsible for it. From the point of view of a technical solution, we can see a data product as an analog of a microservice in the data world. In addition to making data available, the data product embeds code related to data transformation, cleaning, or harmonization. It also exposes interfaces for automatic integration with the data mesh environment and platform by providing, among other things, the following:

- *Input logic and output ports*—Form and protocols used to ingest from the source and expose data to consumers
- *Operational metrics*—Number of users, throughput, amount of data fetched, etc.
- *Data quality reports*—Quantity of incomplete data, format incompatibilities, statistical measures of outliers, etc.
- *Metadata*—Specification and description of the data schema, domain description, business ownership, etc.
- *Configuration endpoint*—Means to configure the data product in run time (e.g., setting the security rules)

These are a few examples of what can constitute a data product as a technical component.

1.4.3   *Federated computational governance*

The third principle is to *federate and automate data governance across all participants of the data mesh*. This principle aims to provide a unified framework and interoperability to the ecosystem of largely independent data products. Its purpose is to make the autonomous data products work in an actual data *mesh* (not just as standalone products).

Federated computational governance requires two inseparable elements: the governing body and a means of rule enforcement. Overarching rules and regulations should be agreed upon by a body composed of data product owners, a self-serve data infrastructure platform team, security specialists, and CDO/CIO/CTO representatives. This body would also serve as a place for discussion regarding, for example, development of new data products versus adding new datasets to existing data products, methods of ingesting new external data sources, or central platform development priorities.

Effective data governance is crucial, as data security is one of the main concerns of CDOs/CIOs in companies covering all sectors and sizes. Also, most large enterprises need to introduce controls on data security and governance that are enforced by governmental or business regulations such as the GDPR, Health Insurance Portability and Accountability Act (HIPAA), Payment Card Industry Data Security Standard (PCI DSS), and Sarbanes-Oxley Act (SOX).

FEDERALIZATION OF DATA GOVERNANCE

At first glance, the data mesh is an additional layer of complexity in an already vast scope of data governance that now also needs to address a shift of responsibilities to data products. Each data product, in turn, needs to be equipped with processes allowing safe and efficient ways of handling business-owned infrastructure, code, and data (and metadata). Moreover, data governance processes need to balance company-wide cohesion of data solutions, usually achieved through standardization, versus autonomy-driven flexibility and creativity offered to data product teams.

It is imperative to understand that there is no silver-bullet solution to balancing central governance and local autonomy! The approach will always depend on the specifics of your organization. For example, what are the needs and the maturity of your data product owners? What is the data-related risk appetite of the organization? What is the level of expertise of your central data governance team? How sensitive is the data you're working with? You need to answer these and other questions before you'll be able to set the responsibilities of central and local teams.

Another set of policies is required to ensure interoperability of data products and the ability of data consumers to join them together readily. Finally, the procedures need to provide the compatibility of various data products without explicitly enforcing an overarching data model. An approach such as this has been proved to create a bottleneck in data operations.

The data mesh tries to answer that need with federalization of data governance. *Federalization* in this context means having a governing structure operating at parity at distinct levels—central and local. The central level of governance, executed by the data governance council (of course, this governance body may use another name, e.g., in chapter 3 we call it simply the *data governance team*), will decide on a minimal set of global rules required to ensure safe and secure discoverability and interoperability of data products.

Data product teams, led by data product owners, are responsible for developing their products with a high degree of autonomy, deciding on all technical and procedural problems (within boundaries of the enterprise technology stack). There is no silver-bullet solution as to the precise division of responsibilities, the structure of the data governance council, and exact rules governing the data world. Instead, each business will have its own set of global rules, leaving domain teams with different levels of control over their data products. Chapter 4 discusses the effects of various levels of domain team autonomy on their agility and overall system complexity.

COMPUTATIONAL ELEMENTS OF DATA GOVERNANCE

The term *federated computational governance* was coined by Dehghani in her de facto data mesh manifesto (see her blog article, "Data Mesh Principles and Logistical Architecture," http://mng.bz/44rV). However, as computational governance is not defined anywhere else, throughout this book we will assume that this term relates to elements of data governance automation enabled through the existence of the central platform (as we call self-serve infrastructure as a platform, presented in a bit more detail in section 1.4.4 and in a whole lot more detail in chapters 7 and 8) serving as a medium connecting different data products.

Data governance elements, which can be automated and embedded into a data platform, include but are not limited to the following:

- Metadata
- Catalog, reference, and master data
- Lineage and provenance
- Validation and verification
- Storage and operations
- Security and privacy

Once again, no silver-bullet solution exists for deciding which of these should be automated. It will require your teams' hard work to identify which data governance tasks create bottlenecks in data mesh development in your organization and to automate them. However, automation will pay off. First, it will offer data product owners the solution that allows them a frictionless connection of their data products. Second, it will enable users to make efficient use of the exposed data. You will learn more about automating elements of data governance when we discuss the details of the self-serve data infrastructure as a platform next.

1.4.4   *Self-serve data infrastructure as a platform*

The fourth principle is to *extract the duplicated efforts of the data mesh into a platform*. This principle calls for the application of platform thinking to the data context. *Platform thinking* means that efforts that are duplicated throughout the company to a larger extent can also be packaged into a *platform*, and thus they are done only once but offered as a *service* to others.

Just as anyone can rent cloud resources on one of the major cloud providers and customize them to fit their needs (taking away the need to duplicate the effort of maintaining your own cloud), this idea can be shrunk to efforts inside a company. Building and maintaining data products is resource intensive and requires a set of specialized skills (ranging from computational environment management to security). Multiplication of the required effort by the number of data products would endanger the feasibility of the whole data mesh idea. The idea behind the central platform is to centralize repeatable and generalizable actions to the degree necessary (yet again, depending on the context of the company!) and to offer a set of tools abstracting away specialized skills. It would reduce entry and access barriers for both data product developers and data product consumers.

You may start with the requirements of your first data product owners and iteratively build the setup up to meet your organization's needs. The infrastructural support can be offered as on-premises computing power or in the cloud, depending on the enterprise policies. Its elements can be available in infrastructure as a service (IaaS), platform as a service (PaaS), software as a service (SaaS), or their hybrid models. A data mesh platform could, for example, support the following:

- *Governability*—All data computation related to data governance processes needs to be incorporated and automatically enforced on every data product connected to the data infrastructure.
- *Security*—The infrastructure solution should ensure that all data products offer freedom of operation for users whose access allows them to meet their information requirements and ensure safety from unauthorized access. To do that, a set of ready-to-use processes, tools, and procedures should be accessible to data product creators and users.
- *Flexibility, adaptability, and elasticity*—The infrastructure needs to support multiple types of business domain data. This means enabling various data storage solutions; extract, transform, load (ETL) and query operations; deployments; data processing engines; and pipelines. All that needs to be scalable to serve business needs as they arise.
- *Resilience*—Smooth operation of data-driven businesses requires high availability of data. Therefore, the infrastructure should ensure redundancies and disaster-recovery protocols at the design level of each infrastructural element.
- *Process automation*—From injecting metadata at the data product registry to ensuring access control, the data flow through the central infrastructure needs to be fully automated—possibly using machine learning (ML) and artificial intelligence (AI) to ensure efficient data processing, quality, and monitoring.

Now that you have a short summary of the four key data mesh principles, let's revisit Candace and see how she scores on these principles.

1.5   *Back to snow shoveling*

In Candace's business, you might identify a few *expert domains*. Seems like shovel procurement is one, but the two streets also seem to be separate domains. They definitely are different in some key elements, and local knowledge is needed to work effectively. Let's look at how the business has evolved over time:

- In Candace's first year, her team does not own the data even though they own their *domains* in the sense that they are responsible for operations there as well as creating domain data. There is no data governance mentioned and not much of a platform to help them do anything with data. Data is a by-product of their work.
- In Candace's second year, she makes a key change. She gives Adam and Eve data ownership in their domains. She also extends their responsibilities in general, and this is something that happens in many companies before transferring data ownership. However, there is still no data governance or platform, and not much data is being treated as a product.
- In Candace's third year, she essentially tells Adam and Eve to finally treat the data as valuable not just for themselves but also as a product for others (in this case, Bob). Finally supplied with a proper *data product*, Bob is able to also optimize the costs of the business.

In summary, Candace focuses mostly on the principle of decentralized data ownership and data product thinking. Since her operation is small, she doesn't need to do much governance besides talking with her employees about using data in decision-making. She also does not have to use a large platform or any central platform besides maybe email, simply because there isn't yet a large mesh of data products to connect.

> **KEY POINT**   The value lies in decentralization, not in all four principles. We think that data meshes at the core are just about the decentralization of data ownership into any kind of *autonomous* unit. That can be an individual, a whole department, or anything, depending on the situation. The key principles are guidelines for helping us execute this decentralization process well.

We believe that the data mesh journey might begin at any size of an enterprise if you *feel the pull of decentralization*. We discuss that in more depth in chapter 2.

> **KEY POINT**   Data meshes are for companies of all sizes. The data mesh is a possible tool for companies of all sizes. But that does not mean it is the right tool for every company in its current stage. It can also be the wrong tool for a company (again, independent of its size). We discuss the decision process in chapter 2.

So why did Candace feel this *pull of decentralization*? And why will you feel it too at some point?

1.6 Socio-technical architecture

The data mesh is not a technical solution for data problems. The data mesh solves these problems by using a *socio-technical architecture,* or a socio-technical system design. We believe this is the biggest strength of the data mesh as a paradigm, and we think you should treat the socio-technical architecture as a foundation of your data mesh implementation. You need to apply socio-technical architecture consciously to make it successful.

But first you need to understand what it means, how it originated, and most importantly, the underpinning laws behind it. For that, we look at Conway's law to understand why we won't be able to change technology just on its own. We then look into the Team Topologies framework, which is, in essence, about socio-technical architecture. Finally, we look into cognitive load as one of the main ideas used by the Team Topologies framework.

1.6.1 Conway's law

Conway's law is defined as follows:

> *Any organization that designs a system (defined broadly) will produce a design whose structure is a copy of the organization's communication structure.*

Computer programmer Melvin Conway made this observation in a 1968 paper (http://mng.bz/Qv9j), just a decade after Fortran (the first widely used high-level language) was released. It didn't take us long to see this strong, almost gravitational force in practice. This *force* will sooner or later transform our architecture so it will look like our organizational structure. As architects, we need to be fully aware of the implied consequences.

We should take as an example the martial art Aikido. *Aiki* refers to the martial arts principle or tactic of blending with an attacker's movements to control their actions with minimal effort. The masters of Aikido teach that you should not put your force directly against the force of your opponent. Instead, you should take advantage of the force they are exerting. In the same way, we should be aware and take advantage of Conway's law.

> **Example: Central data warehouses**
> Conway's law is a good explanation of why people say, "central data warehouse" but mean "central data warehouse operated by a central data team." It's because usually when you find a central data warehouse, it's been built by a central data team.

Conway's law simply tells us to take care of the organizational side of things and the technical side. Just changing technical things isn't going to have an effect. The organization will cramp itself into the new technology.

1.6.2   Team topologies

In the socio-technical architecture approach, as the name suggests, we are trying to codesign both the social and the technical architecture elements simultaneously. This way, we are thinking up front about all constraints and concerns.

This section is about the one main architecture method that is used today and within the data mesh community to do socio-technical architecture well. According to its website, "Team Topologies is a clear, easy-to-follow approach to modern software delivery with an emphasis on optimizing team interactions for flow" (https://teamtopologies .com). Matthew Skelton and Manuel Pais created Team Topologies, and they are starting to get some traction in the community because of their simplicity and straightforward application.

Team Topologies is an approach that helps you not to fall into the trap of Conway's law. The Team Topologies framework is designed to optimize the teams inside a company for optimal flow. It relies heavily on the idea of cognitive load to properly split workloads across this flow and separates teams into just a few teams. It also separates interaction modes into ones that are designed to minimize cognitive load. Since Team Topologies is focused on the optimal flow of the company, it will help us to optimize the data-to-value flow inside the company.

1.6.3   Cognitive load

Cognitive load is a term from cognitive load theory and means the number of mental resources (working memory) used by a person. In the beginning, this theory was applied to the teaching field and influenced the way we write instructions so readers can easily digest them. Later it was used in a greater number of areas, including IT.

As socio-technical architects, we should shape our teams so that the total cognitive load is limited and is mostly reserved for the essential, value-creating activities. It is similar to road traffic: you will not maximize the flow of trucks if you fill up every square meter of the road with trucks, cars, and bikes. The traffic moves in the fastest way when there is enough space between vehicles to enable them to travel near the speed limit. It is the same with the teams.

What can we do to make data mesh teams performant? First, we should plan our technology stack to be simple compared to the capabilities of the team. Second, we should embrace platform thinking so as not to force teams to reinvent the wheel every time with yet another monitoring and logging solution. Doing both will allow the team to entirely focus on what is essential—its business domain. To further focus in and not overload the team, we decompose large domains into small, focused domain-oriented data products.

All of the data mesh principles are influenced by socio-technical ways of thinking. Domain-oriented decentralized data ownership and architecture reduce the load by decentralizing responsibility for domains and corresponding data.

Data as a product reduces collaboration between teams to access data by making data findable, accessible, interoperable, and reusable. It limits the load by exposing data in an expected and known format and ports by consuming teams. Self-serve data infrastructure as a platform reduces the load by providing a self-service platform.

Federated computational governance makes collaboration between teams easier by enforcing common standards and patterns. It enables team members' transfers by reducing the possible technology stack within the company.

As you can see, at the heart of every principle is a socio-technical way of thinking. Because of the socio-technical nature of this paradigm shift, it's important to be clear about the benefits that can result from this shift. While data mesh is a socio-technical solution to many problems, some major challenges are associated with it. Let's explore them in detail.

1.7   Data mesh challenges

Data mesh is neither a silver bullet nor a plug-and-play solution. Instead, its successful implementation requires overcoming an array of challenges. This section covers the technological, data management, and organizational challenges.

1.7.1   Technological challenges

The most crucial technological challenge of data mesh implementation is ensuring that proper tooling is available to both domain-focused and central platform data teams. Providing only data discoverability and links between domains may prevent the whole ecosystem from becoming a siloed world.

The other challenge is ensuring that the tooling developed locally can be shared across domains. The flexibility and autonomy of teams should not lead to inefficiencies at the company level and reduced synergy. To effectively develop and maintain their data solutions, domain data teams need safe and secure access to data storage services. Centralizing, for example, maintenance of a cloud computing environment is much more efficient than the multiplication of this effort by each team. In addition, centralized control over cloud storage and computing can also help introduce a proper spending regime. We've seen way too often seemingly rational spending by multiple separated teams sum up to amounts far exceeding levels justifiable at the company level.

With a plethora of distributed, semi-independent data products, the development of consistent monitoring, alerting, and logging procedures becomes a challenge. As a result, both central platform and domain teams need to collaborate closely to ensure continuous insight and control over data quality and security and maintenance efficiency.

1.7.2   Data management challenges

Like the first technological challenge, the critical data-management-related challenge is ensuring that data is easy to locate and comprehensively documented. The importance of a data catalog cannot be overestimated. It is not a challenge unique to data mesh, but as it's based on the decentralization paradigm, the consequences of overlooking it would be much more dire. No central data team will be capable of ad hoc identification of available data assets (not that such ad hoc querying would be an advisable form of interacting with, e.g., data lake contents!).

Another challenge is ensuring control over the duplication of data across domains. With each new business domain needing to be served with repurposed data, redundancy may emerge. This redundancy not only increases the costs of data storage and management, but also introduces lineage and versioning problems. Data consumers may analyze outdated, incomplete, or altered data and, as a result, reach misleading conclusions.

The third challenge is not specific to data mesh; however, we need to remember it when embarking on a data mesh journey. It lies in cross-domain analytics. Because business analysts and data scientists will not have access to a harmonized enterprise-wide data model, they may need additional platforms to aggregate and consolidate the various data products. Work on distributed data sources may also lead to spaghetti data pipelines; this would reduce their efficiency and reusability. Cross-domain access also challenges the data safeguarding and access controls, as many-to-many relationships require simultaneous access to multiple data products.

1.7.3   *Organizational challenges*

Organizational challenges in the data mesh context can be divided into three categories: scope, data practices, and culture. The first organizational challenge is the scope of such a paradigm shift. It requires coordinated efforts from multiple engaged parties from different business areas: IT, business units, and senior management.

Second, it does require a level of maturity in the handling of data by multiple parties. Centralized parties, data creators, managers, and users will need to learn to handle data with a certain level of proficiency.

Third, in most enterprises, going from *data as a by-product* to *data as a product* will be a substantial cultural shift. This shift will involve not only data engineers and IT departments, but also product, management, marketing, and sales departments, and most other departments working with data.

Decentralizing the decision-making process, shaping data product owner positions, developing multiple cross-functional teams, and shifting responsibilities requires a significant restructuring of existing organizational charts. Moreover, such changes come with costs in time, brainpower, and finances.

Federated governance requires the development of novel procedures; this extends from decision-making to communication methods. These responsibilities and principles have to be appropriately identified and federated.

As we come to the end of this chapter, you should now have a better understanding of data mesh as a joint technological and organizational paradigm (as well as its underlying principles). In chapter 2, we will show you how to build a data mesh in your organization within a month.

Summary

- The cornerstone of the data mesh is decentralization—moving ownership and responsibility for data closer to its source. This approach aims to keep data in sync with the subject matter, removing bottlenecks caused by long data pipes and central team inefficiencies.
- The data mesh is a socio-technical architecture paradigm based on principles of domain-oriented data ownership, treatment of data as a product, federated computational governance, and self-serve data infrastructure as a platform.
- Domain-oriented data ownership means the data and its relevant components should be owned, maintained, and developed by the people closest to it (the people inside the data's domain).
- Treating data as a product means a conscious design of the outcome presented to the outside environment, clearly assigned roles for ensuring that outcome availability and quality, and autonomy of development required to produce that outcome.
- Federated computational governance means two things. First, the responsibility for data governance is split between the central body responsible for company-wide policies and standards and the owners of highly autonomous units, usually domain-oriented, responsible for the development of actual systems. Second, rule enforcement should be automatically executed wherever it's feasible.
- Self-serve data infrastructure means extracting the duplicated efforts of the data mesh into a platform; thus it is done only once but offered as a *service* to others.
- The data mesh is not a precisely defined solution. The extent of application of each principle differs widely from application to application, and it will vary depending on your business case.
- When considering the data mesh implementation, you must take into account major technological, data-management-related, and organizational challenges.

Is a data mesh
right for you?

In the first chapter, we explained the meaning of *data mesh*. We also explained why your company should consider implementing it. In this chapter, we answer two other essential questions:

- Should I implement a data mesh in my business (i.e., what are data mesh drivers)?
- How much effort does it take to implement a data mesh (i.e., would the benefits outweigh the effort of its implementation)?

The presence of the first question may surprise you in the context of this book. *Data mesh* has become one of the hottest buzzwords in the industry. But many companies have started to implement it without first considering whether it fits their organizations (or thinking through all of the requirements and ramifications). We have observed several similar rushes toward patterns or practices in the past (including microservices or Agile). A large number of these ended badly, and people blamed the patterns and practices instead of their own implementation mistakes. The truth is, there is no silver bullet. Every pattern or practice has its area of applicability. They come with tradeoffs. Treat a data mesh as yet another tool in your toolbox.

The second part of this chapter focuses on implementing a data mesh. We will show you the possible steps toward this goal and how all the skills and knowledge you will learn in upcoming chapters fit together. But as we said before, the most important thing is to know whether you need a data mesh. So let's start there.

2.1 Analyzing data mesh drivers

To decide whether a data mesh is the right choice for you, we need to analyze the decision drivers behind architecture selection. We split these drivers into three categories:

- Business drivers
- Organizational drivers
- Domain data drivers

Let's start with the most crucial aspect: business reasons.

2.1.1 Business drivers

We think you should start your analysis from the business side. If you can't find a suitable business reason to start your data mesh journey, stop there. You'll already have an answer: you don't need a data mesh.

BUSINESS STRATEGY

Look at your business strategy at the company level or, in the case of big corporations, at the unit level. Search for the answers to questions like these:

- Are we defining our company as data driven or planning to shift our strategy to be more data driven?
- Do we have objectives and key results (OKRs), or any goal-setting methodology, that requires data to be met?

> **NOTE** *OKRs* is a methodology used to define goals for the company (and on the individual level). This methodology is often used as a tool to implement business strategies.

If the answer to these questions is *yes*, you can dig deeper and look for the specific business cases requiring data (which we cover in the next step). If the answer is *no*, your work is going to be more challenging. Business cases for data needs are often hidden in business unit strategies or in specific business processes. Finding what you need will require some laborious searching.

BUSINESS CASE AND ITS COMPLEX DATA NEEDS

To build a viable business case for data mesh, start with answering the following questions:

- Do you have specific business processes that are starting or ongoing with complex data needs?
- Do you need to kick off a product/project with complex data needs to accomplish OKRs?

By *complex data needs*, we mean multidimensional analysis (ad hoc, AI/ML, reporting) running on top of the data coming from multiple sources. If the answers to these questions are positive, you might have a compelling business case.

> **KEY POINT**   A data mesh requires a business case and is useful when there are related complex data needs.

Let's look at the examples of business cases and their data needs.

EXAMPLE 1: SNOW-SHOVELING BUSINESS

In the example described in chapter 1:

- Candace realized that she combined too many business processes into one data flow. In this way, she lost the data context.
- Adam and Eve had no way of supplementing raw data with their knowledge and experience.
- Bob operated detached from his actual stakeholders.

The business case for a *data mesh-ization* of Candace's shoveling business could improve demand forecasting for shovel ordering.

EXAMPLE 2: WELL-KNOWN FAST-MOVING CONSUMER GOODS MOGUL

A nonfictional fast-moving consumer goods (FMCG) company realizes that its R&D efforts across brands are disconnected. Each R&D team produces its data and stores this in a silo. There are also imprecisions and contradictions in the description language used. While performing similar or identical tests, various groups use different standard operating procedures. Their individual results are also described uniquely.

The initial effort of developing a data warehouse is stopped when the central data team fails to develop a harmonized data model. The lack of a common language (and often contradictory requirements) make it impossible.

An introduced data mesh helps in a couple of ways:

- The bottleneck of the central data team's need to cooperate with all the domains is removed. This team focuses on developing the data exchange platform and providing necessary metadata management tools.
- The domain teams no longer have to modify their data structures to multiple other domains. They put their effort into developing extensive documentation of their sources.

After decentralizing the effort, domain teams (having fully documented metadata concerning other datasets) can use to their advantage historical data produced by their counterparts. A spillover benefit also arises. Data harmonization occurs naturally when teams start to use and discuss one another's data. Over time, they also formulate a common language.

As you can see, the business case can range from the strategy-level company-wide cleanup to a single business process improvement. The approach and expected journey scale will differ, but the critical factor (business improvement) needs to be identified and quantified.

2.1.2 Organizational drivers

Organizational drivers are situations, or the state of your business environment, in which the nature of the organization itself becomes a bottleneck. Implementing a data mesh should help remove these by shaking up the organizational structures and culture.

SOCIO-TECHNICAL COMPLEXITY

A socio-technically complex organization owns numerous systems producing and consuming data. These systems have been developed by multiple teams, units, or individuals belonging to different chains of command.

Socio-technically complex organizations could also have a few, but enormous, teams struggling with internal communication (for example, not colocated and without a good remote work culture). We believe that socio-technical complexity along with complex data needs are the main reasons to implement a data mesh.

KEY POINT A data mesh is for socio-technically complex organizations with complex data needs.

DATA MATURITY

For data maturity classification, we find the Gartner Analytics Ascendancy Model handy (www.gartner.com/en/documents/1964015). This model describes four stages of data maturity:

1 *Descriptive*—We record what already happened.
2 *Diagnostic*—We know why it happened.
3 *Predictive*—We predict what will happen.
4 *Prescriptive*—We know what we should do to take advantage of what will happen.

A company introducing a data mesh should at least be scorable using this scale (i.e., it should have data collection, storage systems, and culture, thus enabling reliable access to historical data). If this is not the case, the company should start gradually learning how to use available data rather than aiming to transform significantly. We also think that the more mature you are in this model, the more value you will be able to extract from moving into a data mesh.

KEY POINT A data mesh is for companies with a certain level of data maturity.

SOFTWARE ENGINEERING MATURITY (CI/CD, DEVOPS)

A data mesh is a socio-technical change in company operations. As much as we emphasize the sociological part of the transformation, the technological part needs to be on par with it. To evaluate whether your software development teams will be able to efficiently introduce the necessary changes, you will need to consider their engineering maturity.

The following list is not comprehensive. However, for a good overview of the general state of the teams that will carry the brunt of the transformation, you should be considering the following:

- Level of test automation
- Development operations (DevOps) culture
- Continuous integration/continuous delivery (CI/CD)
- Level of embedding security factors into the development process
- Focus on developing products instead of projects

If these concepts are not the bread and butter for your development teams, implementing good data products will be difficult for them. It could be advisable to focus on improving your engineering maturity before beginning a data mesh transformation.

KEY POINT   A data mesh is for companies with a high level of software engineering maturity.

You need to consider a few more organizational-related drivers when deciding whether a data mesh is right for your company. We present them separately in section 2.1.4 because their weight is much lower than the drivers presented in this and the following sections. Figure 2.1 depicts the summary of main organizational data mesh drivers.

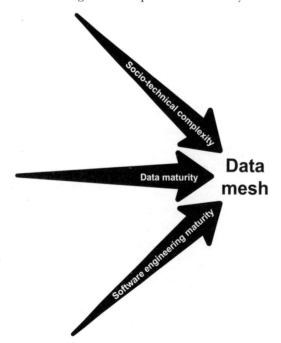

Figure 2.1   Primary organizational data mesh drivers

It's important to keep in mind that none of these drivers represent the necessity or sufficiency of a data mesh implementation. Let's now discuss equally important data-driven drivers.

2.1.3 Domain-data drivers

Domain-data drivers focus on data produced at the domain level. If it's not clear what a domain is, please refer to chapter 1 for a quick explanation, or to chapter 4 for methods of defining domain boundaries. For now, let's approximate a *domain* as an area of responsibility of a single business function. *Domain data* is data produced by each domain. This section specifies factors indicating a data mesh as a solution suitable for exposing data produced in the business domain.

DOMAIN AND DATA MODEL COMPLEXITY

Data models for complex business cases are difficult to develop and maintain. Proper modeling requires expertise in both data modeling and the subject matter. In strongly centralized architectures, especially in big companies, central data teams serve too many domains to secure the required expertise. Their workload is usually too high to allow them to spend sufficient time on resource-intensive tasks of data harmonization and tightly coupled model evolution (we noted these problems previously in chapter 1). Even if we could imagine the cross-functional project of the model development, assuming that the data team is not directly involved in domain operations, then the cognitive load of continuous updating and modifying would strain their capacity.

> **KEY POINT**   A data mesh is for companies with complex domains.

The solution is the decentralization of data ownership. You should consider the implementation of a data mesh because domain-focused data ownership is one of its pillars.

DATA DIVERSITY

Harmonization problems often plague companies operating with data of varied formats and from multiple sources (e.g., a combination of structured, unstructured, and semi-structured sources; or as events, files, graphs, relational and NoSQL databases, etc.). Each new data format and source in parallel increases the coupling and chances that a change will occur. Every change in the source or transitional data model may lead to a cascading, more or less catastrophic failure.

The other often-encountered problem is ensuring that the data can be found and accessed. Keeping the metadata repository up-to-date becomes a challenge. The same holds true for the maintenance of granular access rights to hundreds of data assets, especially if data comes with varying levels of protection depending on its origin (e.g., the European Union versus Bolivia).

> **KEY POINT**   A data mesh is for companies with diverse data sources.

Suppose the company struggles with consistency, harmonization, and abundant data sources. In that case, a data mesh may be a viable solution because of its focus on data productization, loosening the data coupling, and domain-focused shift in ownership.

DATA VOLUME

Companies working with high volumes of data may experience bottlenecks in cost and time as data is transformed and transferred. These bottlenecks are harrowing in the case of centralized architectures, as data needs to be imported from all the sources into a central lake to be transformed and queried.

If your company operations require time minimization between data generation and analysis or consumption (that is scalable and near real time), then ownership decentralization and data productization may work for more-efficient high-volume data processing. Figure 2.2 depicts the summary of domain-data drivers for a data mesh.

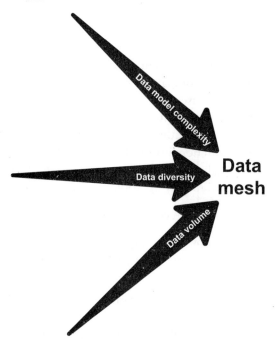

Figure 2.2   Domain-data-related data mesh drivers

It's important to remember that these drivers, even in combination with organizational drivers presented in section 2.1.2, represent neither necessity nor sufficiency of a data mesh implementation. To make your consideration even more thorough, you should take into account other additional minor drivers. We explain them in the following section.

2.1.4   *Minor organizational drivers*

Minor organizational drivers are not critical for your journey (but could be considered when evaluating how costly your journey would be if you decide to start it). We believe that the data mesh is the next stage in architecture evolution. So, if your organization enjoys the benefits of well-developed maturity levels of governance, engineering, and domain-driven design, as well as data-savvy engineers, then the goal of your business case can be achieved relatively easily. The transition should also be relatively frictionless.

If these areas in your company are underdeveloped, but the major drivers described in sections 2.1.2 and 2.1.3 still push you toward a data mesh, then you need to consider the additional effort of required cultural change management. The following factors influence estimating costs and the effort needed to perform a transformation. Nevertheless, it should give you a solid starting point.

DATA GOVERNANCE MATURITY

One of the pillars of the data mesh is federated data governance, which we describe in detail in chapter 6. Irrespective of your current data governance model, the higher your data governance maturity level, the easier the transformation will be.

To evaluate your data governance maturity, we propose using the Gartner Data Governance Maturity Model, not to be confused with the Analytics Ascendency Model we referred to in section 2.12 (see http://mng.bz/XZl6). It divides governance maturity into six tiers:

- *Unaware*—No ownership, security, or systems defined for data
- *Aware*—Project-oriented strategy, efforts to document the data-related risks begun, siloed information consolidation
- *Reactive*—Formalized objectives for information sharing, localized integrations, and point-to-point interfaces
- *Proactive*—The data governance team established, data-related policies adhered to, locally maintained data models aligned with central architecture guidance
- *Managed*—Cross-functional information problems addressed by the data governance body, enterprise-level approach to information needs
- *Efficient*—Automated data governance seamless information flows

If your company is at early maturity stages (e.g., either aware or not), implementing federated data governance may require a lot of time and effort.

> **KEY POINT** Data mesh is easier to implement in companies of high data governance maturity.

DATA-SAVVY SOFTWARE ENGINEERS

Even if your software development teams are mature, their world is separated from the world of data in many companies. In such a case, the (mis)communication between these worlds often creates bottlenecks in data operations. If your company engineers are already data savvy, the evolution of data products from existing systems should be a quick and easy process. Otherwise, when planning a transition to a data mesh, you need to consider the competence gap you'll have to fill.

Suppose your company already hires apt data engineers. You will still need to develop a strong platform team to prepare a user-friendly environment for joint software and data development teams to form. You will also need to build a strong enabling team to mentor these teams.

If your software development team has insufficient experience working with data, and you also lack experienced data engineers, you may need to consider recruiting data-savvy engineers. This cost can be added to your calculations.

KEY POINT   Data mesh is easier to implement in companies in which software is developed in close cooperation with data experts.

FOLLOWING THE DOMAIN-DRIVEN DESIGN APPROACH

Domain orientation is at the core of data mesh. Even if your teams do not consciously use the *domain-driven design* approach, you might consider how closely they follow its principles in their day-to-day operations. To evaluate the cost in effort of turning your teams' focus to domains, ask these three key questions about their activities:

- How close are they to the core of the domain? How closely does their work follow domain logic?
- Do they base their software and data designs on domain models?
- Do they collaborate with domain experts?

We covered some of these questions separately when considering other drivers. However, putting them together may provide a clear picture of the difficulty in implementing the domain ownership principle in your organization.

KEY POINT   A data mesh is easier to implement in companies that are following a domain-driven design approach.

None of the described drivers, alone or in combination, give you a clear go/no-go answer as to when you should start your data mesh journey (neither does their combination). To understand whether a data mesh is the right path for your organization (or even the right solution to solve your business case), you need to compare it to the alternatives.

2.1.5   *Is a data mesh a good fit for me?*

You need to ask yourself one critical question: is your current socio-technical architecture capable of supporting your current and planned business operations sufficiently? That is why, at the beginning of this chapter, we encouraged you to consider the business case. There is a chance a data mesh could help you if one or more of the following apply to you:

- Your operations are slowed by data not being easily findable or accessible by consumers.
- Your data consumers spend too long aligning with software and/or data engineering teams.
- Your central data team has an arm-long backlog of problems to deal with (e.g., maintenance of data models and catalogs, deciding on access rights, or costs of to-and-fro data transfer).

If any of these issues apply (but only to a minor degree; or if the inconveniences they cause are not significant), data mesh is less likely to be a worthwhile investment. However, suppose that you observe any combination of the previously mentioned problems in your company. Additionally, suppose that your organization has a strong business reason for needing a data mesh, including to derive value from data, a complex socio-technical architecture, complex data needs, or requiring scalability for planned growth. In that case, the chances that data mesh will be right for you are high. However, to make the final decision, you should not only understand what the expected final effect could bring but also what the journey would entail.

2.2 Data mesh alternatives and complementary solutions

Solutions described in this section can be considered as either complements or alternatives to a data mesh. This depends on whether we look at them as technology or socio-technical architecture, respectively. Therefore, we will describe popular patterns and architectures not only from a technical perspective, as it is usually done, but also from a socio-technical one.

We hope that this discussion will help you decide whether any of these solutions is sufficient for your organization's needs. You can also select them as technologies to be used as elements of your data mesh.

> **NOTE** A data warehouse, lake, lakehouse, or fabric can be complementary solutions. These architectures are not necessarily alternatives, but they could be treated as complementary solutions. You simply need to navigate away from their standard socio-technical architectures and align them with data mesh's socio-technical architecture. The way to do that is to decentralize ownership.

Each architecture we describe here comes in many flavors. In each organization, they undergo many tweaks, adjustments, and improvements. But we will keep our description simple and will not consider all possible variations. In our comparison, we will refer to the standard, most popular ways of their implementation.

2.2.1 Enterprise data warehouse

The *enterprise data warehouse* is an approach to storing data in the central data repository that the central data team owns. Data is ingested to the data warehouse by using the extract, transform, load (ETL) or extract, load, transform (ELT) approach, usually directly from systems-of-record databases. Data is harmonized into a canonical model that is stored in the data warehouse. Data is either directly consumed from the data warehouse or through simpler data marts usually focused on just one business function (figure 2.3).

In the example data warehouse in figure 2.3, you can see that teams A, B, and C are producing data and do not own the pipelines used to extract data from their sources. A central data team owns the pipelines. It is expected that the central team also owns BI and reporting. BI/reporting and data analysis in figure 2.3 are depicted

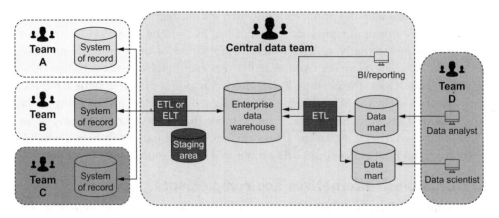

Figure 2.3   In this enterprise data warehouse socio-technical architecture, the boxes represent areas of responsibilities of different teams, the "ETL or ELT" and "ETL" rectangles are data transformation components, and the arrows indicate direction of call—from caller to callee.

as being owned by separate teams. But that's often not the case, and they also may be owned by the same central data team.

The following illustrates when you should consider implementing an enterprise data warehouse instead of a data mesh:

- Most of the sources of the data are structured.
- Your current data use cases are well known and not likely to expand or evolve.
- You extract value from data using mainly BI, reporting, and data analysis.
- You rely on a small number of unchanging source systems.
- Sources are owned by a small number of teams.
- Your central data team has expertise in data warehouse technologies.

As we stated in the beginning, the enterprise data warehouse is a socio-technical approach, but a data warehouse is an underlying technology. The technology itself is not an alternative to a data mesh. However, it might be one of the technological solutions used to build a data mesh. But remember, in such a case, a data warehouse should not try to aggregate data from the whole organization. A data warehouse's usefulness as a technological data storage solution should be decided by each domain on a case-by-case basis.

The following shows when you should consider using a data warehouse in addition to a data mesh:

- At least one of your domains has mostly structured data sources.
- You are extracting value from that domain's data by using BI, reporting, and data analysis.
- Your data engineers have expertise in data warehouse technologies.

2.2.2   *Data lake*

We mentioned data lakes in chapter 1. Here we will go into greater detail. A *data lake* is quite similar to a data warehouse; for example, both rely on a central data repository. The main difference is in the way a data lake stores data: in raw format. Data engineers transform the data into more structured and cleansed forms. They then move it into different zones along with its lineage and versioning.

A data lake has numerous *zones* (e.g., *process zones* used to store data already processed but not yet ready for production or accessed by end users; or *access zones*, with data already curated and ready to be accessed by consumers; see figure 2.4). A data lake is often described as a schema-on-read, in contrast to the data warehouse, which is described as a schema-on-write. In a data lake, incoming data is not forced to conform to the specific schema and data model. Instead, we force the data to conform before end users access it in different zones.

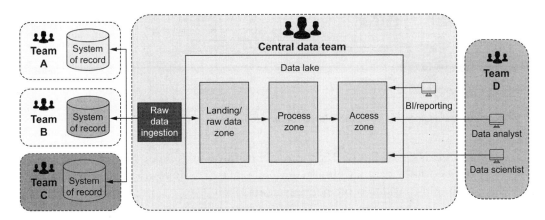

Figure 2.4   Data lake socio-technical architecture

A data lake is often described as more than a storage pattern. It also offers many related capabilities (ingestion mechanisms, security, metadata, catalog, processing engines, access mechanisms, and many others).

The common socio-technical architecture of the data lake is almost the same as the enterprise data warehouse. As shown in figure 2.4, all data-related components are owned by the central data team. Here's an example of when you should consider implementing a data lake:

- You deal with big data (volume, velocity, and variety).
- You have structured, semi-structured, and unstructured sources of data.
- It is hard to foresee all your data use cases.
- Data sources are owned by a small number of teams.
- Consumption patterns are not yet established.

2.2.3   *Data lakehouse*

A *data lakehouse* is a combination of a data warehouse and data lake (figure 2.5). It is built on top of data lake with added features like these:

- Atomicity, consistency, isolation, and durability (ACID) transaction support
- Schema enforcement and governance
- BI support on top of the same data source

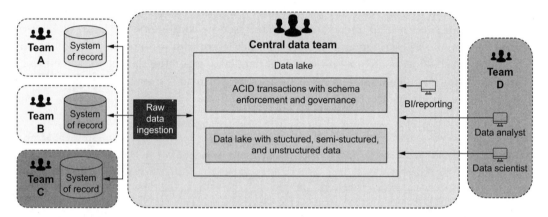

Figure 2.5   Data lakehouse socio-technical architecture

As you can see in figure 2.5, the socio-technical architecture is the same as the one described for a data warehouse and data lake. The following are examples of when you should consider implementing a data lakehouse:

- Some use cases are well known and rely on structured data.
- You are extracting value from data by using BI, reporting, and data analysis.
- You have structured, semi-structured, and unstructured sources of the data.
- It is hard to foresee most of your data use cases.
- You are dealing with big data.
- Sources are owned by a small number of teams.
- Consumption patterns are not entirely established.

> ### On the consequences of similarities of data lakes, warehouses, and lakehouses
>
> Data lakes, warehouses, and lakehouses, in their standard implementation, rely heavily on a central data team. In our experience, this is their fundamental weakness when the company has a lot of data sources and complex usage patterns.
>
> From a purely technical point of view, these three architectures may pose an excellent computational environment for a data mesh. This is because the elements of a data mesh may be constructed with existing infrastructure.

A data mesh will not require you to replace the technology into which your company has already invested millions. A data mesh will ensure that organizational inefficiencies of over-centralization do not throttle down your platform's potential.

The three previously described solutions have a common element—namely, the centralized data team. The next solution is on the other extreme of the centralization scale.

2.2.4   *Data fabric*

A *data fabric* is a technology-centric solution for data management. It provides a low-code or no-code platform to connect data sources with consumers alongside governance applied on top of it. This approach aims to simplify the integration and delivery of the data in a heterogeneous data environment across many platforms.

Data fabric solutions utilize AI/ML and knowledge graphs in addition to metadata to make an integration and delivery process as automated as possible. A data fabric is a vague concept, and, unfortunately, it is next to impossible to find a precise definition. As Gartner defines it (see http://mng.bz/yvjq and http://mng.bz/M5Gn), an ideal data fabric should have the components shown in figure 2.6.

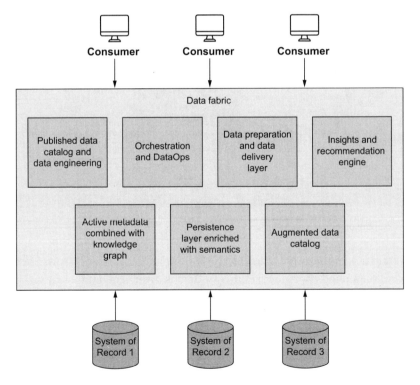

Figure 2.6   Data fabric components

By definition, a data fabric has no implicit socio-technical architecture. This is why it is hard to consider it as a data mesh alternative. We look at it more as a possible way of implementing our data platform. Data fabrics are offered by Cinchy (www.cinchy.com) and Talend (www.talend.com/products/data-fabric/). Here are examples of when you should consider implementing a data fabric:

- You have structured, semi-structured, and unstructured data sources.
- You are dealing with big data.
- There are many data sources, and they are owned by many teams.
- You are dealing with many different ways to consume the data.

2.2.5   *Data mesh vs. the rest of the world*

We've summarized the comparison between popular data architectures and the data mesh in figure 2.7. This Venn diagram uses bubbles previously described in sections 2.2.1, 2.2.2, and 2.2.3.

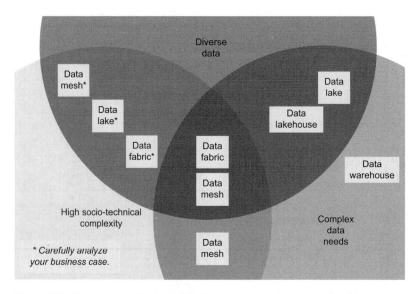

Figure 2.7   Comparison of data architectures

As you can see, a data mesh is a solution for complex organizations from both a socio-technical and data needs perspective. If your data is diverse, a data mesh is also a good fit. You can consider combining a data mesh with a data fabric for an organization that checks all three boxes. Remember that a data lake, lakehouse, or warehouse implemented classically is not the best fit for complex socio-technical organizations but when combined with a data mesh, they can thrive.

The main conclusion from figure 2.7 can be summarized as the following key point.

KEY POINT   A data mesh is for socio-technically complex organizations with complex data needs.

If you decide that the socio-technical and data complexities in your organization may justify giving data mesh a shot, the following section will show you what takes to implement one.

2.3   Understanding a data mesh implementation effort

If you performed the driver analysis described in section 2.1, you should know whether the implementation of a data mesh would bring value to your organization. Now is the right time to consider the requirements to make it happen and whether they are worth the effort. To answer this question, we will walk you through the steps we propose to take and the structures to apply on the organizational level to implement a data mesh.

We will not get into details of technological solutions and their associated costs. There are simply too many possibilities to list them all here. However, we believe that after reading this book, especially chapters 7 and 8, you will be able to create a reasonable estimation for your situation. For now, let's see an overview of the implementation process.

2.3.1   The data mesh development cycle

In our experience, a data mesh implementation works best if its development is similar to CI/CD-based software development. Small steps taken in cycles ensure quick wins, rapid feedback and correction ability, and flexibility in reaction to changes. Figure 2.8 shows the high-level overview of the development process.

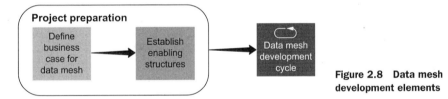

Figure 2.8   Data mesh development elements

Before you jump headlong into the transformation, you should prepare foundations for the change. Figure 2.9 focuses on elements of the preparatory phase.

We previously discussed the importance of the business case, which will serve as a reference for all other decisions. The second element of your preparatory work is ensuring that you have enabling structures in place. The three key elements that you should consider are as follows:

- Enabling team
- Governance team
- Platform team

The latter two are optional and will depend heavily on your setup. To learn more about these topics, read chapters 6 and 7, respectively. In our experience, however, the quality of the enabling team is critical to a data mesh implementation success. You

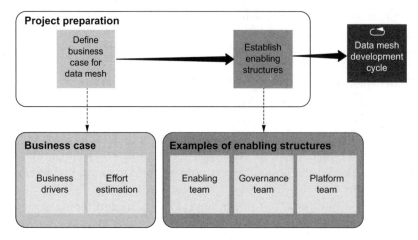

Figure 2.9   Data mesh development elements—project preparation details

can form your enabling team as a group responsible for the change management, a community of practice, or a governance team. We will expand on their roles and responsibilities in section 2.3.3.

With an initial structure in place, you can start your development cycle. Figure 2.10 focuses on elements of the development cycle.

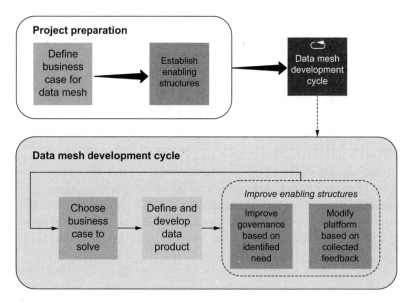

Figure 2.10   Data mesh development elements—data mesh development cycle details

The cycle should always start from a business case that can be enabled with data. Choose the business goal with clear measures of success.

On the other hand, the modification of enabling structures should take place at the cycle's end. This is when all misalignments or inadequacies are well defined.

The development of data products needed to solve the business case is at the core of the data mesh development cycle. Figure 2.11 details the data product development cycle.

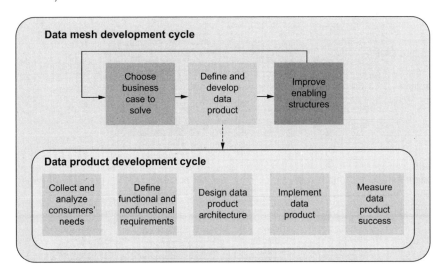

Figure 2.11   Data mesh development elements—data product development cycle details

You should start with a good understanding of consumer needs. This results from the business case. Then you should translate these needs into the developed data product's functional and nonfunctional requirements. As a next step for the data product, design boundaries, assign ownership, and align with governance policies. Only then is it time to start the actual data product software development. An integral part of the data product development cycle is monitoring its success. This will not only help the data product owner to further improve it, but will also allow the developer to identify required changes to the enabling structures.

With the business case solved, the data product in place, and enabling structures modified (if needed!), rinse and repeat. All elements of a data mesh development are presented in figure 2.12. If this process seems daunting, see chapter 3 for an example of a simple minimum viable product (MVP) implementation.

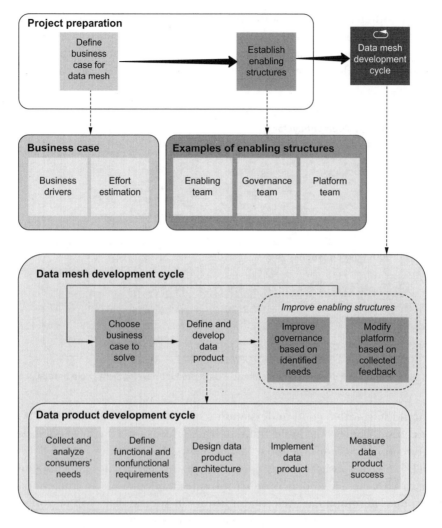

Figure 2.12   Detailed view of data mesh development elements

2.3.2   *Development cycle in the shoveling example*

In the first chapter, we described how Candace introduced a data mesh into her organization's work:

1 She identified the business case: profits were low, and data utilization was overly complicated and inefficient.
2 She prepared for the project.
   a She appointed herself as an enabler and read *Data Mesh in Action* from cover to cover.
   b She divided her business into domains and pushed ownership of data, information, and some decisions to the main domains of her operations. Instead

of collecting their raw data to later transform and analyze, she presented domain owners the problem. They collectively agreed that Adam and Eve would work with their data and come up with a decision-pricing model for their streets.

It's worth noting that she profited even before the first development cycle started! The next year, the team went through the first development iteration:

1. The business goal was developed to improve the procurement forecast.
2. The data products were defined: Adam's and Eve's shovel use estimations.
3. The data products were developed: online spreadsheets for Adam and Eve.
4. She reviewed the results and planned the next cycle iteration.

As you can see, the first data mesh implementation cycle doesn't have to be long or strenuous, or encompass all the data mesh properties to bring the business value. We will expand on this topic in chapter 4. There, we use the example of Messflix to show how a data mesh MVP could be implemented within a month. For now, let's learn a bit more about cycle elements.

2.3.3 *Enabling the team*

Irrespective of the scope and range of your planned data mesh implementation, you need to ensure that there is a person responsible and accountable for its progress. Because the data mesh boundary encompasses both data and software worlds, identifying the right person to lead this effort may not be easy. However, that person should have experience in both environments.

Considering the nature of the data mesh implementation drivers, we expect that a data mesh will usually be implemented in high socio-technical complex environments. This means one person almost surely will not be enough. Additionally, the enabling team will have to be interdisciplinary. The team members can be recruited from communities of practice, guilds, or chapters.

ENSURING DATA GOVERNANCE

Your organization may or may not have a governance structure. If it suffices to achieve your goal, you may choose to let sleeping dogs lie for the first iteration. The frictions and possible improvements will be discovered during the feedback collection phase. Your next goal may become improving on governance. However, it is advisable to ensure that relevant data of the data products you designed is under the owner's responsibility.

FACILITATING DATA PRODUCT DEVELOPMENT

The enabling team needs to support domains in developing its data products. The team members should facilitate cooperation between subject-matter experts, data engineers, and software developers. This part of their job is depicted in figure 2.13.

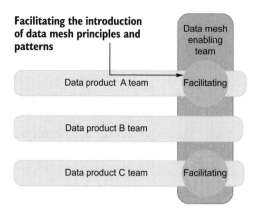

Figure 2.13   The role of the data mesh enabling team in data product development

FACILITATING PLATFORM DEVELOPMENT

The enabling team must be able to support the platform team (should one be developed). This means the enabling team will have to conceptually align data product teams' requirements and the platform's capabilities. This alignment will help the data product team communicate its needs in the language of platform capabilities. It will also help the data platform team communicate platform features, expectations, and limitations to data product developers (figure 2.14).

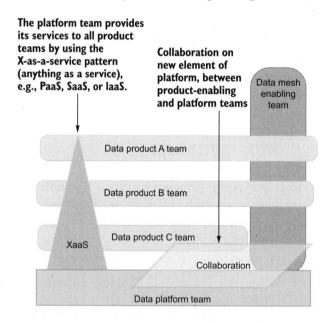

Figure 2.14   The role of the data mesh enabling team and data platform team in support of data product development teams

The platform team should provide its services by using the X-as-a-service pattern (anything as a service), and so it might be PaaS, SaaS, or IaaS. When a platform team is developing new platform features, it should collaborate with one of the other teams to test-drive new functionalities.

FACILITATING GOVERNANCE

Depending on your organization's governance model and maturity level, facilitating governance can be the most challenging part of enabling teamwork. A data governance team needs to have the gravitas to carry out its duties. Advising these team members against their habits can be somewhat tricky.

The key to success is to clarify the governance role and area of responsibility in your data mesh. Parties leaning strongly toward extreme governance centralization or decentralization will have to understand the benefits of a federated model before being ready to accept it as a solution.

We list the main advantages of federated governance in chapter 6. It would assist your enabling team to know them well before approaching potential governance team candidates. The collaboration with the governance team requires at least some enabling team members to possess not only technical knowledge (related to both software development and data engineering) but also the infamous *soft* skills (figure 2.15). Otherwise, the governance team meetings may turn into a shouting match instead of discussing policies and practices.

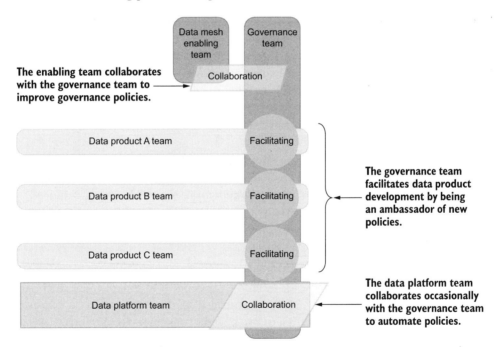

Figure 2.15   Team topologies of the governance team

As you can see, the enabling team will be extremely busy throughout the transformation. Let's look at the development cycle this team will support.

2.3.4   *Development cycle in detail*

The data mesh development cycle is focused on achieving business goals by using data. The cycle includes a definition of the goal, data required to achieve it, development itself, and, if the situation requires it, adjustment of the data governance environment or central platform modification.

It probably won't be the case in the early data mesh development stages, but when your data mesh spans multiple domains, each domain will have its own development cycle. These domains will, however, have to align their development with the works of central teams: data government and platform.

CHOOSE A BUSINESS GOAL TO ENABLE WITH DATA

We described the drivers, which may help you identify the pain points you may wish to remove when using a data mesh. However, just naming them may not be enough. To describe your business goal in sufficient detail, you need to understand the objectives of defining it.

First, you need to explain why you think it is even worth achieving your goal. What is the added value to the business? Your goal could be described using one of the frameworks—for example, OKR or SMART (which stands for specific, measurable, attainable, relevant, and time-based).

Second, you need to make sure your goal is presented in the context of the work required to achieve it. And we are not talking only about balancing the benefits of achieving the goal and the effort needed to achieve it. Teams engaged in your project will need to be able to relate their tasks to the goal in front of them. Achieving the goal should be the final factor in deciding whether a team should pick up a given task and, if so, with what priority.

Third, your business goal should have an associated responsibility assignment matrix—such as RACI (responsible, accountable, consulted, and informed), PARIS (participant, accountable, review required, input required, sign-off required), or one of the scores of other similar participation models. Having a matrix will ensure that your goal remains relevant to the business and its realization does not lead to a dead end.

DEFINE THE DATA PRODUCTS NEEDED

We mentioned earlier that your goal needs to be presented in the context of the work required to achieve it. Now it's time to dig deeper into one of these work areas: defining what data is critical to achieving your goal and how it should be transformed into data products to allow its efficient use by data consumers driving business value.

We propose you start with identifying data use cases. This can be done quickly and efficiently by answering these questions:

- Who are the actors critical in achieving your goal? (If you described your goal correctly, answering this question should not be hard.)
- How do these actors use data?
- What is the data they use?

- Where do they get this data?
- Where is the actual source of data they use?

You should end up with a list of data sources and their access systems. The knowledge and techniques presented in chapter 4 could be used to identify which of these sources could belong to the same domains. These sources are candidates to be merged that can reduce the number of data products to develop.

The other problem is the data access systems used by your actors. They can be combined or transformed into consumer-oriented data products. If the source data products will be able to provide data in an instantly usable form, these systems can be avoided completely.

DEVELOP DATA PRODUCTS

Whatever method you'll use to define their boundaries, chapter 5 will help you turn data sources into data products. Developing data products does not differ much from developing any other IT product, except that software engineers, domain experts, and data engineers are engaged in the whole process. Also, the whole data product platform, source, and data are owned by the data product owner. It should be their and the development team's responsibility to choose the best development framework for their needs and style.

COLLECT FEEDBACK ABOUT THE PLATFORM AND ANALYZE SHARED NEEDS

This step is essential for the long-term success of your initiative (second only to the business case selection). Even if you make errors in your data product design or implementation, they can be corrected with good feedback loops.

The most important thing for you to remember is that in your feedback collection, you need to put the same emphasis on discovering the pain points of two distinct, but at this stage, equally important, groups:

- Data consumers
- Developers

The importance of understanding the needs of data consumers (actors responsible for delivering business value) is, hopefully, obvious. However, it doesn't mean that the problems encountered by developers are any less important. The data mesh aims to create a decentralized environment, allowing scalable and efficient operations of decentralized units. Early identification and removal of blockers of their potential are critical to ensure that they can fulfill their role in the system. Problems solved at the first iteration of the first data product's development will not plague the development and maintenance of the future data products, because that's the core of the scalability.

If you're unsure how to collect the feedback, you may use any combination of the following methods and their variations:

- *Email and chat*—Both methods are equally convenient for feedback givers but unwieldy and require manual processing of results by the feedback collector.

- *Team meetings*—These allow you to chain questions and clarify answers but might be hard to organize and considered an unappreciated distraction from work. Also, some of the feedback content may be forgotten by stakeholders between meetings.
- *Feedback reports*—These provide a convenient way of collecting structured qualitative and quantitative feedback but at the risk of losing details of atypical situations.

Or you can try one of the feedback collection platforms, designed to extract and aggregate the required information, but which come at the cost (financial and time) required for stakeholder training. You should look at the feedback data and search for repeating problems and clusters of problems with a high synergy of developed solutions.

ESTABLISH COMMON POLICIES AND IMPROVE GOVERNANCE

You should always ensure that identified problems are solved systemically. Occasionally, the development and dissemination of best practices will suffice. Sometimes additional training or facilitation will be required to secure a smooth transition. Also, at times, the problems are simply too serious to leave solutions to chance and the goodwill of the stakeholders. In that case, you should try to ensure the solution's permanence by implementing it in the form of a policy guarded by the governance structure.

In our experience, this is a drastic measure. Devising policies for each and every minor concern leads to either paralysis or, in the best case, a slowdown of operations and possibly the quiet disregard of policies. Unfortunately, in the latter case, the chances of the policy becoming disregarded do not depend on its insignificance but on a generated inconvenience. Your governance team should help decide whether the problem justifies using centrally controlled measures and verify that the desired solution aligns with applicable internal and external regulations.

DEVELOP THE PLATFORM

This step of developing the platform depends on the specifics of your business case and the nature of the data environment. If the derivation of business value requires modifying the existing platform or building a new one, now is a good time to undertake this task. We describe platform development in detail in chapter 7 and compare implementation options in chapter 8.

Keep in mind that throughout the whole data mesh development cycle, the platform in a data mesh should be treated as a product that can enable two things:

- Connecting data products and data consumers (in any required configuration)
- Automating the implementation of governance policies

Before the round of data product development and feedback collection, it is next to impossible to decide on the required scope of work on the platform. The platform development team will be properly equipped to plan its work for the next development cycle with the feedback that both data consumers and product development teams collected and analyzed.

In this chapter, you learned about the business context of a data mesh and the groundwork required for a successful kickoff of a transformation project. The next chapter will show how you can prove the assumptions related to a data mesh business value with a quick MVP.

Summary

- A data mesh is not a business goal. What is your company's strategy? If it emphasizes deriving value from data, a data mesh may be useful.

- Identify your business case with complex data needs. Next, consider whether a data mesh would help solve otherwise persistent problems, and then work from there. Remember that a data mesh is not suitable for every context.

- There are alternatives more suitable for different business needs. A data mesh should work well in an environment with high socio-technical complexity, complex data needs, and diverse data.

- Identify all transformation drivers: organizational (e.g., socio-technical complexity and data and software development maturities); as well as related to domain data (e.g., the complexity of domains and their data, and data diversity and volume).

- Lay the groundwork of your data mesh (i.e., develop your business case and set up governance and enabling teams). Also, ensure that data products, data governance, and central platform development will be sufficiently supported and facilitated.

- Develop your data mesh in cycles built around adding new data products to the mesh and collecting and analyzing feedback, and modify platform and governance only if needed.

Kickstart your data mesh MVP in a month

This chapter covers

- Selecting part of your organization for building your first data products
- Choosing the right people to work on your project
- Setting up the governance of your data mesh
- Discovering and describing your first data product
- Creating the minimal viable infrastructure as a platform (aka the central platform)

In chapter 1, you learned what a data mesh is and what its elements are. In chapter 2, we provided a framework for analysis in terms of whether a data mesh is suitable for you and your business. If you're here, it means you're ready to put that knowledge into practice.

You may use this chapter as a learn-as-you-go experience and, following your Messflix alter-ego example, build your data mesh *minimal viable infrastructure as a platform*, constituting an MVP of your data mesh, within a month. You'll learn how to map your organizational environment and select partners, enabling smooth project development, as well as how to use the most straightforward technical tools to develop a data mesh.

The minimal mesh

The *mesh*, at its most fundamental, is a graph—in the discrete mathematics understanding of the word. As such, it has two main element categories: nodes and edges.

A *data product*, in this case, can be perceived as a node. The *central platform*, offering the capability of connecting two nodes, forms an edge.

The central platform uses the standardized port of the data product. (Some sources use *data quantum* instead of *data product*, but as *data quantum* comes with its own theory and constraints, to keep our definition simple and inclusive, we intentionally avoid this terminology.) The minimal mesh will then be two data products connected by the central platform.

On the other hand, getting less mathematical and more practical, we could think of a single data product connected to a self-serve infrastructure as a platform. As long as such a simple setup would add business benefit, it could serve as a helpful example from a data mesh perspective.

If proven to bring a clear business benefit, even such a small data mesh seed may become a prime success story for expanding the data mesh concept within your organization. To illustrate how a data mesh can bring tangible benefits to an organization, we will show you how the MVP of a data mesh can unlock the potential of data interoperability and enable ML, creating entirely new business capacity at Messflix.

By the end of this chapter, you'll have a firmer grip of data mesh principles, the means for implementing them, and their associated challenges. However, because we are creating an MVP, you'll learn to achieve success using as few resources as possible and with only a small group of people. Such an approach means taking a lot of shortcuts, so think of duct tape and zip-tie solutions as you go. The rest of the book will give you tools and perspectives on how to address those challenges in depth.

3.1 Getting the lay of the land

Before starting your project, you need tools to navigate through the organizational and infrastructural landscape present in the company. To succeed with your tight MVP deadline, you need to identify the path of least resistance while not forgetting about the need to add value to company operations.

> **NOTE** In chapter 2, when describing data mesh development, we put a lot of emphasis on the business case. It's the same when it comes to a data mesh MVP. It doesn't differ from any other MVP in this sense. It needs to show, in a measurable way, the benefits of the new solution.

You may use the following examples as templates, allowing efficient mapping of the environment of your project.

3.1.1   *Drawing a system landscape diagram*

As a chief architect at Messflix, your first instinct is to put pen to paper (or a sticky note to a whiteboard) and map the company's systems, actors, and development team (figure 3.1).

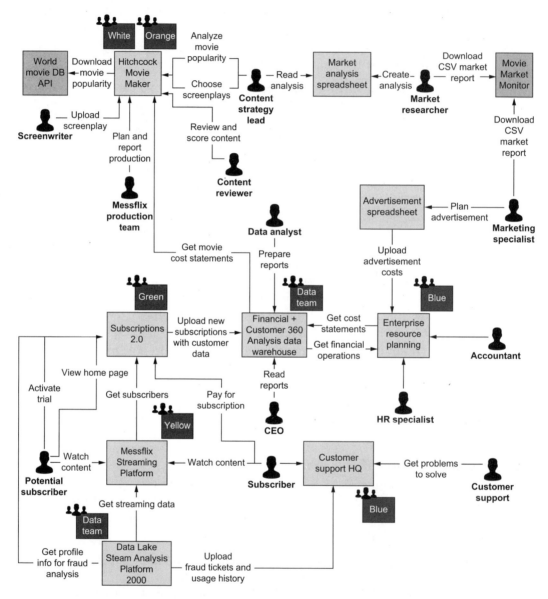

Figure 3.1   This landscape diagram of the Messflix architecture depicts Messflix internal systems, external data sources, teams, and users.

You will notice that, remaining loyal to the Messflix name, the current setup is rather *complicated*. That's one of the reasons a data mesh may just be the tool required to untangle this mess.

You take the following four steps to develop a system and development team landscape diagram:

1   You start with whitespace (whiteboard, piece of paper, or digital whiteboard) and place the internal IT systems and the external systems used by users or internal systems.

2   You add all the other actors interacting with systems to your working space.

3   You order the system and user indicators (sticky notes, shapes) and draw arrows indicating interactions between the collected elements.

4   You decide that to help you with the implementation team selection, the landscape needs to be enhanced with an additional element not usually present in such a diagram: you add teams responsible for the development and maintenance of all IT systems.

We will use this landscape, summarized in table 3.1, to decide on an MVP environment. Later, we will fill in the table as we discover the pros and cons of engaging each team.

Table 3.1   MVP environment selection sheet

System	Users	Development team(s)	MVP pros	MVP cons
Hitchcock Movie Maker (Production-specific data storage)	Messflix production team Screenwriters Content reviewers Content strategy lead	Orange team White team		
Market analysis spreadsheet (Market information)	Market researcher Content strategy lead	Market researcher		
Advertisement spreadsheet (Cost reporting)	Marketing specialist	Marketing specialist		
Subscriptions 2.0 (Management of user subscriptions)	Potential subscriber Subscriber	Green		
Financial + Customer 360 Analysis data warehouse (Data warehouse harmonizing and storing financial, production, and ERP data)	Data analyst CEO	Data team		
Enterprise resource planning (Third-party ERP system)	HR specialist Accountant	Blue		
Messflix Streaming Platform (Content-streaming platform)	Potential subscriber Subscriber	Yellow		

Table 3.1   MVP environment selection sheet *(continued)*

System	Users	Development team(s)	MVP pros	MVP cons
Customer HQ	Customer support	Blue		
Data Lake Stream Analysis Platform 2000		Data team		

It is worth noting that this exercise requires a lot of information collected from multiple people from different company areas. However, it is also an excellent opportunity to learn who is who, which is the knowledge you'll utilize in your next step.

3.1.2   *Performing stakeholder analysis*

As Messflix chief architect, you've been given the organizational chart of the company. You use the chart to identify the actors for your system landscape diagram. The result is presented in figure 3.2.

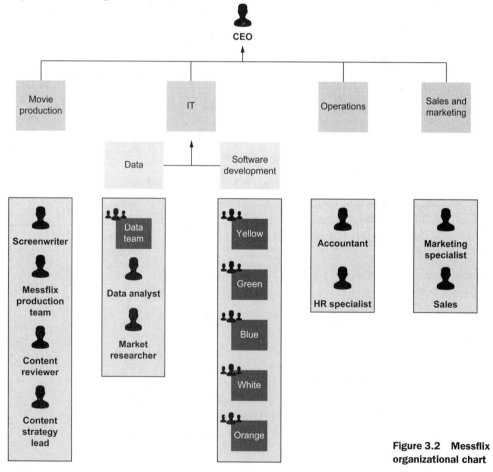

Figure 3.2   Messflix organizational chart

This chart is not very helpful for deciding whom you should cooperate with if you want your project to have the desired effect. Because you are still new to the company and can't rely on personal experience, you decide to use a popular structured approach called *stakeholder mapping*, or *stakeholder analysis*, to help you make this decision.

> **DEFINITION** According to the ISO 21500 standard, a *stakeholder* is a "person, group, or organization that has interests in, or can affect, be affected by, or perceive itself to be affected by, any aspect of the project." It is crucial to note that even the perception of being affected is enough to be considered a stakeholder and that the perception of being affected can be either positive or negative.

The idea behind stakeholder analysis is to identify stakeholders and their relation to your project so you can strategize how to maximize your positive effect on them and minimize their hindering effect on the project wherever applicable.

This exercise is next to impossible to complete on your own, assuming that you are working in a socio-technically complex environment. Your direct stakeholders and contacts may have other stakeholders and constraints you may not be aware of. Our advice is to use your experience from discussions related to the system landscape diagram and secure help from many people across your organization.

Ruth Murray-Webster and Peter Simon, in "Making Sense of Stakeholder Mapping" (http://mng.bz/aJ2B), propose a stakeholder mapping framework that's perfectly applicable to our needs. It's based on evaluating stakeholders according to three main criteria: power, interest, and attitude, and then mapping their position on axes to create a stakeholder matrix.

The stakeholder's place on the matrix defines their category. Different stakeholder categories have different advised ways of interaction. Let's look at Murray-Webster's and Simon's explanation of the analyzed dimensions:

- *Power* is defined as the ability to direct or influence the organization.

    The middle manager of a team of five has less power in the organization than the C-level executive. However, someone who weekly plays golf with the CEO may have more actual power than that person's position in the organizational chart would suggest. You want to capture the real, not the nominal, power of your stakeholder, if only for your personal use.

- *Interest* is defined as the stakeholder's level of active engagement in the project.

    The chief data or information officer in the company holds a lot of power over the long-term future of the data mesh initiative. Therefore, the CDO/CIO might voice considerable interest and be willing to support the data mesh approach after it has been proven to work. However, unless you are that person (or the CEO), you can't expect their active involvement at this stage. Thus, stakeholder interest at this stage is low!

- *Attitude* is defined as the expected type of engagement in the project: supporting, resisting, or remaining neutral toward it.

This criterion goes beyond the apparent feeling of positivity or negativity toward your initiative. For example, someone may feel positive about a data mesh per se but compete with you for resources, because they may be implementing a noncompatible solution.

With those criteria in mind, you position each Messflix data mesh stakeholder's power and interest on a scale and indicate their attitude toward your project by assigning each a color. You end up with the matrix presented in figure 3.3.

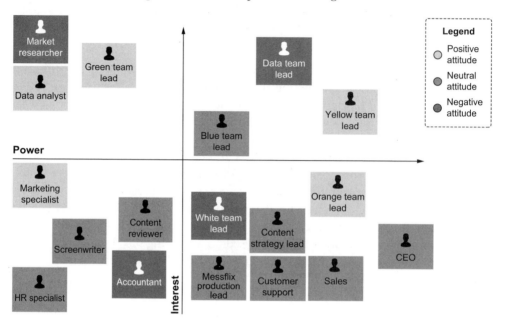

Figure 3.3   Messflix stakeholders map

The first glance reveals a vital conclusion: most people don't care about the data mesh. As we just mentioned, Murray-Webster and Simon suggest interaction patterns with various stakeholders, depending on their position within the matrix. For a quick reference of stakeholders' types and interactions, refer to figure 3.4.

The top-right quadrant is your primary focus. Your *saviors* should be well informed about your progress and, if possible, involved in your activities (e.g., as members of the governance body, described in section 3.2.4). Dealing with *saboteurs* is an art in its own right. The best way to neutralize them is to find a way to understand the threats they perceive and either explain why the reality differs from their perception or, if the danger is real, try to identify a way to create benefits outweighing the losses. The same transparent and proactive attitude may allow you to neutralize *time bombs* (lower right) before their involvement results in unexpected distractions.

On the opposite spectrum, *trip wires* and, surprisingly, *acquaintances* should be intentionally avoided to avert losing energy on managing their involvement.

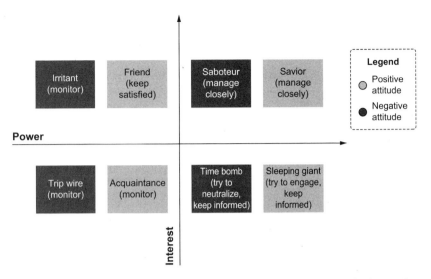

Figure 3.4   Stakeholder type and advised interaction based on position in the matrix

Monitoring that their position on the map hasn't changed should suffice. This is also true for *irritants*.

Your *friends* and *sleeping giants* may become your assets if appropriately engaged. Securing their involvement will strengthen your project.

Armed with a system landscape diagram and the stakeholder map, you're ready to plan your project. In the next step, you'll learn to decide which team members you should partner with. Proper partners will make the system and dataset selection process much easier and may help you identify the potential benefits of your project.

3.2   Identifying candidates for the MVP implementation team

We have said a couple of times already that your success will depend on choosing the right people for the right job. Let's consider the qualities you should look for in your development and governance teams.

3.2.1   Choosing development teams

The ideal situation would be to identify a team that has data already well documented and organized with consumers in mind. This might have come through the necessity of already serving their data for further downstream consumption. Or they've experimented with domain-driven design, and thus have already constructed a domain-centric model for their data.

If the team's data meets these criteria, try to learn about the team itself, particularly its inner dynamic. You can talk to team members or their stakeholders. Team members should be agile and goal-oriented if you are going to make a change within a month. This means team members should be willing to compromise and go with good-enough solutions to maintain momentum. When choosing, ask yourself and the team members for their approach toward mistakes. Are mistakes acceptable, or even better, a chance to learn? You will embark with them on a journey to an unknown land, so you are bound to err.

The team members selected must have a good track record and be on top of their schedules. Again, a discussion with their stakeholders should allow you to get this metric. This is doubly important. A team feeling on top of its game is more willing to take risks and more enthusiastic about trying new things. At the same time, they also enjoy more leeway with their surroundings, allowing them more tolerance and freedom of movement based on the trust built beforehand. The likelihood of project success and positive perception within the company may increase if you identify a group that already does experimental-like projects such as prototyping or strategic analysis.

Knowing what the perfect team looks like is one thing. Making do is another. So let's walk through selecting the good-enough team(s) from the pool of available ones. In our selection process, we'll consider the following criteria:

1 *Long-term perspective*—In the future, beyond the first month, will this team member be an ally and a great example in the quest to introduce the data mesh to the rest of the company?

    Look at the stakeholder map: the Yellow team is your savior, and with its high interest and power, fulfills this criterion for sure. The Orange team's power and Green team's interest should also suffice if other factors analyzed later in this chapter will position them as potential partners.

2 *Immediate perspective*—Will the data mesh add value by solving this team member's pressing problems (e.g., data access or interoperability problems)?

    If you have such knowledge, use it to your advantage. As a new employee, however, you may not have this luxury.

3 *Short-term perspective*—Consider the following questions:
   - Is their work focused on a single business domain?
   - In their domain, is the IT team working closely with the business?
   - Is their data organized enough to need just a bit of focused work to expose it in the form of a data product?
   - Is their system easily adaptable?

To consider the third criterion, you need to look closer at figure 3.1 and examine systems developed by the three teams meeting criterion 1 (because you're not equipped to narrow the selection by using criterion 2). Table 3.2 summarizes the selection criteria.

In your Messflix position, as a first approximation, you decide to develop MVP around the project involving the Yellow or Green teams first.

Table 3.2   Updating the MVP environment selection sheet

System	Users	Development team(s)	MVP pros	MVP cons
Hitchcock Movie Maker	Messflix production team Screenwriters Content reviewers Content strategy lead	Orange team White team	A lot of datasets to choose from	White team lead's negative attitude. Orange team lead's low interest caused by the work overload of that team.
Market analysis spreadsheet	Market researcher Content strategy lead	Market researcher	Simple, concise dataset	No development team.
Advertisement spreadsheet	Marketing specialist	Marketing specialist	Simple, concise dataset	No development team.
Subscriptions 2.0	Potential subscriber Subscriber	Green	Simple, concise dataset	Its data includes personally identifiable information (PII), so a lot of scrutiny would occur from the cybersecurity side. Relatively low power of Green team lead.
Financial + Customer 360 Analysis data warehouse	Data analyst CEO	Data team	A lot of datasets to choose from Multiple integrations (possibility of reducing workload) The system is used directly by the CEO	The Data team is overworked. The Data team lead is categorized as a saboteur.
Enterprise resource planning (ERP)	HR specialist Accountant	Blue	A lot of datasets to choose from	ERP is a third-party solution, hard to modify. The Blue team lead's interest is just about average; the lead is not yet a data mesh supporter.
Messflix Streaming Platform	Potential subscriber Subscriber	Yellow	Simple, concise dataset	
Customer HQ	Customer support	Blue	Simple, concise dataset	The team uses PII data, so a lot of scrutiny would occur from the cybersecurity side. No clear business case at this stage. The Blue team lead's interest is average; the lead is not yet a data mesh supporter.
Data Lake Stream Analysis Platform 2000		Data team		The Data team is overworked. The Data team lead is categorized as a saboteur.

3.2.2   *Choosing the cooperation model*

Having two teams, Yellow and Green, to potentially cooperate with, you need to consider structuring your project and selecting a cooperation model. The three basic cooperation models for such projects are as follows:

- Select a single team responsible for all datasets you plan to turn into data products.
- Create a cross-functional team, temporarily connecting members of multiple teams under your lead (you would serve as a team leader, but your team members would work in your team temporarily).
- Coordinate work of multiple teams (you serve as a facilitator to other team leaders).

In the Messflix environment, the Green team is a bit more agile and willing to take risks, but the Yellow team offers more maturity and experience. Therefore, Green and Yellow team leaders advise that you leave the team management to them, focusing on coordinating the effort. You appreciate the offer, knowing that forming a new team is a task probably exceeding the complexity of the development of a data mesh MVP itself.

In the meantime, because data governance is one of data mesh's principles, you shouldn't forget one more essential human-factor-oriented exercise: forming your data governance team.

3.2.3   *Choosing a data governance team*

If your organization already has a data governance body, you should probably start there! Building a parallel reality may lead to confusion, contradictory policies, and a plethora of problems. We will continue this subsection with a working assumption that, like Messflix, your organization does not have any data governance in place.

WHY DO YOU NEED A DATA GOVERNANCE TEAM?

A *data governance team* is a group of people who will decide on data-related policies. They'll have to make decisions, driving the data products' design into interoperability with existing systems and with each other. We will explain the role of the data governance team at the MVP stage in section 3.3, and we'll expand on that in chapter 6.

WHOM DO YOU NEED ON A DATA GOVERNANCE TEAM?

You want people who understand the data journey, from data generation/acquisition to its actual business use. Therefore, it's of paramount importance to include stakeholders from multiple areas of the organization—from IT to affected business departments to management. Of course, you want to have at least one representative of your implementation team, but you don't want your governance team to be just a different label for your implementation team.

All that is no more than four or five people. Fewer participants create the perception that your governance is overly centralized (we do our best to avoid words like *dictatorship*), and more would be impractical to coordinate. Even a kickoff meeting between more participants could take more time than the promised month. Ensuring the time availability of prospects is of paramount importance.

> **NOTE**   Throughout this chapter, we will avoid specifying your central data governance team with a particular naming convention or in an exact position in the organizational chart. Instead, in chapter 6, we propose a central governance structure based on three separate bodies.

How do you select a data governance team?

We would like to start with you stopping for a second and resetting your thinking about the teams and their roles in implementing the MVP.

Initially, our focus will be on the top-right quadrant, representing stakeholders with significant power within the organization and high interest in your project. Residents of this quadrant in the stakeholders' map require close management. And what would be a better opportunity to manage relations than the development of a joint project?

In your Messflix stakeholder analysis, you identified the Data team lead, Yellow team lead, and Blue team lead as top-priority stakeholders. Please note that during this exercise, we do not care about the systems owned by stakeholders! The relative importance of the systems they manage is represented by their power. All three Messflix high-priority targets are system owners, but that doesn't have to be the case in your company.

Now, a bit of practical advice. The order of invitation matters. Figure 3.5 depicts the path you pick to navigate through Messflix stakeholders.

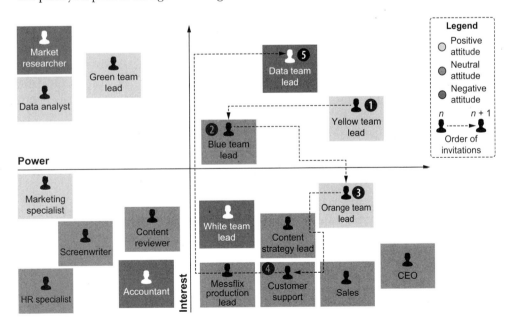

Figure 3.5   Messflix stakeholders map

Why choose this order? You want to achieve a snowball effect:

1 You start with the Yellow team lead. She already agreed to work with you on MVP implementation, so there are two arguments for starting with her. First, you have a high chance she'll accept the invitation. Second, her presence will ensure implementation team representation in the data governance team. As a bonus, you have an opportunity to discuss governance problems with someone deep inside Messflix IT. This conversation leaves you much better prepared for the following discussions.

   One down.

2 The Blue team lead expresses above-average interest in your project, but previously his attitude wasn't positive enough for you to risk inviting him to the implementation team. However, the Yellow team lead's relative power helps you build credibility, so you can try to engage him. Fortunately, you manage to leverage the Blue team lead's curiosity toward your project and secure his involvement. This is excellent news, because if you improve his attitude, you may turn him into a full-fledged savior!

   Two down. The last stakeholder in your top-interest quadrant is the Data team lead. You decide to expand the selection criteria at this point.

3 The Orange team lead holds a lot of power, and his attitude is positive. Unfortunately, his team is too overworked to participate in the MVP implementation. However, the arguments you coin during discussions with the other two team leads allow you to convince him that your initiative is worth his attention and that a relatively low workload expected from the data governance team will not affect his other activities. The Orange team lead's engagement means that you have secured an opportunity to wake up a sleeping giant.

   Three down. Congratulations! You've successfully invited two out of three top-priority targets and supplemented them with one more high-power system owner. Job well done! Well, not yet. We cannot overemphasize how important it is to have business representation in your governance body.

   Neither the Yellow nor Green team's systems have direct users from the business side. However, the Blue team has contact with three of them. There is no silver bullet. Finding a business case requires you to talk to all of them.

4 After to-and-fro discussions, you identify common ground with Customer Support. That department's representative ensures that your data governance team isn't limited to the IT world. Customer Support even comes up with a proposition for the MVP business case, which we'll describe in section 3.4.1. Win-win.

   Job well done? Can we get to work? Hold your horses. You may be inclined to limit the invitation list to friends, saviors and, if an opportunity arises, to add someone neutral or two, but preaching to the choir will not serve your long-term strategy well. A data mesh is a collective effort, and the MVP is there to prove its value. The voice of scrutiny may help you understand the worries and reservations of the resistance. Transparency of your actions and active engagement of the data governance team members may help defuse the situation and earn you allies.

5   As the last step, you invited the Data team lead. The collective power of your data governance team is now too great for him to ignore the invitation. Now you can keep your friends close . . .

With that, you finish your governance team selection.

In this section, you've thought about how to identify the best candidates for the initial implementation team (and learned that it's a chicken-and-egg type of problem, with IT teams in the role of the chickens, IT systems and datasets in the role of the egg, and for good measure, business benefit thrown in as an omelet). We also discussed setting up the right sort of data governance team.

> **NOTE** Even if you choose your governance team well, the people selected may still raise concerns about whether they should join your initiative. In our experience, the key is to introduce the data mesh as a socio-technological architecture, not as yet another technical solution. Including people with key business roles, and shaping the team early on, are critical for its proper functioning.

All of this will make the implementation process for data mesh much smoother, but the right implementation team still needs materials to work with. So in the next section, let's look at how to design and implement the building blocks of your data mesh: your data products.

3.3   Setting up MVP governance

It could seem that setting up governance is the least of our problems and that it could wait for all the important (technical) solutions related to the central platform to be in place or data products to be developed. But that's not exactly true. You don't want your governing body to be an afterthought.

Neither the platform nor data products you will develop at the MVP stage are likely to last, but your governing body will, at least in some capacity. You've chosen the data governance team members for their experience and influence. It would be a grave mistake to start your collaboration by reducing their role to rubber-stamping whatever you prepare for them.

What you can and will do is clearly state the purpose of your data governance team. To lay the cornerstone of data mesh data governance, this team will achieve two goals within the MVP span:

- To develop a value statement related to data governance policies and rules (we present the definition of a *value statement* in section 3.3.1)
- To set up initial rules and policies to govern the central platform and data products

Depending on the composition of your data governance team, you may decide that other goals are more relevant to your project. If so, in chapter 6, we suggest decisions that could be channeled to different central governance bodies. You may look to that chapter for inspiration.

At Messflix, you decide to follow the two primary goals we've presented. The first one provides a good base for a long-lasting data mesh effect, and the second makes the selection of technologies behind your central platform and data products easier.

3.3.1   *Defining data mesh value statement(s)*

The first goal of your governance body—defining value statements—is not technical; it is vital nevertheless. It not only sets the tone for the data mesh but also may bring new quality to data governance in your company even if you decide to pursue another approach.

What is a value statement? Many equally good definitions exist. However, for this exercise, we use the one describing a value statement as an assertion of causality between a business action and the resulting business value.

Robert S. Seiner, in *Non-Invasive Data Governance* (Technics Publications, 2014), presents a general structure of a value statement as follows:

> *Organizations that [take some action] demonstrate [business value improvement].*

What is the added value of a value statement? Isn't it just a buzzword? If done well, it isn't. It's the backbone for all the decision-making, to be referred to as context for what to do next. The value statement is supposed to be the final word when setting priorities.

You may ask, "Isn't it enough that we choose more efficient technical solutions? Why do we need to waste time discussing value statements?" You just made a value statement. Let's rephrase it:

> *Companies that simply choose more-efficient technical solutions demonstrate less time wasted on buzzwords.*

Wasn't that hard, was it?

However, in your MVP, you may want to test your value statement against business reality. Is the efficiency of IT solutions the most important value in your organization? Or maybe some efficiency can be sacrificed for the sake of user experience? Or sustainability? Or maintainability?

We're not saying that all of these contradict each other. We're just noticing that in some cases, they might. And we believe that companies that have a lighthouse allowing them to navigate through unobvious decisions fare better—which is one of the value statements of this book.

That is the role of data value statements: to serve as the final word when in doubt. They won't affect your lives as often as the selection of this or that technology stack—just as seatbelts do not save your life every day. It's just that when they are needed, they are hard to substitute on the fly (pun intended). Therefore, value statements should not be taken lightly because they set up the expectations of the whole data environment of the company.

Discussion about data mesh value statements serves a double purpose:

- Deepening understanding of the data mesh within your governance body
- Providing a clear understanding of the data governance team's expectations from the data mesh (even if they won't end up in a final value statement list)

Defined value statements themselves are a powerful tool too. First, they allow you to discover organizational-level value added by data mesh development. Second, they will guide your implementation team members to prioritize development if time constraints won't allow them to finish all planned data products or the central infrastructure platform features.

At Messflix, your governance team has a long debate on the value statement. The team members list key areas of their operations as follows:

- Technical efficiency
- Financial efficiency
- Operational resilience
- Customer satisfaction

For MVP purposes, they decide to focus on the latter. They declare the following:

> *Organizations that put effort into using data to improve their understanding of their customers demonstrate a higher return on data investments.*

With this focal point in place, they begin to think about how to align their business processes to reflect this value statement. Policies are the best tools to shape business processes at any governance body's disposal, so let's see how they work in practice.

3.3.2 Defining data governance policies

The list of all potential policies and aspects they may govern is long and never exhaustive. Trying to define and execute all of them may lead to a highly inflexible environment and is not advised. Finding the right balance between the control of the central governing body and the autonomy of data product owners is not an easy feat. Chapter 6 covers this topic, and there is still more to this art than that!

However, focusing on just the technical aspects of the data mesh and leaving data governance policies out of the MVP would be a mistake, as would be treating them offhandedly. We touched on this topic in this section's introduction. We have seen data mesh projects losing momentum because the data governance team was composed of people not capable of making policy-level decisions. Their influence on the organization was simply too limited to turn an MVP success into a company-wide commitment.

On the other hand, if you invite senior management to participate, you shouldn't expect them to spend their time deciding minor details. Make sure that the meeting agenda focuses on problems requiring policy-level solutions. Setting this expectation will enable the worthwhile engagement of senior nontechnical staff.

TIP Pick your battles wisely! The role of the MVP governance team is not to create a parallel universe but to shape business processes in a way that ensures the company is moving toward its goals. Trying to fill the gaps in the existing governance structure will create less friction than fighting the inertia of existing solutions.

In your discussion with the Messflix data governance team, you decide on an overarching policy that the data introduced to the data mesh will be FAIR. The data governance team agrees with all FAIR principles, as defined by Mark D. Wilkinson et al. in "The FAIR Guiding Principles for Scientific Data Management and Stewardship" (www.nature.com/articles/sdata201618). However, for your MVP, the two following principles are selected as non-negotiables:

- *Findability*—The requirement for (meta)data to be assigned a globally unique and persistent identifier and to be registered and indexed in a searchable resource
- *Accessibility*—The requirement for (meta)data to be retrievable by its identifier, using a standardized communications protocol and the protocol to allow for an authentication and authorization procedure, where necessary

Ultimately, the first policies adopted in your organization will be your data governance team's decision and will depend on their value statements.

3.3.3 *Federating data governance*

We shouldn't forget that data governance in a data mesh will be federated. Chapter 6 presents a list of critical elements that may be considered when deciding on the governance authority and split of responsibilities. In *federated governance*, some decisions are made at the central government level, while others are left at the discretion of autonomous local governing bodies.

As usual, there is no silver-bullet solution. However, depending on your situation, some decisions can be made centrally or locally, depending on your organization's needs.

At Messflix, you have created the data governance team operating at the central level, defined the value statement, and specified policies to be respected by data product owners. The technicalities of policy implementation will depend on data product owners, whom you'll appoint only after selecting datasets to be turned into data products.

3.4 *Developing minimal data products*

With your Messflix implementation teams selected and the data governance team's decision on governance principles, it is high time for you to start work on data products. To do that, you need to do the following:

1. Identify candidate datasets.
2. Appoint data product owners.

3   Ensure that data products adhere to your data governance policy:
  – Prepare data product searchable descriptions.
  – Expose the data in a controlled manner.

This section walks through each of these steps and identifies techniques for effective execution.

3.4.1   Identifying domain-oriented datasets

At the MVP stage, to select datasets to be exposed in the form of data products, you should identify data already fulfilling or close to fulfilling the minimal data product requirements. The heuristics for the selection of a suitable dataset can be based on the following criteria:

- It's focused on a single domain.
- It's richly described with metadata.
- It has clearly defined access ports.

To improve the business impact of data product candidate selection, you can add more criteria. For example, you may decide to focus on adding value to your MVP by selecting, for example, systems regularly exposing the data for use by other systems or datasets underutilized in the business because of findability/access concerns.

> **DEFINITION**   A *domain* in domain-driven design, which is conceptually closely related to a data mesh, is defined simply as an area of interest. For now, think of domains as cohesive business areas. For example, the domain may be sales, accounting, or procurement.

As Messflix chief architect, you started with selecting the teams to cooperate. You assumed you want to proceed with the Yellow and Green teams responsible for the Messflix Streaming Platform and Subscriptions 2.0 systems, respectively. This approach significantly reduces the number of systems and datasets to select as your data product candidates.

Suppose while implementing the data mesh in your organization, your choices are overly limited in terms of initially identified teams and datasets. In that case, you may need to pause and get a more detailed map of all datasets available for a bigger picture, and rebalance the benefits and tradeoffs of each team-dataset combination.

You will need such a map at some point, but at this stage, when time is of the essence, you may as well start with datasets generated by your selected teams. If they fulfill the requirements, you will save time by not analyzing all the others. Datasets selected for your MVP should allow decentralization of ownership and transformation into data products in an assumed time frame, not necessarily production-ready. With that assumed, let's focus on defining *domain-oriented dataset.*

The full details of the process leading to the design of domain-oriented data products are described in chapter 4. This section presents a simplified method for discovering the datasets consistent with the domain(s) you selected as a training ground.

KEY POINT A *domain-oriented dataset* is not a domain-containing dataset! Throughout this book, we emphasize the role of data products in exposing business domain data. However, it is worth noting that your data product does not have to cover the whole domain. It just should not span over multiple domains. Especially at the MVP stage, you want to start small.

Let's see how cohesive the systems are that are operated by the teams you want to work with.

The Yellow team's responsibility is the Messflix Streaming Platform, serving the purpose of distributing content generated by Messflix. First, let's see how the content distribution business process aligns with the Messflix Streaming Platform datasets.

To quickly analyze a business process, try to depict it using big blocks representing input, output, and actions leading to another. Next, try to add the data generated at each step. Finally, note the systems used to capture the data (figure 3.6).

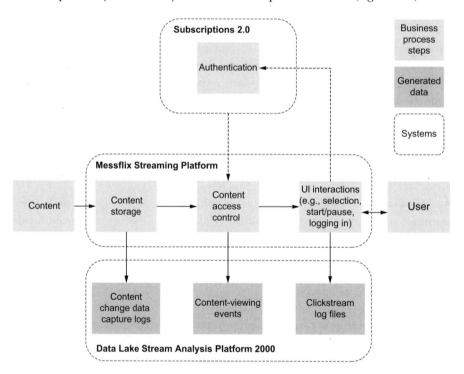

Figure 3.6   Quick process map developed for Messflix content distribution

The Messflix Streaming Platform data, even though it's generated in the context of the content distribution process, is transferred to Data Lake Stream Analysis Platform 2000, managed by the Data team, which claims it belongs to their analytical processes.

Subscriptions 2.0 is a relatively small system focused on simple functionality, so you decide to draw its container diagram rather than a business process. Figure 3.7 depicts the result.

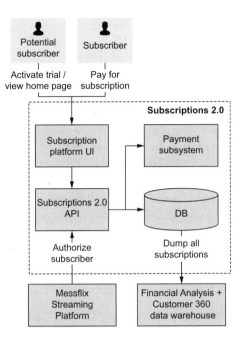

Figure 3.7 The Subscriptions 2.0 system architecture diagram depicts the building blocks of the system (inside the dashed rectangle), actors using the system (top), and other systems interacting with Subscriptions 2.0 (below the dashed rectangle).

All the logs are sent to the Financial + Customer 360 Analysis data warehouse, also managed by the Data team.

Now, consider the data captured by systems in your company. Is it, or could it be, used in any other domain? In conjunction with other data? If so, where does this other data come from? What is the business process generating it?

Identification of domain-oriented datasets is often an iterative process. Think of walking through a graph of business processes, trying to identify the edge between nodes of business processes composed of linked data. A piece of practical advice: if circumstances allow, try to stay clear of sensitive data at this stage. Security takes time.

ADDING BUSINESS BENEFIT TO THE MIX

You need to decide the purpose of the data mesh you developed, who will use it, and what added value it will offer them. At the core of the data mesh is its ability to connect otherwise distributed data products.

Which of your stakeholders put the most emphasis on connecting previously separate data? What are the goals that the stakeholder wants to achieve? The following presents two exemplary goals that are possible to achieve with the connected data products:

- *Integrated analysis*—For integrated efficiency monitoring, reporting, or R&D activities
- *Development of new data products*—Through generating feature vectors for ML, offering processed views of cross-domain data, or modeling cross-domain processes

TIP The data mesh is not just an IT solution. Work with the business! You will save a lot of time and effort if you ask for help from people actively engaged in the business side of the analyzed processes. The functioning of each data product requires close cooperation between IT and business anyway, so why not invite them to the party early? They may know who from other business areas pops up now and then asking questions about their data.

Let's look at the utilization of data generated by systems that you want to work within Messflix. At first glance, both Messflix Streaming Platform and Subscriptions 2.0 data are dealt with well enough. That data is dumped on the lap of the Data team, which knows best what to do with it, right?

Maybe. Full utilization of data potential requires close collaboration among data engineering, data science, and business teams. If a data team creates an environment allowing such partnership, then . . . maybe.

Unfortunately, Messflix doesn't have such luck. The lack of an interface allowing simultaneous access to data from the Data Lake Stream Analysis Platform 2000 and Financial Analysis + Customer 360 data warehouse should be considered a huge red flag.

Let's quickly go through an example of what a business benefit search can look like. The area that often struggles with access to well-defined data is ML. The area that is usually hungry for ML is customer support.

A quick discussion with Customer Support staff reveals that Messflix is half-blind in its churn control, relying purely on customers' average lifetime. Churn, given the continuous interaction with the customer, is relatively straightforward to predict. Messflix Streaming Platform clickstream data and content-viewing history offer plenty of information.

As an ML enthusiast, you also realize that the feature vector used for prediction should be enhanced with the customer purchase history generated by Subscriptions 2.0. After consideration, you decide that the Green team will be tasked with developing a data product exposing required purchase history data from the Subscriptions 2.0 system. However, to satisfy MVP requirements, you decide to limit Yellow team involvement to developing a data product exposing content interaction history from Messflix Streaming Platform. These two data products are also used to feed analytical systems managed by the Data team. The Yellow and Green teams accept this proposition enthusiastically because managing the direct connection with ever-changing analytical systems takes a considerable amount of time.

3.4.2 *Choosing data product owners*

When you selected purchase history and clickstream logs as two candidate datasets, you needed a data product owner for each of them to turn them into data products. Fortunately, both the Yellow team lead and Green team lead accepted the proposition of extending their responsibility range.

Now, why did you ask them? To prove the approach's feasibility, you need to connect two separate dots of data products. If the two systems fitting the bill have the same product owner, it would be advisable to reconsider the selection. The data mesh is all about interoperability, not the ability of a single individual.

The data product owner may or may not be the product owner of the underlying system; however, at the MVP level, *less is more*, so we advise asking current system product owners, who will join your implementation team, to take on additional responsibilities resulting from adding the *data* prefix to their current role description.

However, think it through and make that decision consciously. Depending on other factors, sometimes it's better to choose someone else. For example, if the current product owner is generally busy and delegates most of their work to a local product owner, then, as you've already guessed, the latter person is a better choice. Any subject matter experts or analysts are also a good fit here. The critical factor is smooth cooperation between the product owner and the data product owner.

From now on, the data product owner's responsibilities will include the following:

- Adhering to policies decided by the data governance team
- Envisioning the final form of the data product (e.g., metadata documentation, data models, access ports)
- Closely cooperating with the business to ensure the completeness and clarity of collected data
- Identifying and understanding the needs of the data product users and how to answer them with the domain's data

Now that everything is prepared, we'll start creating your first data products. Because they are minimalistic, as this section's title suggests, we'll focus on two primary aspects. First, describe your data products so they can be found and understood by clients. Second, expose your data products' datasets in a read-optimized way.

3.4.3 Deciding on the minimum viable data product description

You have selected systems that will form the first Messflix data products and have chosen a data product owner for each of them. However, to satisfy the policy of making your data products FAIR, you need to pay close attention to metadata related the data product description.

Each data product, like any other product, needs to be packaged in a way that will allow users actually to use it. This means adding the *self-described feature* to your product, as mentioned in chapter 1.

Take a moment to consider how you learn about products you buy every day, like groceries, electronics, and home appliances. Hopefully, they are packaged in a way that tells you everything you need to know in order to use them. Usually, the package itself presents the product and its primary use. The package also lists its unique features and benefits for you. Last, it mentions who produced it, what it is called, and its key parameters (e.g., power, maximum weight, precision, or color). Usually, any limitations are mentioned, too, like age restriction or maximum capacity. Furthermore, you'll usually find a user manual inside that further explains the product: how exactly to use it, how it is constructed, how to recycle it, and if there are any cautions when using it. You get the idea.

We need to replicate that experience with your data product. Again we'll take some shortcuts here. Take a look at table 3.3 with a sample description of a data product exposing the purchase history dataset.

Table 3.3   Example of data product metadata

Key	Value
Unique identifier	2eb399fd6453172c8b22422e51f59f55
Data product name	Purchase History DP
Project URL	https://messflix.com/DPs/purchaseHistory
Terms of use	(Free text)
Keywords/tags	Purchase, subscription, user
Data product owner	John Smith
Data product owner contact	john.smith@messflix.com
Responsible technical team	Green team
Technical support contact person	john.doe@messflix.com
Business unit	Sales
Data product business description	Customer purchase history
Security management	Access grantor, access policy update
Conceptual model	Link to conceptual model describing relationships with other data products
Data model	A detailed description of every field, including logical explanations, enabling searchable descriptions (its completeness and accuracy are critical to fulfilling FAIR requirements!)
Users of data product	TBD
Status	Experimental
Storage type	CSV

Looking closer at the table, you'll discover that it tries to answer three main questions. The FAIR principles require answering two of them, and one relates to business value:

- *What is the data product?* We explain what data is inside, its origin, related business cases, structure, etc. (In table 3.3, e.g., keywords/tags, data product business description, conceptual model, data model, users of data product.)

- *How do we access the data product?* We provide technical guidance on getting access to the raw data, credentials, URLs, technologies, etc. (In table 3.3, e.g., project URL, storage type.)
- *How does the data product fit into your organization?* Who's responsible for it, how can you contact them, where within the organization is it located, how do you get tech support, etc. (In table 3.3, e.g., business unit, data product owner, data product owner contact, technical support contact person.)

Reuse as much as possible from the project's existing documentation. This might be the case for logical and physical data models. The data products' models may differ, but if you have selected the project for your MVP, the differences may be negligible or nonexistent. Reusing the documentation material is key to proving that the data mesh implementation does not require rebuilding a company's IT infrastructure from the ground up.

Gathering all that information in one place, maybe in the form of a table, is the simplest way of educating your clients about your data product. So feel free to use that template (appendix A) and fill it with your data products' information. We tried to include the fields we believe could be helpful for a data product description in a broad spectrum of businesses, but it's only a template. Feel free to add any other information you think is necessary from your business point of view. Remember, the end goal is to make your clients understand the data product you will serve.

For Messflix purposes, to make the description suitable for automated governance needs, you need to ask data product owners to transform this description into JavaScript Object Notation (JSON) format. Then, they can use it to register their data product in the central platform.

Data product owners also take on the responsibility of aligning their data products' data models and metadata vocabulary. Ensuring data interoperability and reusability is one of the policies they are required to adhere to, but the choice of tools is left to their discretion. Nevertheless, they decide to use one or another type of doc-automation to minimize maintenance overhead and reduce errors.

3.4.4 *Developing the simplest tools to expose your data*

As you learned earlier, the purchase history data from the Subscriptions 2.0 system and the clickstream history data from Messflix Streaming Platform are sent directly to their respective analytical systems. Unfortunately, the development of the full-blown systems for exposing the data exceeds the timeline of your MVP project, so you decide to utilize the simplest possible versioned storage system you have at your disposal: the Git repository of the company. You use the Git repository as a place where the data in CSV format will be stored for use by interested parties.

Section 3.5 explains the selection of Git in a bit more detail. We show there that it offers mechanisms allowing it to serve as a provisional central platform.

When preparing your first data products, consider the following criteria:

- From the users' perspective, what is the most common way they consume the data in bulk? A data warehouse or data lake? A relative or maybe a document database? Perhaps just plain old files?
- With what technologies are your teams proficient? Are they experts in writing web applications or microservices and exposing data as RESTful APIs? Or maybe stream processing is their thing, like Apache Spark, Flink, or Kafka Streams? How about ETL pipelines in Apache Camel, NiFi, or Kafka?
- Is it possible to offload hosting and upkeep? Certainly, in your company, tools and platforms are bundled with support. But right now, you are aiming to deliver value quickly and not building infrastructure or devising backup strategies.

Naturally, you'd like to please the users first. However, remember that you are under time pressure here. Hence it's paramount to identify solutions within the technical proficiency of teams involved in your project development. For example, if you already have an operational data warehouse in your domain, there's no reason to reinvent the wheel. At this stage, the rule of the thumb is to introduce as few changes as possible.

The significant differentiation is that the data product focuses on the external users' consumption perspective, not the source system logic. This means that you are not expected to give users access to the internal storage of your source system. Instead, you need to develop a table (or a set of them) in a read-optimized form (e.g., denormalized if needed, utilizing column encoding and compression, catching aggregate tables, lowering isolation level, etc.) that is easily consumed in bulk.

> **TIP** We encourage you not to lose time overengineering and overthinking your MVP early on. Keep things simple and grounded in the team's experience and in-house services. In the grand scheme of things, the final solution might be as basic as a series of ETL scripts in a repository being periodically executed, and dumping the results into your standard storage system. Just make sure your solution is automatic and repeatable. The MVP, at its core, most likely will not go into production. All the elements are likely to be replaced. It's also in the spirit of data mesh—think about exposing *data*, not underlying technologies.

With the first data products developed, we're ready to talk about connecting them into an actual data mesh in the next section.

3.5   *Setting up the minimal platform*

The self-serve infrastructure as a platform as an element of the data mesh will help your teams with various data-related tasks, including standardization and lineage, quality metrics, and monitoring logging and alerting. It's impossible to get all these tasks done within the scope of an MVP project, so focus on elements crucial for your business.

At Messflix, you decide to start with Git as a solution that will store CSV files containing purchase history and content interaction history generated by Subscriptions 2.0 and Messflix Streaming Platform. The solution you design is depicted in figure 3.8.

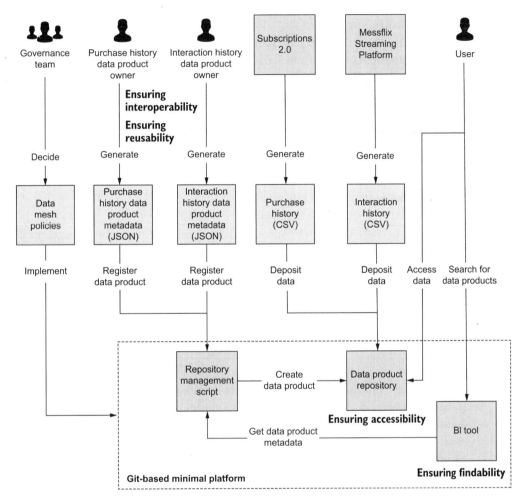

Figure 3.8   Messflix minimal platform setup

Let's see if we can make your minimal platform connect your data products, allowing automated policy enforcement.

3.5.1   *Ensuring platform-forced governability*

The property we need to consider is the ability to implement automated enforcement of policies and rules imposed on the data mesh by the Messflix data governance team. Platform properties like flexibility, resilience, and automation are not less important;

however, you decide that they require much more work than you can spare during MVP development.

The general policy is to adhere to FAIR data standards. However, to ensure implementation feasibility, the MVP is supposed to provide just a subset of them, as described in section 3.3.2.

Using the Messflix Git repository offers an excellent opportunity to fulfill data mesh requirements with a minimal workload to prepare the solution.

Whenever the Yellow or Green team leads, as data product owners, want to add or modify their data products, they first have to submit a JSON-formatted data product description. Then, the resource management script developed and maintained by the Yellow team automatically validates all fields required by the governing policy. Then, if the requirements are met, the script creates the data product repository.

Findability of the data stored in data products can be achieved by deploying a simple BI tool, storing the provided metadata in a Structured Query Language (SQL) table, and making it searchable by users.

This way, your platform ensures the accessibility and findability of data products. For example, there are ways to automatically check that two submitted datasets do not contain columns with identical data, supporting automation of enforcing interoperability and reusability. Still, their deployment is yet again beyond the MVP scope.

3.5.2 *Ensuring platform security*

At Messflix, your situation is relatively simple. Git ensures accessibility to the files to anyone with the necessary access rights. If you decide to use other solutions, don't forget that ensuring system security and data product access control is an essential property of the data mesh.

This step optimally should be planned and executed in coordination with the cybersecurity team. If you took our earlier advice and avoided working with the most sensitive data, your data products should not be under too much scrutiny. We don't want to say you should take security lightly. Just propose a reasonably straightforward solution, allowing quick evaluation.

The exact structure and granularity of access control could be modeled on the basis of the following:

- The nature of the data offered in your data products (e.g., open, internal, confidential, sensitive, PII related)
- The ways the data is planned to be used, or can be used for misuse, for modeling and anomaly detection

Your access control will test privileged access management features:

- *Who is accessing data*—Based on the role defined in a corporate directory.
- *How they will identify themselves*—Following the rule of the thumb regarding maximizing the reusability of existing solutions, utilizing authentication solutions implemented in your company will be the preferred way.

- *What they are allowed to do with data*—For maximum security, the system should follow the principle of least privilege (unless otherwise specified, a role will be assigned the least amount of access possible to a system).
- *Where they are accessing the data from if forced to work with sensitive data*—For example, you may want to change permissions depending on IP addresses allowed to access a given data product or limit virtual private network (VPN) users to read-only access.
- *When they access data*—You can set up yet another maximum security setting, limiting suspicious connections, or simplify control of temporary staff access, for example.
- *Why they access data*—To reduce the effects of stolen credentials or phishing attacks, you may limit the allowed actions of users based on their role.

Depending on the previous list, and the technology you'll use to store your data products, you may restrict access to data at five granularity levels:

- *Data product*
- *Dataset* (table, file, etc.)
- *Attribute* (columns, file types, etc.)
- *Record* (row, files, created in a given time frame)
- *Value* (the crossover of attribute and record)

The task of ensuring platform security may seem daunting, but remember: there are solutions to take the burden of the work from your shoulders. Involve your security team early in the MVP design phase and, hopefully, you'll have a massive part of this work done for you.

Summary

- Preparing for data mesh MVP development starts with mapping existing systems and stakeholders. Connect your MVP with a business case.
- Selecting proper implementation teams, both for software development and data governance, is extremely important. Think about what operational and cooperation models will ensure effective collaboration.
- Implement all or a subsct of data mesh elements required to achieve the business goal. The critical factor is ensuring the decentralization of responsibility for data.
- Ensure that your governance structure covers all critical elements from the beginning. The selection of strategic elements like value statements or policies to be designed by the governance body will depend on the business case.
- A data mesh MVP, like a fully blown data mesh, is *not* just a technical exercise. It's the development of a socio-technological solution.

Part 2

The four principles in practice

The second part of the book will provide you with the tools to tackle the four principles of the data mesh for advancing your data mesh beyond the first month. In the chapters of this part, we will deep dive into one of four principles.

We will start with the Domain Ownership principle; we will provide you with practical methods of defining domains and business capabilities, and assigning ownership of data.

Next, we show you how to change your perspective from "data as a by-product" to "data as a product." You will learn how to define and describe data products to make them findable, accessible, interoperable, and reusable.

We will follow with the practicalities of implementing the Federated Computational Governance principle. You will learn the benefits and disadvantages of centralized and decentralized governance models, and how to find a balance between them, well-fitted to your organization.

We will finish with the Self-serve Data Platform principle, the technology enabling the data mesh. We also will provide you with the implementation details of "platform thinking."

Domain ownership 4

This chapter covers

- Designing domain-oriented data products
- Defining domain and understanding how it can be decomposed
- Establishing data product boundaries
- Defining ownership of data products

This chapter focuses on the data mesh's domain ownership principle. *Domain ownership* is about decentralizing responsibility for data and shifting it to business domains. This shift is a stark contrast to the popular model of centralizing data responsibility within the central data team.

What does *decentralizing responsibility* mean for an individual development team? If you take a team that builds a software component allowing users to register, this component creates data—user data. In the old world, a data team would probably query the developer team's database to get the user data for creating user registration dashboards. This is *data as a by-product.* If the responsibility is with the developer team, however, the data team should ask the developers to provide the data in a way that is suitable for the task, and the team owning the data should expose it in the expected way.

The logic behind decentralization is that the people closest to a business area know the most about its generated data and are best suited for tasks related to that business area. You might ask how being closest to the business area is helpful when it comes to data.

Imagine you are a data engineer in the central data team responsible for the Central Statistics Office in your country (or perhaps the US Census Bureau). You are asked to prepare statistics about fire incidents in office buildings. (Last time you were dealing with fire was three years ago at your grandma's house; she has a fireplace.) It seems a simple task: you collect the number of all fire alarms, you calculate the average number for a city, and voilà, you're finished.

However, the number is much higher than in previous years. As a result, the government heavily increased its spending on the fire department. This increase was funded by raising local taxes.

But the truth is, the number of fires has *not* increased. The initial calculation was wrong because of someone's ignorance. If the person responsible knew anything about fire departments, they would know that each office building must perform obligatory fire drills every month and must test alarm systems bimonthly. All of that activity is logged as an alarm activation, but tagged with a different code than that used for a fire. If we could treat fire departments as a separate domain with their own Fire Incidents data product, this situation would probably not happen, because the people responsible for that domain would deeply understand its data.

To learn how to apply decentralization in a domain-oriented way, we will consider how business activities influence the design and ownership of data products. But how does this whole chapter fit into the bigger picture?

The goal of this chapter is to find possible boundaries of data products. This is a recurring, never-ending process. From the time you decide to go in a data mesh direction, you will have to constantly revisit boundaries of already existing data products and look for boundaries of those that you plan to create in the future.

In chapter 2, we showed you a simplified data mesh development cycle:

1 Choose the business case to enable with data.
2 Define data products needed (find the boundaries of data products required to solve that problem and choose owners).
3 Develop the data based on consumer needs and the discovered boundaries, and then treat the data as a product.
4 Improve or extend the platform based on the needs of the data product development team.
5 Establish or revisit governance policies that will enable further improvement of the mesh.
6 Measure whether you are going in the right direction and repeat the whole cycle.

This chapter focuses on step 2 of this process. We will define data product boundaries and then apply ownership.

In chapter 3, we described a simplified way of finding data product boundaries, using the simple business processes and datasets involved. In this chapter, we will give you more tools for your toolbox so that you can find boundaries that better reflect the business and that will be easier to maintain by development teams. Although this chapter provides improvements, the high-level process of building a data mesh generally stays the same as described in chapter 3.

We start the process of finding boundaries by explaining how to understand, capture, and visualize our domain and define *domain* and *domain-driven design*. We will use the domain storytelling technique (section 4.1).

Following that, we will teach you how to decompose your domain by using business capability modeling. We also will explain how those techniques will help you find the boundaries of data products. With the boundaries discovered, we will show you how to use domain decomposition to implement team ownership. We will supplement the learning process of these practical skills with the introduction of the subdomain, business capability, and data domain concepts (section 4.2).

Next, we will show you an alternative way of finding data product boundaries, using data use cases. In the end, you will be able to apply team ownership to data products (section 4.3).

After that, we will explore the concept of heuristics and how to use it to find even more possible boundaries of data products. We will show you multiple heuristics. After reading this chapter, you will know how to apply them in practice (section 4.4).

Finally, we will take a step back to look at the data mesh from the perspective of multiple interconnected domain-oriented data products (section 4.5).

All those steps form a process, illustrated in figure 4.1.

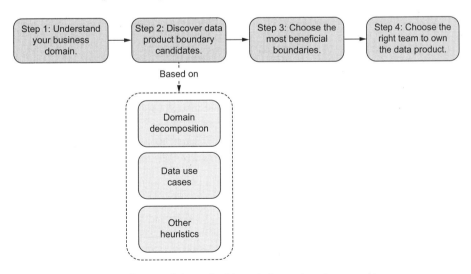

Figure 4.1   Process to discover data product boundaries and apply ownership

You can apply that whenever you need to discover boundaries of data products:

1   Understand and capture your business domain.
2   Find candidates for data product boundaries based on the following:
    a   Business domains and datasets originated in these domains
    b   Data use cases
    c   Other relevant heuristics
3   Compare boundaries discovered using previous methods and choose the most beneficial.
4   Choose the right team to own the data product.

All of these steps can be done using workshop techniques, such as workshops facilitated by a data mesh champion, architect, tech lead, or internal or external facilitator. In fact, anyone who understands this process and has experience with facilitation can lead it. In our example, it will be facilitated by the Messflix chief architect.

After reading this chapter, you will be able to do the following:

- Capture and analyze your domain
- Decompose your domain into autonomous subdomains
- Assign datasets to each domain
- Define data product boundaries using domain decomposition
- Define data use cases
- Assign datasets to defined use cases
- Define data product boundaries using data use cases
- Define data product boundaries using design heuristics
- Apply ownership of data to the right team

The first step to applying domain ownership is to understand your domain. Let's get to it.

4.1   *Capturing and analyzing domains*

This section will teach you what the domain is and how to capture, visualize, and analyze it. This process is a foundation of the domain-ownership principle. The following sections will help you find possible boundaries of data products and distribute their ownership in a domain-oriented way.

The result of this section will be a visualization and common understanding of your business domain that you will use to do the following:

- Decompose the whole domain based on the visualization and captured knowledge into smaller subdomains. Datasets that are originated from these subdomains will be possible boundaries of your data products (section 4.2).
- Based on the visualization, you will be able to look for data use cases in your company and describe them properly. These data use cases will serve as possible boundaries of your data products (section 4.3).

After the enormous success of your data mesh MVP, the Messflix CEO has asked you to solve problems with data ownership. The problem is that the Data team owns all the data, and that team has quickly become a bottleneck.

To understand the root causes of this problem, you talk to business experts and technical leaders. Unfortunately, you quickly find out that you can't understand one another because everyone seems to be speaking different languages. For example, to you, *content* might refer to a blog post used in marketing, but for the subject matter experts, *content* means a movie.

This is your first experience with the entertainment industry, and you don't know how it works. Because you don't understand the domain, you don't know where data belongs. From your perspective, content belongs to the marketing domain, but in this case it might belong to production or distribution.

Because you know it is impossible to propose a solution without understanding the problem and its context, you decide to capture and analyze your business domains. The steps you take are quite simple:

1 Invite the right people.
2 Choose the right tool to discover the domain.
3 Facilitate a workshop session and capture the domain.

4.1.1 Domain-driven design 101

This section presents a deep dive into domain-driven design (DDD) and its core concept: the domain. The principle of domain ownership is about shifting responsibility for data toward those closest to its point of origin. This shift can be implemented only through decentralization.

> **DEFINITION** The Cambridge Dictionary defines *domain* as "an area of interest or an area over which a person has control." In DDD, the domain is the area of interest. It could be a business as a whole or just a part of the business (e.g., a content streaming domain, content production domain, pharmaceutical domain, or private banking domain).

Decentralization is one of the cornerstones of the data mesh. The most effective and scalable way to achieve decentralization is to base it on domains. The concept of the domain in a data mesh is based on DDD. When you better understand DDD, it will be easier to apply these concepts in the data field.

DDD is a software design approach that emphasizes common models and language between business and development teams.

At Messflix, the business people call a paying customer a *subscriber*. Therefore, following DDD principles, the Yellow team developing Messflix Streaming Platform uses the word *subscriber* in its internal conversations, requirements, documentation, and code (e.g., class names).

Achieving a shared understanding of a business, its rules, and policies is at the heart of the DDD approach. Eric Evans's *Domain-Driven Design: Tackling Complexity in the Heart of Software* (Addison-Wesley) introduced that approach in 2003. DDD revolutionized software development. It promoted the idea that we need to understand the problem space to create and model a solution effectively. So it makes sense, right?

DDD as a methodology can be divided into two types of patterns:

- *Tactical patterns*—Design patterns for object-oriented programming
- *Strategic patterns*—Patterns focused on domains, dividing responsibility and ownership, and communication (between systems and people responsible for those systems)

From the perspective of the data mesh, strategic patterns are more relevant, because the goal is to design ownership, responsibilities, and communication. Let's learn how we can utilize DDD domain concepts in practice.

4.1.2 *Invite the right people*

You now know what the domain is. You also know that one of DDD's goals is to set up a common language. But who should you find to discover that language?

During your MVP exercise, you performed stakeholder mapping. However, the scope is much more expansive this time, as is the group of people you need to communicate with. The people who can help you form a complete picture of the domain can be divided into two groups:

- People who can provide you with a business understanding of each domain:
  - Subject-matter experts/business experts
  - Experienced specialists with a broad view of many processes in the company
  - Product owners
  - Business analysts
  - Heads of departments
  - Business or enterprise architects
  - Data analysts or scientists
- Technical leaders who need to understand the problem to propose a solution:
  - Software architects
  - Domain architects
  - Principal or senior engineers
  - Team leaders
  - Chief or lead architects
  - Technical C-level executives

Depending on the company size, domain discovery may require iterative approximation by organizing multiple meetings of various sets of business and technical experts. Some of these people and their teams might own or consume data products you will define in upcoming sessions. Others might be responsible for determining ownership and boundaries of data products. It is not necessary to cover the domain of your whole organization from the beginning; you can start small with just one department or unit. In fact, starting small and then building on that first success is a recommended approach.

Getting the right people in a single room (physical or virtual) and dropping on their laps the question "What is your domain?" or "What is your business area about?" is usually counterproductive. People don't know what you don't know. They will try to avoid stating the obvious (to them), or might get bored and impatient, not seeing how they can benefit from what they'll perceive as going in circles. This is why we advise using workshop techniques to facilitate that discussion.

4.1.3   Choose the correct workshop technique

Multiple techniques can be used to capture business knowledge, but we highly recommend the method that arose inside the DDD community: *domain storytelling*. This method can be handy because it was designed with domain thinking in mind. It can provide well-established heuristics for extracting domains and subdomains. Moreover, this technique is lightweight and well described in easily accessible open source materials. Also, the method is inclusive, meaning that participants are actively collaborating during sessions.

Other domain-capturing techniques

We also recommend two other domain-capturing techniques: rich pictures and event storming. *Event storming*, invented by Alberto Brandolini, is one of the most well-known facilitation techniques in the DDD community. You can use it as a replacement for domain storytelling. Event storming can help you achieve a common understanding of the domain you are responsible for and data use cases that you should solve or help with.

This method works best in a face-to-face environment because of its inherently dynamic nature. Its power comes from discussions of spontaneously forming subgroups. Unfortunately, simulating such group dynamics in a virtual meeting is difficult. If you want to learn more, *Introducing EventStorming* (by Brandolini) is the right book for you; at the time of writing, the book is a draft available on Leanpub.

The *rich pictures* technique, developed as part of Peter Checkland's soft systems methodology (SSM), is straightforward and isn't focused on any formal notation. Instead, this technique is a way to discover, define, or capture an idea in the form of diagrams. The outcome of this exercise is an initial mental model. This model can depict various things: a process, the operation of an organization, a system, or a problem. This method uses simple drawings, sketches, words, mind maps, cartoons, and many other illustration options.

Because of its simple nature, the rich pictures technique can work in any kind of environment: remote or in person. It is a great tool to complement other exercises. It can be run before domain storytelling or event storming, as an introduction to explain the scope and share a common understanding of the business area that you are focusing on. You could use this exercise as an alternative to event storming or domain storytelling. However, you need to be aware that it would probably lead to a shallower understanding of the domain compared to the other two.

Let's look at domain storytelling in a little more detail. We do not delve into this technique's mechanics or facilitation methods here, because other books cover these topics. We recommend *Visual Collaboration Tools* by João Rosa and Kenny Baas-Schwegler et al. (available as a draft on Leanpub) and *Domain Storytelling* by Stefan Hofer and Henning Schwentner (Addison-Wesley, 2021).

DOMAIN STORYTELLING

Say you choose domain storytelling to perform domain discovery for Messflix.

> **TIP** To make a workshop efficient, it is critical to invite the right people and the correct number of them. From our experience, you should not exceed 15 people; otherwise, you will not be able to keep them engaged. When just a few people are engaged and the rest are left out, the energy of the whole group drops. The list of roles mentioned previously is quite long, but you don't have to invite all of them at the same time! For simple domains, you could have a group as small as two or three people.

You ask the participants to tell specific stories from their business perspective, and while they are doing it, you try to visualize those stories.

Figure 4.2 depicts an example process visualization resulting from your efforts. This is how domain storytelling represents Messflix's market research function. This is just a part of the bigger picture, depicting steps 12 through 16. On yellow sticky notes you can see people (actors), and on blue sticky notes you can see objects. In this particular story, the market researcher is sending a final screenplay to independent reviewers to gather their feedback. Then the researcher is sending promotional materials to

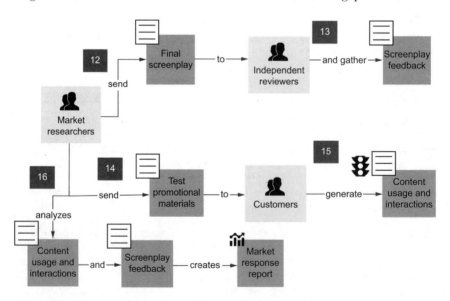

Figure 4.2 Market research captured during a domain storytelling session

customers who are generating data about content usage and interactions. In the end, the market researcher is analyzing this data to prepare a market response report.

The philosophy underlying domain storytelling is that people naturally like to tell stories and that stories can drive our understanding of things, concepts, or processes. Telling stories is natural to humans. Our brains evolved to digest this form of information ever since the first words were uttered by early Homo sapiens, probably some tens of thousands of years ago.

A significant advantage of domain storytelling is how easy it is to understand its results, even for those who didn't participate in the exercise. It is also an excellent base for domain decomposition, because it's easy to identify groups of noninterconnected stickers, which often indicate separate subdomains.

A word of warning, though: make sure not to let the most extroverted members of the team hijack the whole meeting. It's your role to ensure that even the shyest participants have a chance to tell their stories! You may need to moderate discussion, divide the group into a smaller groups, or encourage participants to work individually in silence for some period of time.

At Messflix, you decide to proceed with domain storytelling because it doesn't depend on the physical presence of the participants; it's single-phase. It's also simpler to facilitate than event storming.

Because you find a common language with your peers, you're ready to step up your game and move to ownership decentralization. In the next section, you will learn how to use domain decomposition to find data product boundaries.

4.2 Applying ownership using domain decomposition

In this section, we will use domain decomposition based on business capability modeling to find data product boundaries. Then, based on these boundaries, we will pass the domain ownership to the relevant team. From our perspective, this is an efficient way of getting to decentralization using the domain ownership principle.

At Messflix, following your domain storytelling sessions, it's time for a hearty discussion with your technical leaders about their problems. First, you interview senior engineers, technical leaders, and architects of systems of records and operational systems, producing and capturing data. You ask them about the bottlenecks in the development process, technical risks, concerns, and communication problems with other teams. You note a few main points:

- It is tough to evolve systems. The Data team creates data pipelines directly integrated with the system of record databases or spreadsheets maintained by different teams. Development teams cannot easily change database or spreadsheet schema, which requires weeks of communication with the Data team. For example, to prepare financial reports, the Data team downloads the movie production cost spreadsheets created by the Messflix Production team and stored in the Hitchcock system, maintained by the Orange team.

- Every release requires testing and a sign-off from the system of record and the central data teams.
- System developer teams are overflooded with bugs raised by the Data team (e.g., data pipelines break if someone from the business team makes an error filling out the spreadsheet).

Then you interview the Data team and ask about their collaboration with system of records teams. This is what you hear:

- The Data team members don't understand the data they are responsible for. It's impossible to be an expert in all aspects of various data types: financial, content production, market, etc.
- It is hard to extract meaningful data from other teams' databases or files, because schemas are not self-explanatory. For example, the movie production cost spreadsheet uses unexplained acronyms as column names.
- The work is tedious because of the need to constantly fix broken data pipelines.
- The Data team is asked to prepare analyses on top of the company data. Still, that data is hidden inside the systems, and extracting that data slows new initiatives. Good examples are the scripts and cast datasets hidden in the Hitchcock system. This data could be used to automate the ideation phase of content.

In figure 4.3, you can see Messflix's system landscape. In this chapter, to keep things simple, we will focus on just part of it: Hitchcock Movie Maker and its surroundings. Starting from the top left, Hitchcock Movie Maker is developed by the Orange and White teams. Hitchcock is responsible for producing new content.

Hitchcock is responsible for storing and reviewing scripts/screenplays, visualizations of movie market trends, managing the production of the movie (cast, production costs, etc.). It is connected to the API of an external system called World Movie DB. Moving to the right, we can see that marketing specialists use an external system called Movie Market Monitor to plan advertisements. This system is also used by a market researcher to perform movie market analysis.

In the bottom-center, you can see that Messflix built a big data warehouse, storing all financial data from the production and ERP system, which is used in the form of reports by the CEO to plan future steps of the company. The aforementioned ERP is consuming cost statements that originate in Hitchcock; the ERP system also is used for accounting and human resources purposes.

To apply ownership using domain decomposition, you need to follow these steps:

1 Decompose your domain.
2 List related data to each domain.
3 Pick the correct boundaries of the data product.
4 Choose the team that should own it.

We will look at these steps in detail in subsequent sections. However, before we jump into details of the solution, we need to introduce some crucial concepts taken from DDD and business architecture.

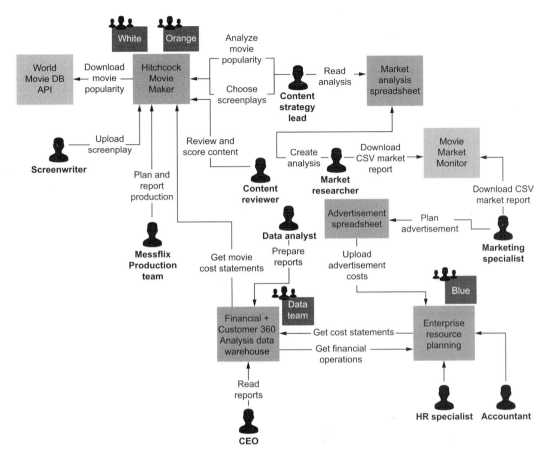

Figure 4.3 In this Messflix system landscape, enhanced with system ownership, we'll focus on Hitchcock Movie Maker and its surroundings.

4.2.1 Domain, subdomain, and business capability

As stated before, the *domain* is an area of interest or an area someone controls. The *subdomain* is a child domain contained within another domain, as illustrated in figure 4.4. In the Messflix example, Execute Production is a subdomain of Produce Content.

Domain and *subdomain*, however, lack precise definitions, which makes them hard to apply. We (the authors) discovered that a much better fit for domain decomposition is the concept of *business capability*, derived from the world of enterprise and business architecture. We believe that domain, subdomain, and business capability can be treated as equivalent concepts, although *business capability* has a more precise definition than *domain* or *subdomain*. We explained the concepts of domain and subdomain first to avoid confusion, because Zhamak Dehghani uses those terms in her data mesh principles.

In figure 4.4, you can see the relationships between domain, subdomain, and business capability. A subdomain is a part of the domain; a domain may contain multiple subdomains. Every subdomain can be further split into more granular subdomains.

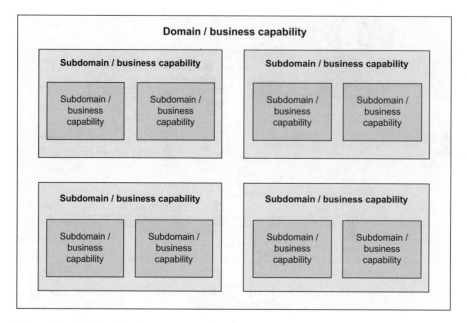

Figure 4.4   Relationships between domain, subdomain, and business capability

Finally, each subdomain can be treated as a domain on its own. In summary, depending on changes in granularity of the view, every domain may become a subdomain, and vice versa. Because we believe business capability is an equivalent concept to domain and subdomain, as you can see in figure 4.4, it can be used interchangeably.

Now that you've seen an abstract diagram of these relationships, let's look at a specific example. Figure 4.5 depicts a Provide Pharmaceutical domain and its subdomains: Discover Drugs, Distribute Drugs, Perform Clinical Trials, and Develop Drugs.

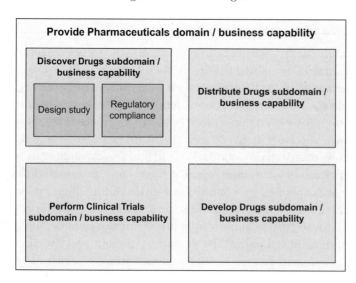

Figure 4.5   Domains and subdomains of a pharmaceutical company

Let's see what makes *business capability* a more precise definition in our context. A *business capability* is what a business can do. It focuses on *what*, not *how* or *who*. It is defined by its *outcome*, which is usually expressed as a qualitative rather than quantitative measure. *What* we are trying to do or achieve in business changes slowly, while *how* we are doing it or *who* will be doing it can change often. This is why *business capability* maps are time resilient.

By focusing on the *outcome,* we give ourselves the freedom to do and change whatever is needed to deliver as much business value as possible. Therefore, we should also focus on the *outcome* (qualitative), not the *output* (quantitative). For example, if we organize a birthday party for children, it doesn't really matter how many cakes, toys, chairs, and tables we prepare (quantitative output). What matters is happy and smiling kids after the party (qualitative outcome); how we achieve that is of secondary concern.

Business capability should be phrased as a verb-noun combination, and this structure will help us focus on the *activity* and its *outcome*. Table 4.1 shows how to phrase business capabilities correctly, as well as common mistakes, such as answering the wrong questions.

Table 4.1   Correct and wrong business capability names

Question	Capability name	Correctness	Explanation
What?	Produce Content	Correct	*Produce Content* tells you about the needs and expectations of the business; it helps you understand what is essential, making this capability autonomous in terms of its implementation.
How?	Film Content with a Digital Camera	Wrong	Answering this question leads to one possible implementation. You are not open to ideas on how to deliver value in a better way; maybe there are better ways to film content than with a digital camera?
Who?	Produce Content Using Cool & Fancy Studio	Wrong	Answering this question leaves only one possible company to deliver value; you cannot optimize the process or the people involved.

It is vital to define the name of a capability *and* its desired outcome (not output). Table 4.2 shows an example.

Table 4.2   Correct and wrong business capability outcomes

Outcome	Correctness	Explanation
Produce good-enough quality movies and series desired by the audience.	Correct	This is a proper outcome. It is a qualitative measure and is focused on the impact that should be made (a series *desired* by the audience).
Produce 100 movies a year.	Wrong	This indicates the output, not the outcome. The fact that we produced 100 movies does not tell us anything about these movies' significance. Maybe nobody will be watching them.

A well-defined business capability can be approximated to a standalone product or service that could be sold or outsourced. Such a decomposition gives us a stable structure composed of autonomous and usually loosely coupled parts. These parts can be optimized separately, with little to no overhead costs of reintegration with the rest of the organization.

Let's look at how it works at Messflix. The Produce Content domain, presented in figure 4.6, can be split as follows:

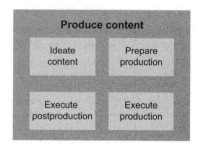

Figure 4.6   Part of the Messflix business capability model

- *Ideate Content subdomain*—The outcome is a list of screenplays that the audience should enjoy.
- *Prepare Production subdomain*—Prepare everything needed to start shooting, including cast, audience, locations, and equipment.
- *Execute Production subdomain*—The outcome is raw shots that are ready for postproduction.
- *Execute Postproduction*—Process the shots, add special effects and the soundtrack; the outcome is audiovisually engaging content.

The business capability model is hierarchical and time resilient (business capabilities usually change only when the business model changes), with autonomous capabilities focused on providing business value. All these properties make business capabilities a perfect base for forming the following:

- The structure of the organization
- The structure of data ownership

4.2.2   *Decompose domains using business capability modeling*

In the previous section, you learned *why* boundaries of business capabilities help design boundaries of data products. However, you still don't know *how* to find boundaries of business capabilities. This section describes the methods and steps to achieve this. These skills are crucial for correctly assigning domain ownership. Because we want to decentralize data ownership based on business domains, we need to decompose our whole business domain to find these domains.

As stated before, we believe that the domain, subdomain, and business capability can be treated as equivalent concepts; *business capability* has a more precise definition than *domain* or *subdomain*. We also think that the best way to decompose a domain and visualize its decomposition is to use the business capability modeling technique. Previously, we showed just a tiny part of the Messflix business; let's see how the big picture looks. In figure 4.7, you can see the Messflix business capability model. (You don't have to become familiar with its details; it is just an example of how this model could look for the whole company.)

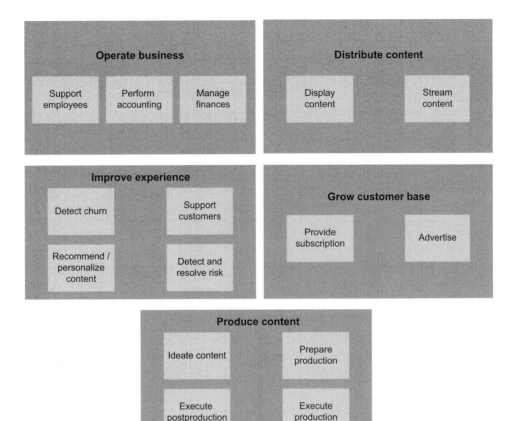

Figure 4.7 Business capability model of Messflix

As you can see, we divided Messflix into five major business capabilities: Operate Business, Distribute Content, Improve Experience, Grow Customer Base, and Produce Content. Each capability is further divided into smaller capabilities; for example, Produce Content is divided into Ideate Content, Prepare Production, Execute Production, and Execute Postproduction.

Business capability modeling is a technique widely used by business architects and enterprise architects. It is an excellent foundation for reorganizing businesses. For example, if you structure your company hierarchy, including IT, based on the business capability model, both will be firmly focused on providing business value. At the same time, you will have defined clear responsibilities for your data domains.

4.2.3 How are domains and business capabilities related to data?

We introduced some concepts from DDD and business architecture, but how are these definitions related to data? You can think of data as a by-product of business-as-usual operations of the domain or business capability, or sometimes as a fuel needed to deliver business capability.

For example, the Ideate Content capability produces a list of ideas for films, with scoring (by-product) and scripts chosen for production (output). This data can be human input (film ideas, scripts) or algorithm/machine output (scoring). You can find this example visualized in figure 4.8. Domains are exchanging data to fulfill business needs. For instance, the Prepare Production domain is consuming scripts chosen for production from the Ideate Content domain.

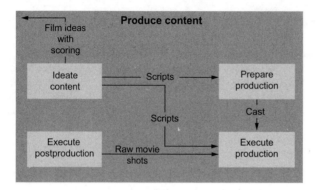

Figure 4.8   The flow of data between business capabilities

What we can learn from figure 4.8 is the premise that all data in our business is either produced or used by business capabilities. Therefore, we can safely assume that every dataset belongs to a business capability, giving this dataset a context of usage and reason for existing. This is why business capability is an excellent blueprint for the boundaries of one or more data products.

DOMAIN, BUSINESS CAPABILITY, DOMAIN DATASET, AND DATA PRODUCTS

Because of the close connection between data and business capabilities, we can think of a capability as a *boundary*, or a home, for the associated data. In this case, a business capability becomes a boundary for one or more domain datasets (a domain-oriented dataset consisting of a cohesive model and having an autonomous business meaning). Domain datasets can be grouped on their cohesiveness and packaged inside the data product. This grouping would result in one or more data products living inside the domain/business capability (figure 4.9).

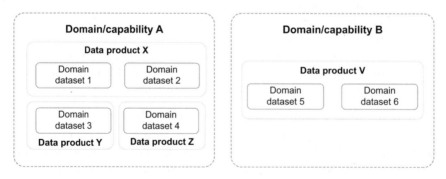

Figure 4.9   Domain/business capability, domain dataset, and data product

As you can see, domain A has three data products inside it: data products X, Y, and Z. A data product can have one domain dataset (data product Y with domain dataset 3) or multiple domain datasets (data product X with domain datasets 1 and 2).

Let's wrap up. To discover data product boundaries by using domain decomposition, you need to take these steps:

1 Find business capabilities.
2 Match data flows between them. We are looking for cohesive datasets with their own business meaning.
3 Identify data product boundaries by checking the origin of domain datasets. If few domain datasets originate from the same source and are coupled and cohesive, they could be grouped into one data product.

APPLICATION TO CASE STUDY

At Messflix, you decide to use the business capability model to discover and define data products. Let's look at how it works for the Produce Content domain.

For each capability, you list all domain datasets' outputs, by-products, or fuel. As a result, you get the map presented in figure 4.10.

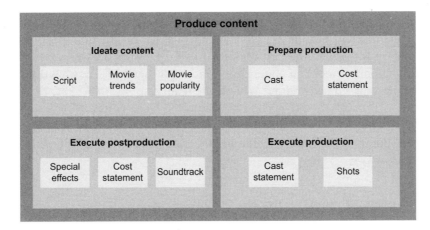

Figure 4.10 The Produce Content business capability with related datasets

TIP Each of the identified domain datasets is a natural candidate for a data product. However, sometimes it makes sense to group multiple domain datasets. Such a grouping becomes much easier if you consider relations between domain datasets in the context of their parent business capabilities. It makes sense to group datasets when they are strongly coupled; for example, expenses, income, and transaction descriptions could be parts of one finance data product.

After brainstorming with relevant business and IT teams, you decide to create five data products for the Produce Content domain, as explained in table 4.3.

Table 4.3   Data products

Data product	Reasoning
Scripts	Autonomous dataset with precise business meaning related to one business capability. One possible usage of such a data product is automatic tagging.
Movie Popularity	Autonomous dataset with precise business meaning related to one business capability. It's separate from movie trends because of different granularity; popularity is about specific movies, and trends are about movie categories.
Movie Trends	Same as movie popularity.
Cast	Separate from the other human resources datasets because of their different nature; e.g., hiring a stuntman is required for each key actor.
Cost Statement	Merged cost statements come from preproduction, production, and postproduction because of their similar nature, attributes, and usage. All of them are related to the higher-level capability of Produce Content.

You decide not to include special effects, soundtrack, and shots because you can't figure out how to use that data outside its in-domain use of movie production/postproduction.

You end up with clear ideas and boundaries for Messflix data products. This creates a foundation for deciding about decentralized ownership. But what does it mean that the team owns a data product? What is the team responsible for?

4.2.4   *Assign responsibilities to the data-product-owning team*

Figure 4.11 shows several responsibilities that the team owning the data product should take care of:

- Data
- Data pipelines, software, and source code
- Quality, cleansing, and deduplication
- Enriching and aggregations
- Domain data model
- Terminology
- Ontology
- Domain knowledge
- Metadata

This chapter covers just the first four items. The rest are covered in other chapters. Let's look more closely at each.

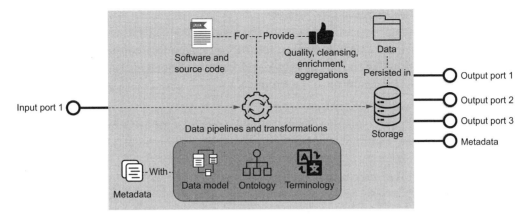

Figure 4.11   Scope of ownership of a data product

DATA

We've decomposed our data landscape into data domains and established their clear ownership. We are responsible for the data that resides in our data domain. But does this mean that pieces of that data enriched or transformed into different model cannot be hosted, served, and owned in other data products? The answer is no; sometimes we need to aggregate data from other data products into a new data product, perhaps because of different business purposes or consumer personas. So, *data duplication is not forbidden.*

To be more precise, the data-owning team is responsible for data persistence (database, documents, files), the way that data is modeled (schema), and how and for whom data is exposed (API, ports, security, privacy). So if there is a requirement to expose the production cost statements (currently stored as a spreadsheet) in the form of a REST API available only for management, the data-owning team should upload that data periodically into the database, expose it through a REST API, and apply authentication and authorization to make it secure. If you are interested in a more technical perspective (for example, how the data might be synchronized between systems and data products), see chapter 9.

DATA PIPELINES, SOFTWARE, AND SOURCE CODE

The massive difference between other approaches and the data mesh is that the team owning the data is also responsible for all of the *code* that created the data and its specific formats. So the team is responsible for the code of data pipelines, transformations, batch and stream processing, and migration scripts.

But source code is not enough to create working software. The team needs to follow DevOps culture and describe and spin up the required infrastructure and software delivery pipelines. The team members need to expose logging, monitoring, and tracking. In a nutshell, the team is responsible for the whole software delivery process, from understanding data the user needs, to code development and deployment, to feedback collection, to fixing production bugs and adding improvements.

QUALITY, CLEANSING, AND DEDUPLICATION

For specific purposes, data needs to meet a certain quality level. In the data mesh paradigm, the owning team is responsible for understanding consumer needs and providing the data that meets quality requirements. The data implementation team is responsible for cleansing and deduplication.

ENRICHING AND AGGREGATIONS

Sometimes users need a more aggregated form of information or information enriched with additional data. Some of these enrichments and aggregations are also in your scope.

Let's look at the production cost statement example. A cost statement could be created weekly. However, suppose there is a requirement to prepare a yearly summary of all costs. In that case, the team owning that data product should create batch processing that periodically calculates all costs for a year and exposes it in the required form.

As you can see, with this approach, more responsibility is moved closer to the data-producing teams. In the following subsection, you'll see how a similar shift in ownership and responsibility works at Messflix.

4.2.5   *Choose the right team to own data*

Now that you've identified domain boundaries, you decide to analyze the Messflix systems architecture and form the teams that should own the newly established data products.

Figure 4.3 represents the broad landscape of Messflix; figure 4.12 provides a more detailed view of one system: Hitchcock Movie Maker. As you can see, the system has a few separate parts:

- *Scripts*—Involves writing and reviewing scripts using a microservice with its own database.
- *The main Hitchcock application*—Involves movie producing and choosing the right movies to be created using a monolithic application with its own database.
- *Cost statements*—Involves tracking spending during production, which is captured in spreadsheets.

There are also two integrations, with the following:

- *World Movie DB API*—An external application with movie popularity data
- *Data warehouse*—An internal Messflix application

Each part is owned by a dedicated team. For example, scripts are handled by the White team, production cost statements are handled by the Orange team, and the data warehouse is managed by the Data team.

In the Produce Content capability, we discover five data products: Scripts, Movie Popularity, Movie Trends, Cost Statement, and Cast. Movie Trends are excluded from your consideration at this point, because they are not part of the Hitchcock system.

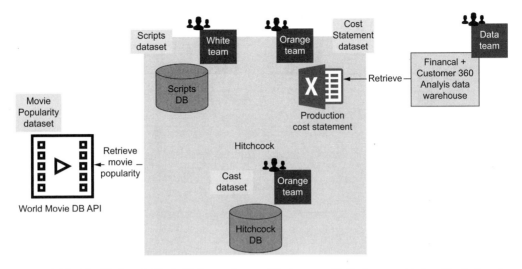

Figure 4.12 The Hitchcock Movie Maker system and its teams, with their ownership (positioning) and datasets

The Cost Statement dataset is an excellent example of strong coupling with the Data team. This dataset is needed in two places: the data warehouse for reporting and analysis purposes, and the ERP system for accounting. Because integration using spreadsheet files is complex and error prone, the Data team is asked to ingest that data into the data warehouse integrated with ERP.

The Orange and White teams don't feel responsible for this integration. The Orange team, which owns the production cost statement, doesn't intervene when the Movie Production team quite often changes the format of the submitted file. This means the pipeline is broken most of the time, costly errors occur in accounting, and financial planning and forecasting often don't correctly take into account the spending of the Movie Production team.

The solution for this problem is to create a data product out of cost statement data and move it to the Orange team, which is already responsible for the Produce Content capability in Hitchcock. The Orange team would be responsible for keeping the schema stable in time and exposing the interface consumable not only by the Data team and data warehouse but also by the Blue team owning the ERP.

As you can see in figure 4.13, inside the scope of the Cost Statement data product, a script is used to transform the spreadsheet into an easily consumable and well-described format and storage for output files.

Movie Popularity is an example of an external dataset that an organization is paying for. Making a data product out of it brings a couple of benefits to the company:

- Optimizing the cost of data consumption (payment for single access)
- Ensuring data accessibility for other departments
- Reducing the number of times the same transformation has been performed on the data

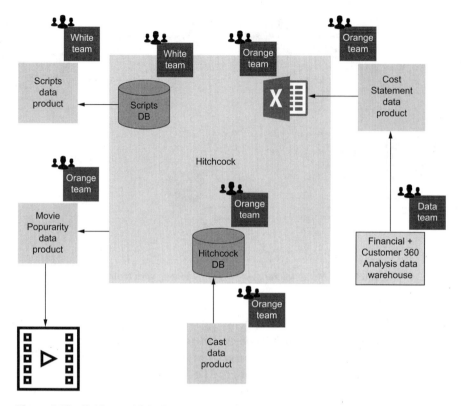

Figure 4.13   Newly established data products in Hitchcock Movie Maker and the teams with the data products' ownership

You choose the Orange team as the owner, because Movie Popularity is used primarily by that team's system. At the same time, you notice the growing responsibilities of the Orange team and make a note to consider moving that responsibility somewhere else. The Orange team, in this case, is responsible for maintaining the connection with the World Movie DB API (a microservice downloading data from the API) and the storage in which the data is cached for future use. (To not pay twice for access to the same data, the legality of this approach is confirmed with the World Movie DB by Messflix lawyers.)

The Cast and Script datasets are good examples of data products created for new business possibilities. These datasets are hidden deep in Hitchcock's monolith database, where we have to access them directly through the database (which is problematic for many reasons). Messflix could start working on the engine to recommend scripts automatically instead of manually by exposing the Cast and Script datasets as a data product.

In the next section, we will use an alternative method to discover boundaries of data products: data use cases.

4.3 Applying ownership using data use cases

This section presents the Messflix data landscape from a different angle. We will focus on analytical and data-heavy use cases to establish boundaries of needed data products.

Even though some data responsibilities have been moved to source systems, the Messflix Data team is still too big. The team members also struggle to establish true collaboration with dashboard owners, data analysts, and data scientists. The model they created in the warehouse was complex and hard to maintain. They want to split it somehow, but don't know how. At the same time, they are responsible for maintaining data pipelines and data processing in the data lake. Domain knowledge needed for these operations is very diverse.

It's hard to decide on priorities when we have just one team with too many goals. Moreover, business stakeholders have ideas on using the already captured datasets to be more competitive, but the Data team can't handle additional responsibilities.

Here are the steps of the solution:

1. Find data use cases.
2. List data related to each use case.
3. Group data use cases into data domains.
4. Choose a team to own each domain.

4.3.1 Data use cases

An excellent way to discover data domains is to analyze the consumers and use cases of the data. Here are some examples of our use cases:

- The data analyst looks at film rankings and popular hashtags to find current trends in the market.
- The market researcher analyzes mentions and interactions with the published content to prepare a market response report.
- Marketing staff members analyze the Financial Analysis + Customer 360 data warehouse to create customer segmentation.

If you look at figure 4.14, such use cases could be derived easily from domain storytelling, but they would be existing data use cases. You need to talk to the business stakeholders to understand their plans for data application.

In the case of Messflix, company leaders are planning to utilize the existing data for automatically recommending scripts for production.

Let's try to write down required use cases in a more descriptive manner. That will help us analyze them later. Business stakeholders, such as CDOs or senior data scientists, usually provide such use cases. Or you may reverse engineer them from domain storytelling or descriptions of currently existing solutions.

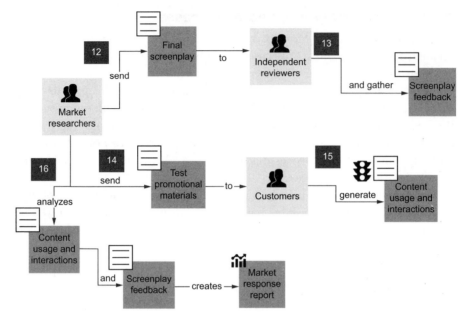

Figure 4.14   Domain storytelling at Messflix

USE CASE DESCRIPTION TEMPLATE

To make the description of a data use case self-explanatory, you need to capture at least the following:

- Who is using data (role)
- How the data is being used (activity)
- What data is involved (datasets)
- The reason for doing something with that data (reason)

To make sure everything is captured, you use a template similar to the one for a user story:

> As a [role]
> I am/want [activity]
> Using [datasets]
> So that [reason]

Here's an example:

> As a *data analyst*
> I am *analyzing current film trends in the market*
> Using *film rankings and popular hashtags datasets*
> So that *I can recommend categories of films that should be produced*

Using such a template helps truly understand a data use case. The business reason behind the use case is apparent in this example: data is used to recommend movie categories for production. As a result, movies of these categories are expected to gather a bigger audience and generate a more significant profit.

You write down a few more Messflix use cases:

1. As a *CEO*

    I want *to analyze financial reports*

    Using *production cost statements, financial data from accounting and subscriptions*

    So that *I can decide if the current company strategy is working*

2. As a *content strategy lead*

    I want *to analyze new scripts and select promising ones, which should be filmed with a proposed cast*

    Using *movie popularity, movie trends, scripts, cast*

    So that *I can produce movies that will gather more audience*

3. As a *content strategy lead*

    I want *to find trends in the movie market*

    Using *movie market reports*

    So that *I can decide what movies should be produced next*

4. As a *marketing specialist*

    I want *to find trends in the movie market*

    Using *movie market reports*

    So that *I can target marketing content better*

Having these use cases, you can try to align their boundaries with the boundaries of data products. For the analyzed use cases, you define four data products:

- Financial Analysis/Reporting data product
- Script Recommendations data product
- Content-Producing Movie Trends data product
- Marketing Movie Trends data product

You define possible data products in your domain. However, by looking at the associated datasets, you can see that data comes from multiple sources, and some overlap exists too! What should you do about the ownership in such a case?

To answer this question, we must first look at two more concepts from DDD: model and bounded context.

4.3.2   *Model and bounded context*

Domains, subdomains, and *business capabilities* are terms used to describe the business. At the same time, they form a good blueprint for system boundaries, data, and teams. They describe the *problem space*. However, it is not enough to define a problem; we also need to identify a solution!

Model and *bounded context* in DDD come from the solution space. We create the *model* to solve the problem. These two terms are essential to a data mesh. Data use cases (analytical use cases) are usually different from the software use cases, so we need to design other models for these purposes.

A *model* is a simplification and abstraction of a fragment of reality. Models are always created for a specific purpose and to solve a particular problem. For example, a floor plan is a model of a part of the building. It is created to arrange a floor, place internal doors, and partition walls, but it should not be used to calculate the building's structural strength! These are the boundaries of its usage; such boundaries are called in DDD the *bounded context*.

Figure 4.15 shows the relation between *model, bounded context,* and *domain.* The floor-plan model, and the building construction model, are separated by boundaries of their bounded contexts: floor-planning bounded context and design-building bounded context. Both contexts are located in different domains: the Plan Floor domain and Design Building domain.

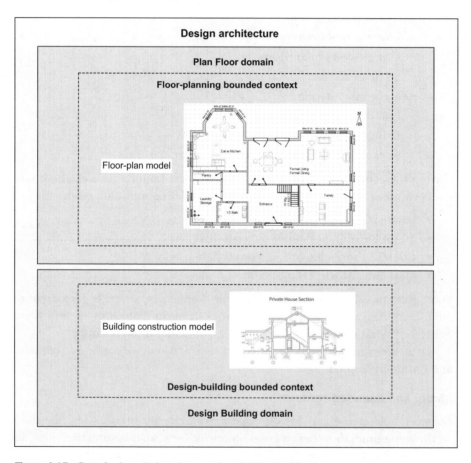

Figure 4.15   Domain, bounded context, and model (dashed box)

In the DDD approach, we base our software solution on a domain model emerging through analysis of business and its needs. The *model* can have multiple representations, such as application source code, documentation, graphical (e.g., Unified Modeling Language, or UML, diagrams), dictionary, tests, and data model.

In a data mesh, we can treat a data product as a bounded context. Finding the proper boundaries is always a decision between a more generic, reusable model and a specific, single-purpose one. It is always a balance. Having DDD in mind, we should prefer a specific model over a generic one. But in some cases, it makes sense to use and maintain one model for two different domains with similar underlying datasets. You can decide when a more generic model does not lead to ambiguity or loss of meaning of the data.

With that knowledge, we can revisit the boundaries of use-case-driven data products.

4.3.3 Set up boundaries of use-case-driven data products

In this section, we will think about the models needed to fulfill data use case needs. We will see if this concept somehow influences the boundaries of data products, and we will consider the responsibilities of teams owning them. In section 4.3.1, we defined the following data products:

- Financial Analysis/Reporting data product
- Script Recommendations data product
- Content-Producing Movie Trends data product
- Marketing Movie Trends data product

The Financial Analysis/Reporting and Script Recommendations data products remain unchanged, but we decide to merge two other data products into one Movie Trends data product. The reasoning behind that change is described next.

FINANCIAL ANALYSIS/REPORTING DATA PRODUCT

The Financial Analysis/Reporting data product will be an aggregation of data coming from multiple sources: production cost statements, financial data from accounting, and subscriptions. However, it won't be a simple data cloning.

For example, if you want to run financial analysis across the enterprise, you need to design a model fit for that purpose. In a relevant data product scope, there would be code responsible for transformations, aggregations, and storage. The team owning this product would not own sources, such as the production cost statement. It would just use the data coming from that source.

SCRIPT RECOMMENDATIONS DATA PRODUCT

The Script Recommendations data product will support the decision-making. Its outcome should be a stream of recommendations. It makes these recommendations based on the ML model. But ML needs data to be preprepared and transformed into a specific model. So the team responsible for this data product will take the movie popularity, movie trends, scripts, and cast data, and create a code and pipelines responsible for the transformations and aggregations needed to prepare the input for the ML model.

This team will also not be responsible for data sources, such as movie popularity or movie trends. These datasets should be provided by other teams, preferably as data products. This ensures that the data is available in an easily consumable form and expected quality.

MOVIE TRENDS DATA PRODUCT

Section 4.3.1 presented an idea to create two data products: a Content-Producing Movie Trends data product and a Marketing Movie Trends data product. However, the underlying models are so similar that it makes sense to generalize and harmonize them, enabling the development of just one: a Movie Trends data product. In addition, this is a cost-effective approach.

The team owning this data product will consume data from the external system: Movie Market Monitor. This team will then be responsible for this data download, storage, transformation into movie reports, and ensuring access via the API.

4.3.4   *Choose the right team to own data*

The method of finding data product boundaries does not change the way you should assign the ownership of the resulting data products. Again, the data product should be owned by the team closest to the data. This time, it will be a team implementing the use cases (preferably end to end).

For the Financial Analysis/Reporting data product, ownership lies with a team owning and supporting financial BI tools used by the CEO.

The Script Recommendations data product should be managed by a dev team writing and releasing the ML algorithm recommending scripts.

Finally, the Movie Trends data product should be maintained by a team already familiar with the movie market domain. Possibly, that could be the team owning the script recommender.

The domain decomposition approach and data use cases are the most practical, but at the same time, these are just two possible heuristics that can be applied. The following section explains what a heuristic is, other possible heuristics to be used, and how you can apply them if these two approaches do not meet your requirements.

4.4   *Applying ownership using design heuristics*

This section uses a more systematic approach to choosing proper ownership: heuristics. This chapter summarizes a variety of possible ways to apply domain ownership to decentralization. As you will see, not all of these heuristics are exactly domain oriented, but for the sake of comprehensiveness, we introduce all of them.

At Messflix, you've applied domain decomposition and data use cases, and yet, after all the work is done, you still have some datasets not assigned to any data products. The central data team is one that still owns some unrelated datasets.

How do we find proper owners of this data? Follow these steps for a solution:

1 Create many options using design heuristics.
2 Establish tradeoffs, and weigh pros and cons.
3 Select the best options.

4.4.1 What is a heuristic?

A *heuristic*, as defined by the Oxford English Dictionary, is "a method of solving problems by finding practical ways of dealing with them, learning from past experience."

This is a technique of choosing a solution based on past experiences. It gives you some options on how to solve a problem; although the results are not guaranteed to be optimal, they should be good enough in most cases. It is an iterative way of working, involving trial and error.

If you want an example of a heuristic approach, think of rules of thumb. You apply them whenever it makes sense. The two-pizza rule is an excellent example of a heuristic: you should not organize a meeting for a group too large to be fed with two pizzas. It sounds reasonable, but there are clear exceptions, like a company town hall meeting.

The most simple heuristic in our case is to create a data product for every domain dataset identified in our domain.

4.4.2 Using design heuristics

You can think about heuristics as different lenses through which you can look at the same problem. When you switch lenses, you will see the problem from a different perspective and discover alternative solutions. After applying other heuristics, you will end up with different designs and generate many options. Based on these options, you can make a comparison, look for pros and cons, combine some of them to make them even more beneficial, and, in the end, hopefully make a genuinely conscious decision.

4.4.3 Designing heuristics and possible boundaries

This subsection presents the heuristics we believe are the most useful for this book's purposes. The list is not complete, and we hope that you and your community will find more interesting and beneficial ones. With every heuristic, we are trying to show you how it could be used.

ALIGN DATA PRODUCTS WITH DOMAINS/BUSINESS CAPABILITIES
This is the most important heuristic. It should be your default solution. As we showed you in sections 4.1 and 4.2, domain or business capability boundaries are very natural boundaries for one or more data products.

ALIGN DATA PRODUCTS WITH POSSIBLE USAGE OR USE CASES
As we described in section 4.3, the other most widely applicable boundary is the group of related use cases. The best way to group use cases is to collate them by their purposes and business value. Data serving this group of use cases is a good candidate for data domain and data product boundaries.

ALIGN DATA PRODUCTS WITH PERSONAS OF CONSUMERS

Another heuristic related to the previous one is to group use cases based on the persona/actor/consumer performing the analysis or for whom those analyses are done.

The Movie Trends data product is an excellent example of how this heuristic can be applied. We established that we have two consumers: a marketing specialist and a content strategy lead. If we use this heuristic, we could create a Content-Producing Movie Trends data product and a Marketing Movie Trends data product. This setup has one advantage over a single Movie Trends data product: there is no risk of model ambiguity, where one entity means different things in marketing and movie production contexts. When we have two different consumers, the model could become too complex and hard to maintain. Although choosing heuristics usually requires a tradeoff, we choose between consistency and cost-efficiency (a single data product should be cheaper to maintain).

ALIGN DATA PRODUCTS WITH THE SOURCE SYSTEM

In most cases, source systems are owned by teams that know the most about the data they produce. This is why it makes sense to create one or more data products derived from the data coming from each system and give the ownership for these data products to the team governing the source system.

The Hitchcock system is an example of the application of this heuristic. Two teams are involved in this system development. The White team is responsible for the script service, and the Orange team is responsible for the Hitchcock main application. We align the Scripts data product with the script service and the team that owns it. We do the same thing with the Cast data product, as you can see in figure 4.13.

ALIGN DATA PRODUCTS WITH THE CONSUMING DASHBOARD/VISUALIZATION/BI TOOL

Quite often, dashboards and visualizations are designed with a specific business purpose in mind. Therefore, it is possible that data served on dashboards can be formed into data products. Let's have a look at the example in figure 4.16.

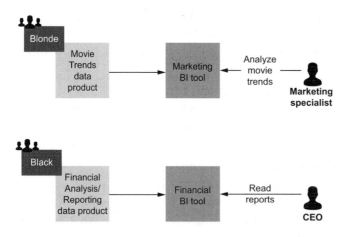

Figure 4.16 Movie Trends and Financial Analysis/Reporting data products with corresponding BI tools

We can align the Movie Trends data product with the marketing BI tool, and the Financial Analysis/Reporting data product with the financial BI tool. This heuristic applies if the BI tool, dashboard, or visualization serves a single purpose or similar purposes. However, you need to be careful not to align data products with a tool used by tens of actors with tens of various goals in mind. Otherwise, you may end up with a canonical model in a centralized data warehouse, losing all the advantages of the data mesh.

BUILD THE DATA PRODUCT AS A REGISTRY FOR A CORE BUSINESS ENTITY

Another way to define a data domain is to look at core physical entities used by various levels of your business. An example of such a data domain could be Customer 360, which describes the physical entity of each customer.

However, you need to be highly cautious when defining boundaries by using this heuristic. It often leads to centralized data warehouse solutions. In the case of Messflix, we could think about tracking the subscriber or customer life cycle in such a data domain. Such a domain could also be responsible for taking care of global identity and deduplicating two entities with the same identity. So you should consider it: if identification, deduplication, or consistency across the organization are crucial concerns, you could consider this heuristic. In other cases, it's probably not the best approach.

CREATE A DATA PRODUCT FOR A COHESIVE GROUP OF DOMAIN DATASETS

Domain datasets stored in a data product should form a cohesive model. Therefore, whenever you notice that some datasets in the data product are not related, it is a sign that you should think about dividing the data product into smaller pieces.

A good example is a data product that stores aggregated financial data and, at the same time, customer 360–type of data. In such cases, we can't refer to a specific customer in aggregated financial data, and there is no shared business goal. Therefore, we should avoid such a situation.

At the same time, we should also avoid creating data products for just a part of the domain dataset. Domain datasets, by our definition, are the most granular datasets that still have a business value of their own. Dividing data products further would force us to integrate multiple data sources, even for the most straightforward use cases.

Imagine you create two data products: Subscriber Details and Home Address. In the Home Address data product, you store country, state, street, and home number. However, you cannot use the Home Address data product on its own. It has no value without knowledge about subscriber details. In this case, we should have a single data product, keeping both datasets.

This heuristic implies that the smallest viable data product is the size of the domain dataset. This could often be a good default solution, but you need to consider its feasibility. For example, managing thousands of data products might be more complex and less effective than doing the same for hundreds of them.

AVOID DATA PRODUCTS WITH A CANONICAL MODEL OF THE WHOLE ENTERPRISE

The canonical model of the entire enterprise usually leads to losing the context of the stored information and architecture of the centralized data warehouse responsible for storing that canonical model. This design is the reverse of a data mesh architecture that is meant to be decentralized.

ALIGN WITH USAGE CONTRACT

Datasets in a data product should be shared under the same usage contract. Because a data product will be an autonomous component in most cases, it will be much easier to enforce contracts and authorization on the data product level.

An example of such a contract is personal data under the European's Union GDP. We should separate the Subscriber data product (which stores such data). Otherwise, any less regulated data combined would be hidden behind stringent security and privacy rules.

ALIGN WITH ORGANIZATIONAL BOUNDARIES

In big corporations, we need to think about teams and systems, as well as the company hierarchy and departments. Crossing organizational boundaries is often impossible because of budgeting, for example. In this case, we may be forced to split our data products between organizational or geographical parts of our company.

Let's imagine that Messflix is a massive company, with branches in many countries and regions. Messflix has set up subsidiary companies in some of these regions to comply with local tax regulations. It would make sense to have separate Financial Analysis/Reporting data products for every branch, and probably an additional one, reading data from all the regional ones, for the global headquarters.

With this example, we completed a variety of techniques that you can use to define boundaries and ownership in a domain-oriented way. In the next section, we will take a step back to see a broader perspective and the landscape of data products that we just designed.

4.5   *Final landscape: The mesh of interconnected data products*

In this section, we want to show you how we imagine the result of applying previous heuristics and principles. We will look at the broader domain from a high-level view.

4.5.1   *Messflix data mesh*

In this chapter, you learned multiple ways of dividing our landscape into data products. Of course, you already know that these numerous options always have various tradeoffs. Depending on which we choose, we can end up with different types of meshes. Let's take a quick look at figure 4.17, illustrating the system landscape before the changes for comparison.

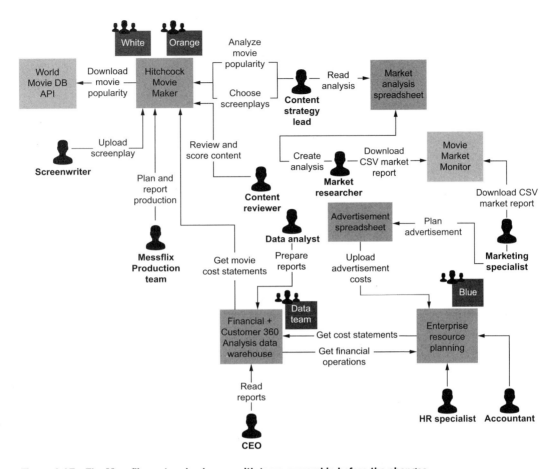

Figure 4.17 The Messflix system landscape with team ownership before the changes

Now let's compare that diagram with figure 4.18, illustrating a possible landscape of Messflix data products.

Before the changes, Messflix was struggling with tight coupling between systems owned by system of records teams, the Data team, and teams developing dashboards. Any change introduced to any system was problematic, because tight connections between systems created an overhead cost to adapt all upstream systems. Systems had to evolve together, slowing them all to a standstill. In addition, the Data team workload created a bottleneck affecting the whole organization.

As you can see in figure 4.18, you divide the responsibilities of the Data team among teams that were closest to the data. You enable the reuse of data—for example, the Movie Trends data product used by marketing is reused as an input for scripts recommendation by ML. You release data from silos. The Cast, Movie Popularity, Scripts, and Movie Trends data products enable the creation of the script recommender, enabling new business opportunities. You change chaotically stored production cost statement files into a data product. That simplifies the integration with other systems,

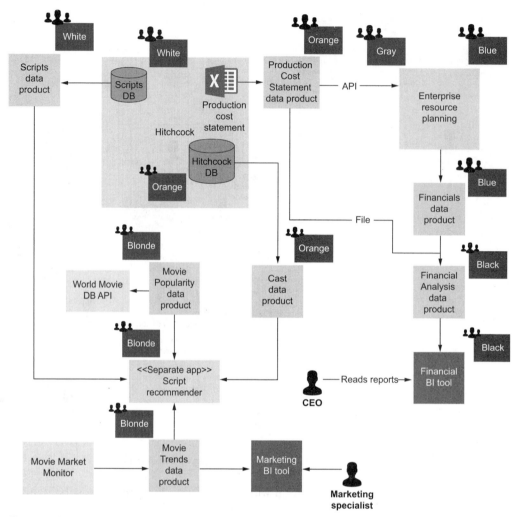

Figure 4.18   Mesh of interconnected Messflix data products

such as the ERP and Financial Analysis data product (formerly the data warehouse). You analyze use cases and notice that customer 360 data unnecessarily squeezes into a Financials data product. There is no actual use for customer 360 data, so you can simply remove it and leave the Financials data product with a single purpose.

These changes simplify integration from a technical perspective and improve team collaboration from a social perspective. The changes make the overall architecture a well-working, optimized, and decentralized socio-technical architecture.

4.5.2   *Data products form a mesh*

As you can see in figure 4.19, data products have input and output ports. In addition, some of the output ports can be consumed by one or more data products or other systems. Therefore, data products derived from other data products are a perfectly viable solution.

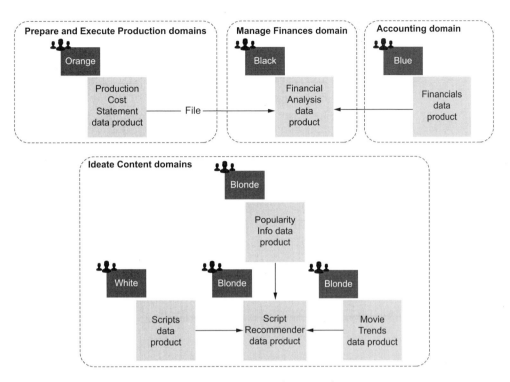

Figure 4.19 Mesh of interconnected data products between domains

Similar to microservices, we can decompose the landscape into smaller pieces: data products. If we orient them around their small subdomains (figure 4.19) and connect their output and input ports, we see that data products form a mesh—a data mesh?

4.5.3 Is it already a data mesh?

We are not there yet. We just applied the first principle: domain ownership. Our data products are still missing product thinking in their design (chapter 5). We need to ensure interoperability and common standards between data products by federated computational data governance (chapter 6). Finally, we need to prepare an underlying platform (chapter 7) for developing and consuming data products.

In chapters 8 and 9, we will tell you how each data product we discovered in this chapter can be implemented and designed. But we already have a frame that will become our domain-oriented foundation.

Summary

- The domain ownership principle is based on domain-driven design.
- DDD is a philosophy that includes domain thinking in every step of the software development cycle.
- *Business capability* is a more precise term for a domain.

- To understand your business domain, use tools like event storming, domain storytelling, or rich pictures.
- Data product boundaries should be designed mainly based on domain decomposition or data use cases.
- You can use business capability modeling to perform domain decomposition.
- You should use heuristics to explore boundary options and find the most optimal split.
- Teams that own a data product not only own data but also its metadata, data model, terminology, ontology, data pipeline, code, and many other things.
- To implement a data mesh efficiently in an organization, we need to design data products and organizational structure (ownership) at the same time.
- We should design team ownership with cognitive load in mind.
- Data products should be interconnected through ports and form a mesh: a data mesh.

Data as a product

This chapter covers

- Applying design thinking to validate legitimacy of the data product candidate
- Selecting the person responsible for its development
- Forming the team that will develop it
- Defining the interfaces of the data product
- Designing the building blocks of the data product
- Complementing the data mesh with data contracts and sharing agreements

In the previous chapter, when discussing the domain ownership principle, we presented sample data products for the business capability Produce Content. We used the term *data product* without specifying what it is and how to create it. It's time to look at what it means to treat data as a product.

Often when thinking about data, we focus on technical aspects such as schema or data relationships. However, we need to remember that other related elements, such as schema description, domain description, definition of access rules, metrics, and quality checks are equally important. Often these individual elements are handled by separate, dedicated, specialized data teams. It turns out that, in reality, these nonfunctional aspects of data do not form an easily managed coherent whole with the data itself.

On the other hand, there are many datasets in organizations that would be valuable to have available in an easy-to-use form. Unfortunately, they are often difficult to access—for example, on a private drive, undescribed, and usually unprepared for consumption (not cleaned or standardized).

Therefore, it makes sense to introduce the concept of thinking about *data as a product*: a well-defined unit tailored to user needs.

In the previous chapter, using the business capability modeling technique, we identified data product candidates from the Produce Content domain. Is what we have done so far enough to say that these will be the final data products? Not yet, because in the data mesh approach, we want to treat data as a product, so we need to make sure that the datasets have the following characteristics:

- Have business value
- Can be easily found
- Are accessible
- Are able to work together
- Can be used in various contexts

We need to make sure that a given dataset is worth making a product, because this activity comes at a price. Moreover, proper analysis allows us to prioritize the work on data products. For this purpose, we will use a technique that has been used for many years in software development: product thinking.

5.1   *Applying product thinking*

Product thinking is a problem-solving technique focused primarily on defining a problem a user wants to solve before we go on to create the product. The goal of this technique is to minimize the gap between user needs and the offered solution. Its two main principles are the following:

- *Love the problem, not the solution*—Before starting to design specific aspects of a product, understand deeply who the users are and the problem you are trying to solve.
- *Think in products, not features*—It is tempting to focus on adding new features and tailoring specific assets. It is important to think about data in terms of a product satisfying user needs. Just exposing existing data is not enough.

The final product should be the result of the process between the users and their needs, the team that solves the problem, and the technology that is the means to solve the problem. Therefore, before you start exposing a dataset, in the spirit of product thinking, ask yourself and your users these questions:

- What is the problem that you want to solve?
- Who will use your product?
- Why are you doing this? What is the vision behind it?
- What is your strategy? How will you do it?
- What are the goals?
- Which features should be included?

Of course, depending on the context and complexity of the data product, the scope of analysis and answers to these questions will vary.

5.1.1 Product thinking analysis

Let's apply product thinking to the data product candidates from the previous chapter: Cost Statement, Scripts, Movie Popularity, Movie Trends, and Cast.

COST STATEMENT DATA PRODUCT

Sometimes the simplest cases are the hardest to define. Many times files in an organization would be worth exposing for wider use.

In the first example, we consider a file with the cost breakdown of a given production run by Messflix. Because no comprehensive solution for this purpose has been implemented so far, the production costs are collected, calculated in an Excel file, and later manually copied and imported into the Financial + Customer 360 Analysis data warehouse. Then some of this data is imported to the ERP system. Figure 5.1 outlines the current situation.

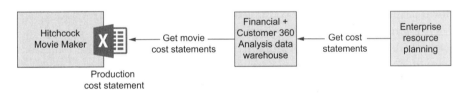

Figure 5.1 Cost Statement data usage before turning into a data product

Let's ask some questions in the spirit of product thinking, as shown in table 5.1. Keep in mind that in this case the dataset already exists, and we are not creating a data product entirely from scratch.

Table 5.1 Cost Statement product thinking analysis

Question	
What is the problem that you want to solve?	Currently, the production cost statement data is used for direct billing between the production team and Messflix finance team. The data file also has costs assigned to categories. This information could be used for more complex analysis and cost comparisons across categories on different productions. Therefore, it makes sense to make this data more widely available for complex analysis.

Table 5.1   Cost Statement product thinking analysis *(continued)*

Question	
Who will use your product?	The data analyst will use it to manually analyze and compile production costs and forecast budgets for new productions.
	The data product developer (data engineer) will use it to import data into the analytical solution.
Why are you doing this? What is the vision behind it?	We will create a dedicated and customized solution to analyze the data for production costs and planning activities. Data engineers can use the original files to import historical data.
How will you do it?	All files need to have exactly the same format. If not, the file should be adjusted to the standardized format.
	It is a good idea to create a simple validator for this purpose, and to make sure that the data formats used are in accordance with the accepted rules of governance (e.g., date format or recording cost in a given currency).
What are the goals?	This data, in the form of a data product, should be available by the end of the quarter so that the first cost summary from the various productions can be done automatically.
Which features should be or should not be included?	Data should be exposed as preprocessed data available through files on the shared drive, and the REST API should be used for integrations with other systems.

SCRIPTS DATA PRODUCT

Movie scripts data is part of the Hitchcock ecosystem and currently a form of microservice used through the UI. However, this data is not shared outside the system, so it cannot be easily used for purposes other than those envisioned by the Hitchcock system. Currently, the process of selecting scripts for production is entirely manual, requiring the intensive work of a specialist. This data could be used to create automated recommendations in combination with information about casts, trends, and popularity of film productions. Table 5.2 shows the product thinking analysis for this data product.

Table 5.2   Scripts product thinking analysis

Question	
What is the problem that you want to solve?	Currently, the process of selecting scripts for production is entirely manual, requiring intensive work. Human preparation can introduce errors, which may cause incorrect script recommendations.
Who will use your product?	The data product developer (data engineer) will use the data in the script recommender application.
	The content strategy lead will generate automated input for production decisions based on the script recommender.
Why are you doing this? What is the vision behind it?	The ultimate vision involving several data products is to create a script recommender system that will automatically pull information from several sources, analyze the data, and make recommendations in the form of a ranking of scripts recommended for production.

Table 5.2 Scripts product thinking analysis *(continued)*

Question	
How will you do it?	As the functionalities concerning scripts are currently implemented in the form of a microservice, creating a dedicated data product should not be difficult, because the relevant data is already domain separated and has its own owner and development team. All that needs to be done is to expose the scripts as a data product to the outside world.
What are the goals?	The creation of this data product is relatively simple, so its release should take place within two months.
Which features should be or should not be included?	Initially, a single REST API port will be provided with all the information about the scripts (e.g., type, number of characters, estimated length, feature film, series, etc.) in addition to the script itself.

MOVIE POPULARITY DATA PRODUCT

At Messflix, data about the popularity of movies is fetched from the paid World Movie DB via a custom-made UI in Hitchcock and used to decide which productions to make. The data is available through the UI in a form that allows only manual use. Similar to scripts, movie popularity data could be used to automate the recommendation process. Table 5.3 is the product thinking analysis for this data product.

Table 5.3 Movie Popularity product thinking analysis

Question	
What is the problem that you want to solve?	Replacing the manual, error-prone process of selecting scripts for production with automated recommendations (analogous to the Scripts data product).
Who will use your product?	Data product developer (data engineer), to use data in the script recommender. The content strategy lead will generate automated input for production decisions based on the script recommender.
Why are you doing this? What is the vision behind it?	Development of a script recommender to automate the selection of scripts for production (like the Scripts data product).
How will you do it?	Currently, data from the World Movie DB is retrieved ad hoc by using the REST API. As we automate the process, this form of access will not be efficient. A solution will be created to download data weekly and store it as files optimized for analytics.
What are the goals?	The development of this data product will be challenging because of the change in approach to data processing, so the release time has been set for the end of next quarter.
Which features should be or should not be included?	The data will be available through the file port and will mainly include production rankings for the week.

The set of questions presented can help us validate the data product's value. As a next step, it is worth making a more detailed analysis of the data product, and this is where the data product canvas tool can be used. It will be useful for looking at the more technical aspects of designing a data product, such as identifying the data sources, the specific data that goes into the product, and the type of data product. This information helps you better understand the nature of the data product and will be helpful when making technical decisions about the final solution.

We recommend using a data product canvas as a supplementary tool to product thinking analysis. We will apply it to the last two data products: Movie Trends and Cast.

5.1.2   Data product canvas

The *data product canvas* is a tool that allows you to structure your data product analysis. It has the form of a visual table with individual sections on various aspects such as name, description, data product owner, and output ports. Because of its visual form, it enables collaborative work in a workshop format. We will use this tool to analyze the next data products.

CAST DATA PRODUCT CANVAS

Information for the Cast data product is shown in figure 5.2.

Name	Description	
Cast	Contains information about actors and roles they play in the specific movie	
Data Product Owner	**Business Capability/ Domain /Bounded Context**	**System**
John Doe	Produce Content	Hitchcock Movie Maker
Classification (source aligned/consumer aligned/shared core)	**Classification (virtual/materialized)**	**Life-Cycle Classification (experimental/stable)**
Source aligned	Virtual	Stable
Input Interface	**Output Ports**	**Security**
Cast relational DB	REST API	Public
Inbound Flow	**Outbound Flow**	**Volume**
Actors Movie roles	Actors Movie roles	10 GB
Datasets		
Actors Movie roles		

Figure 5.2   The Cast data product canvas

As you can see from the example, the data product canvas contains the following sections:

- *Name*—Data product name.
- *Description*—Data product description.
- *Data product owner*—Information about the data product owner.
- *Business capability/domain/bounded context*—The area to which the data product belongs.
- *System*—The name of the system or systems to which the data product is related.
- *Classification*—The nature of the exposed data.
  - *Source aligned*—Data exposed directly from the source system.
  - *Consumer aligned*—Data transformed for meeting consumer needs, often from more than one source.
  - *Shared core*—Data used by many data products and/or consumers.
  - *Virtual*—Data offered to users and computed in the moment of usage.
  - *Materialized*—Data first persisted in a final form and exposed to users.
- *Lifecycle classification*—The stage of the data product maturity.
  - *Experimental*—The data product is under development.
  - *Stable*—The data product is ready to use in production.
- *Input interface*—An interface specifying the data needed from other sources. Its realization uses other systems or datasets to ingest the data.
- *Output ports*—The form in which the data is exposed to consumers.
- *Security*—Security rules applied to the data product's usage.
- *Inbound flow*—Which dataset comes into the data product.
- *Outbound flow*—Which datasets come out of the data product.
- *Volume*—Estimated size of data offered by the data product.
- *Datasets*—Datasets constituting the data product.

MOVIE TRENDS DATA PRODUCT CANVAS

Information for the Movie Trends data product is shown in figure 5.3.

Name	Description	
Movie Trends	Contains information about historical interest in specific movies and ready-to-use analysis of its trends	
Data Product Owner	Business Capability/ Domain /Bounded Context	System
James Spolsky	Produce Content	Movie Market Monitor
Classification (source aligned/consumer aligned/shared core)	Classification (virtual/materialized)	Life-Cycle Classification (experimental/stable)
Source aligned	Materialized	Stable
Input Interface	Output Ports	Security
Movie Market Monitor REST API	REST API CSV files	Public
Inbound Flow	Outbound Flow	Volume
Movie trends	Movie trends	500 GB
Datasets		
Movie trends		

Figure 5.3   The movie trends data product

This product thinking analysis results in the data mesh ecosystem related to the Produce Content business capability shown in figure 5.4.

Having performed the analysis with the help of product thinking and a data product canvas, we define five data products. Three are based on Hitchcock Movie Maker data: Production Cost Statement, Scripts, and Cast. Movie Popularity is based on the Worlds Movie DB API, and Movie Trends is based on Movie Market Monitor.

Each product is used by different systems. The script recommender uses Scripts, Cast, Movie Popularity, and Movie Trends to generate automatic recommendations for scripts worth submitting to production. Movie Trends is used by the marketing BI tool to make decisions related to investments in movie promotion and by the content recommender to generate subject suggestions for upcoming movies. The cost statement is used for financial analysis by the financial analysis system and by ERP to keep track of costs incurred.

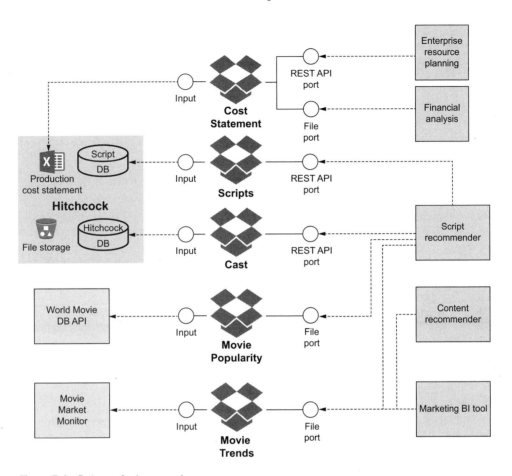

Figure 5.4 Data products ecosystem

5.2 *What is a data product?*

We have used the term *data product* many times so far but haven't provided its definition. Referring to the generic meaning of a product in general, "an effect of a conscious action," it is relatively easy to determine what is *not* a data product. Data that was created as a side effect of another activity is not a data product. If an employee created an Excel file that is freely available, it is not a data product, for the following reasons:

- It was not created with the intention of creating a data product, i.e., no conscious effort was made to prepare it to be a data product.
- It does not address clearly defined user needs.

5.2.1 *Data product definition*

We define *data product* as follows:

> *A data product is an autonomous, read-optimized, standardized data unit containing at least one dataset (domain dataset), created for satisfying user needs.*

Figure 5.5 depicts this idea. In the figure, we see that a data product is an autonomous entity that makes its data available through output ports, from which it can be used by other transaction systems, data products, or end users.

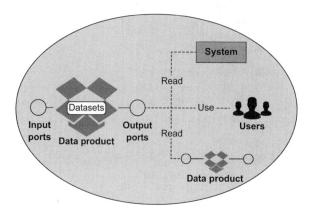

Figure 5.5   Data product
and its context

NOTE   It is also worth noting, to avoid confusion, that the term *data product* already exists in the data world in a different sense (outside the data mesh context). In this case, *data product* is defined as "an application or tool that uses data to help businesses improve their decisions and processes." According to this definition, data products are all the tools that facilitate data processing, especially statistical analysis of data.

Let's look at data products in the Produce Content domain to explain what this definition means in practice:

- *Autonomous data unit*—Every data product is a self-contained system or dataset that can be treated as an independent unit. For example, Movie Popularity is a separate component built in the form of a data lake. It independently retrieves data from an external API, processes it, stores it, and makes it available to its consumers. It can be developed without affecting other Messflix systems and data, as shown in figure 5.6.

- *Read-optimized data unit*—The form of data storage is optimized for analytical functions. In the case of the Movie Popularity data product, the data is stored in the form of files containing the ranking of movies generated every week. Using data engineering tools (e.g., Python language libraries), performing more complex analysis will be easy.

- *Standardized data unit*—The data product must be prepared in the right way, and must be described with metadata, use standardized protocols and ports for data sharing, and use defined vocabularies and an identifier system. You will find more practical examples on this topic later in this chapter.

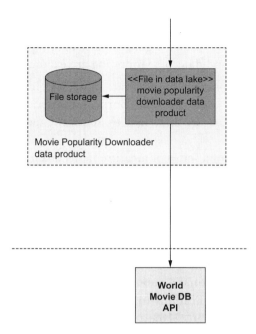

Figure 5.6   The Movie Popularity data product is an autonomous data unit.

- *Node in a data mesh*—The data product naturally becomes part of a larger ecosystem by, among other things, posting the appropriate data catalog metadata and allowing it to be used in a self-serve manner.
- *Containing at least one domain data set*—The product must have a dataset that itself has business value. Movie Popularity contains a dataset of movie rankings from a given week, Scripts contains a dataset of metadata about scripts, and Cost Statement contains a dataset of movie production costs.
- *Satisfying user needs*—The data product was created with product thinking in mind, and it has clearly defined users. In the case of Cost Statement, these are accountants who financially control production costs.

5.2.2   Product, not project

As you already know, the use of the term *product* in a data mesh is not accidental. It is worth contrasting it with the term *project*, commonly used to name various kinds of initiatives carried out in organizations. It is worth emphasizing that the creation of a data product should not be treated as a project. A project is a time-limited activity that is supposed to lead to a specific goal. The project ends and may not be continued.

On the other hand, product thinking makes us look at a data product from a long-term perspective that goes beyond just making it available. This approach also assumes it has further development, adjusting it based on the feedback gathered from users. Product thinking includes the idea of continuous improvement and long-term thinking about quality, as opposed to a one-time project.

5.2.3   *What can be a data product?*

What could be a candidate for a data product? In general, any data representation that has value for users can be a good candidate. The following are examples:

- *Raw unstructured files*—For example, images generated by geological sampling equipment or videos uploaded by users of a video portal. However, to be useful to end users, these files should be accompanied by sufficient metadata that describes them.
- *Simple files*—For example, results of a series of measurements taken on geological samples, Excel reports, or data in CSV format exported from the application. In this case, a description in the form of metadata can also be crucial for further use of the files.
- *A dataset inside a database (or data storage in general)*—Containing a read-optimized representation of data from a source system (system of records).
- *A dataset built based on data retrieved from a COTS-type system (commercial, off the shelf)*—For example, containing information about stock levels.
- *REST API*—Data exposed from applications to read transactional data, optimized for reading, optionally supporting Hypermedia as the Engine of Application State (HATEOAS) to facilitate automated (machine-consumable) data consumption.
- *Data stream representing the history of changes to the application*—For example, events that relate to changes made within a billing account.
- *Data stream representing snapshots of data entities from a transaction system*—For example, information about a system user.
- *Data mart*—Representing data enabling multidimensional analysis of sales results.
- *Denormalized table*—Containing search-optimized information (for example, about the rentals of a particular movie).
- *Graph database*—Reflecting complex relationships between data (for example, specialized for finding movie recommendations).
- *Local data lake or part of a bigger data lake*—Used to build a view used as a basis for analysis of watching movies statistics.
- *MDM-type database (master data management)*—Containing an integrated view on system users (personal information, viewing preferences, viewing time preferences, payment information, rating information, etc.).

As you can see from the examples, there are many possibilities. But of course, these are just examples of the data itself, the core of a data product. A data mesh does not dictate a particular form of data representation or a specific technology.

5.3   *Data product ownership*

Having specified how to define the scope of a data product, its customers, and its business needs, we'll now take a closer look at the human side of a data product—the roles that are responsible for its development. And these are as follows:

- *Data product owner*—The person responsible for the business vision and evolution of the data product. In practice, this can be a person who is also an Agile product owner or a product manager.
- *Data product development team*—A team responsible for implementation, maintenance, and deployment of a data product (in contrast to a central team specialized in data processing).

Let's go back to the Messflix example. The Hitchcock system is developed by two teams, Orange and White, together comprising approximately 30 people. Both teams are mainly concerned with the operational part, because the data is not exposed to the outside world in a significant way. The development efforts are coordinated by the Hitchcock product owner. The assignment of teams to different parts of the system is shown in figure 5.7.

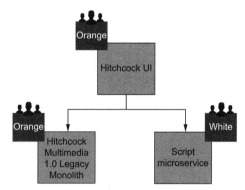

Figure 5.7   Teams assigned to the systems

The introduction of data products changes the system landscape and requires a slightly different organization of teams. Following the principle of domain ownership, we want to make operational teams responsible for data products related to their applications. So the Orange team will be responsible for the Cast and Cost Statement data products, and the White team will be responsible for the Scripts data product. As two new data products and the script recommender application are planned for development, the new Blonde team will be formed, with a few people from the Orange team along with new hires. The target image is shown in figure 5.8.

Data products related directly to the Hitchcock system will be led by one data product owner, and data products related to the script recommender will be led by a second data product owner. In the following sections, we will look at the characteristics of the roles involved in the data product development.

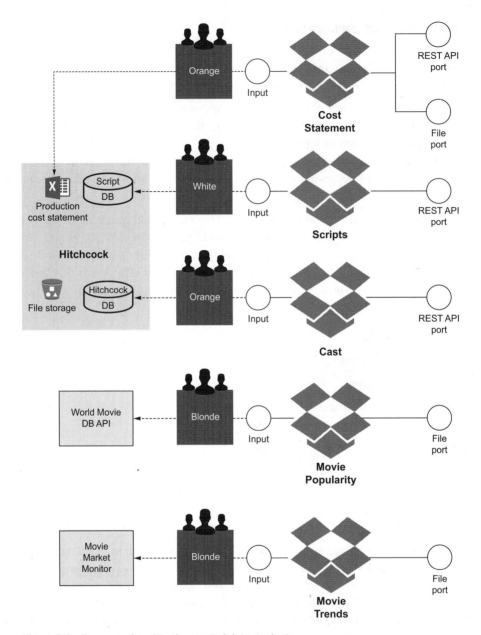

Figure 5.8   Teams assigned to the created data products

5.3.1   *Data product owner*

The role of data product owner is a natural consequence of the *data as a product* principle. Data is becoming such an important resource in an organization that it requires an owner, a person who will think long-term about how to make data even more useful in that organization. This person will not stop at a one-time exposure of data, but will continually collect feedback from users and adapt the content of the data product to changing needs.

An example of such a need might be to extend the data provided with attributes not previously available (e.g., an additional column in the database). Another example could be adding the ability to retrieve data from any point in time, providing a new way to share data, for example, in the form of a reactive data stream or the need to increase the bandwidth of the data being shared.

The preceding examples show that a data product has a life cycle, and that new user requirements need to be managed in a sustainable way. Moreover, having gathered the needs, it is necessary to decide which ones should be addressed first, and which should be done later. Then, together with the development team, the data product owner must plan the implementation of the selected requirements. The data product owner is responsible for all these tasks (and many others).

The role itself is borrowed directly from Agile methods such as scrum. Detailed practices and heuristics can be found in sources describing these methods. For example, a good book on this topic is *Agile Product Management with Scrum* by Roman Pichler (Addison-Wesley, 2010).

The role of data product owner is extremely important, because the manner in which this role is performed will largely determine the success of implementing the data mesh approach. If assigned data product owners strategically develop products and ensure that they are of adequate quality and richly documented, the value of the data available and the benefits of using a data mesh within the organization will be high. A more detailed description of the responsibilities of the role is provided in the next section.

5.3.2 *Data product owner responsibilities*

The data product owner, as the name indicates, should be the owner of the data product. This person has the last word in making decisions and setting the direction of data product evolution. The owner's tasks should include, among others:

- *Defining vision and needs*—Determining the purpose of creating a data product, its users, and their expectations (e.g., using the methods of product thinking).
- *Strategic planning of product development work*—Creating the roadmap, defining key performance indicators (KPIs) for the data product, and ensuring appropriate SLAs.
- *Ensuring that all requirements for the data product are satisfied*—Providing a satisfying level of metadata description, as well as compliance with accepted standards and data governance rules.
- *Making tactical decisions related to the management of the data product backlog*—Prioritizing requirements, clarifying requirements, splitting stories, and approving implemented items.
- *Stakeholder management*—Gathering information from users and management, and clarifying inconsistencies or conflicting requirements.

- *Collaboration with the data product development team*—To clarify requirements and make decisions on problems that may affect the further development and implementation of the data product.
- *Participating on the data governance team*—To influence the introduction of rules in the organization and provide feedback on their practical implementation.

An important rule is that there should be only one data product owner for a specific data product. However, many data products can be owned by one data product owner (if data products are smaller or require less attention).

We have to be aware that data products differ in size and complexity, so specific data product owner responsibilities will also differ depending on the situation. For example, someone taking care of dozens of financial spreadsheets will have other challenges and responsibilities than a person leading a complex data warehouse–like solution as a node in data mesh.

5.3.3   *An Agile DevOps team as a base for data product dev team*

Like the role of data product owner, the idea of a data product development team is borrowed from Agile methods. This cross-functional team works within the domain to which the data product belongs. This also means that the team is not a specialized data team. The rule that applies here is that a given team can look after several data products, but a given data product is developed by only one team.

Let's go back to our example and look at who we will need on each team:

- *Orange*—The team responsible for the backend and UI of the Hitchcock system, and the Cast, and Cost Statement data products. In this team, we need the most diverse competencies: software developers, software testers, user experience (UX) specialists, system analysts, and data engineers. These competencies will be complemented by an operation and security engineer.
- *White*—The team responsible for the scripts microservice and Scripts data product. In this case, the situation is quite simple, because the data product will be exposed in the form of a REST API, and it will be just another representation of already available data, so the classic development team will be absolutely sufficient to achieve this goal.
- *Blonde*—The team responsible for the scripts recommender app, and the Movie Trends and Movie Popularity data products. In this case, the analytics application and related data products are planned for development, so we need a development team supported by data engineers, data analysts, and data scientists.

As we can conclude from the previous examples, the team consists of people who have all the competencies to create a data product end to end. Such a team has characteristics similar to DevOps or DevSecOps teams found in the software development world. These teams consist of people with competencies needed during product development:

- *Data engineers*—To develop data transformations
- *Operations engineers*—For infrastructure, CI/CD configuration, and integration with the platform
- *Software developers*—For more complex programming tasks, if required (e.g., exposing data in a specific REST API HATEOAS format)
- *Data scientists*—To perform complex data analysis
- *Data analysts*—To acquire and analyze the data that is to be the content of the data product
- *Testers*—For verifying the correctness of data transformation
- *Security engineers*—To configure security rules related to the data product

This is a sample list. The competencies associated with the roles are the most important, not the roles themselves. That is, there should be people on the team who can perform different kinds of tasks. Ideally, each team member, at least to some extent, should have the diverse competencies described earlier.

5.3.4   *Data product owner and product owner*

Quite naturally, the question may arise: how do the roles of product owner and data product owner relate to each other? In the case of the Hitchcock system, script recommender, and associated data products, the product owners will also be the data product owners, because the data products themselves have relatively low complexity compared to the systems from which they are derived.

In general, however, this configuration depends quite significantly on the specific situation. We can distinguish between the three situations shown in table 5.4.

Table 5.4   Data product owner and product owner setups

Case	Characteristics
The data product owner is also a product owner. The data product development team is also the product development team.	This setup makes the most sense when the data product is a natural extension of the source system. At the same time, it is not so complex that it requires separate development. For example, a subscription purchase module that provides data about those purchases.
The data product owner is also a product owner. The data product development team is different from the product development team.	This setup will apply when the analytical data provided from the application is so extensive that it requires a separate backlog and team to execute it. An example is a subscription purchase module that will provide analytical data supported by an ML model to enable predictions of purchase behavior.
The data product owner is not a product owner. The data product development team is different from the product development team.	This setup will be useful when the data product is a complex solution that requires independent development, such as building a data mart supported by an ML model to predict purchase behavior.

Now that we've defined the data product and selected skilled people, we can focus on design and architectural aspects of creating a data product.

5.4   *Conceptual architecture of a data product*

In the previous sections, we showed how to validate and define a data product, and how to assign a product owner along with a data product development team. This section focuses on a high-level view of the data product structure from the perspective of the data product user (external architecture view) and the implementer (internal architecture view).

5.4.1   *External architecture view*

In figure 5.8, showing data products in the Produce Content domain, the key elements of the data product's external architecture were presented: external and internal ports. An excerpt for the Cost Statement data product is shown in figure 5.9.

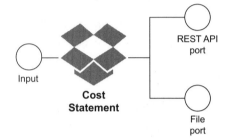

To be fully functional, a data product requires more components to become an autonomous element of the architecture. We

Figure 5.9   Cost statement data product interfaces

should consciously design the entire set of interfaces that will make up the full data product. For the Cost Statement data product, these interfaces are depicted in figure 5.10.

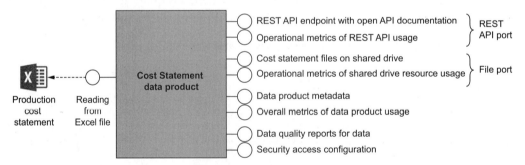

Figure 5.10   The set of interfaces exposed by a data product

As part of the designing process, we decide to provide the following interfaces:

- *REST API endpoint with OpenAPI documentation*—API that will allow consumers to directly use the data
- *Operational metrics of REST API usage*—REST API metrics, such as the number of active users, amount of data retrieved, and number of requests processed
- *Cost Statement files on shared drive*—Processed data exposed as files

- *Operational metrics of shared drive resource usage*—Metrics from the file-sharing system, including active users count, number of downloads, and number of requests processed
- *Data product metadata*—Information describing the data being shared, such as business description, contact persons, and responsible persons
- *Overall metrics of data product usage*—Metrics that are the sum of the metrics from individual ports
- *Data quality reports for data*—Reports on the quality of the data provided, such as information about the time of the update and any data gaps
- *Security access configuration*—A tool for setting up access to data, mainly exposed for a self-serve platform

The generalized external architecture of the data product is shown in figure 5.11.

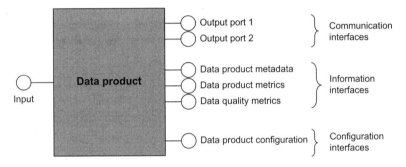

Figure 5.11 The main groups of interfaces of a data product

We can divide all of the data product interfaces into three main groups:

- *Communication interfaces*—Input interfaces and output ports, which define the format and protocol in which data can be read (e.g., files, API, database, and stream)
- *Information interfaces*—Interfaces that can be used by users to monitor and retrieve additional information such as metadata, lineage, current metrics, or quality indicators
- *Configuration interfaces*—Interfaces, mainly platform specific, that enable the data product to be included in the data mesh ecosystem (e.g., security options and parameters, data sharing agreement statements)

Specifically, the self-serve platform uses configuration and information interfaces to configure, catalog, monitor, and visualize the relationships between data products. Interfaces must be standardized for the interoperability to be possible. This standardization is part of computational governance, which is described in more detail in later chapters.

In the next subsection, we will take a closer look at external ports, which are the data product's primary means of exposing data.

DATA PRODUCT PORTS

A data product is created with the end user in mind, and as we know, users have different needs and preferences. For example, a data scientist might prefer to have data about movies rented in Latin America in the form of a well-described file. A data engineer might like to have that same data as a bunch of files to be processed with a crafted Python script. A programmer might prefer to use a REST API.

A data product is not only a form in which data is stored but also the various ways that data can be accessed. In the case of a data product, we call these *ports*.

A data product can have one or more *output ports*, and the infrastructure should make it easy to expose the same data using different forms. Next, we present examples of output port representations.

DATABASE-LIKE STORAGE

One of the primary ports that will come into play when developing data products is database-like storage, i.e., SQL databases, NoSQL databases, or data warehouse data marts. In many cases, this may be the only type of port provided by a data product. As a result, it offers excellent opportunities, especially in the analytical processing of large amounts of data, including the big-data area.

This type of storage can be queried with SQL language or its analog, giving basically unlimited possibilities of further processing. But, of course, they are addressed mainly to technical users who can work with this type of storage and use SQL language.

FILES

The second type of port, which will be familiar to less technical users of data products, is files that can be imported into tools such as Excel, Google Sheets, or used by data scientists. It is worth remembering that data engineers often feel confident working with this type of data source. Files allow working with large amounts of data, and many algorithms implemented in libraries of such languages as R or Python are perfectly optimized for file processing.

Files, in the case of smaller sets, can represent the whole dataset. And for large amounts of data, in most cases, a subset of the data will first be selected, through an appropriate query or configuration of various filters and then exported to a file.

(REST) API

Another type of port is the REST API. We use HTTP REST here as an example of the protocol that is most popular at the time of writing this book. Nevertheless, we mean here a type of interface that is mainly intended for consumption by other systems.

This type of port is mainly suitable for working on small subsets of data, because it is usually inefficient for large collections. If we add GraphQL support to this type of port, we get the ability to perform complex and customized queries on the data. And with the addition of HATEOAS, you can gain additional capabilities for automating data browsing using ML/AI.

NOTE *GraphQL* is an open source data query and manipulation language for APIs, and a run time for fulfilling queries with existing data. *HATEOAS* is a part of the REST specification stating that in addition to the result data, responses should include dynamic metadata allowing clients to browse and interpret the results in a hypermedia way (like links in classical web pages).

So this port is great for automating data processing and for relatively low-intensity analytics that do not require large amounts of data.

STREAMS

By *streams*, we mean messaging-based systems that store information as single messages (e.g., message queues). This type of port is not very popular in the world of data yet, especially as a form of sharing data, because tools for its analytical processing are still under development. Messaging systems are great for distributed processing of large amounts of data, especially when we want to process data in near real time. An example is systems that continuously analyze stock-price changes and generate recommendations for purchases. Near real-time analytical results may be one reason to consider using streams.

The second reason to consider streams in the data world is to use event sourcing, known from the software development world. Event sourcing stores the changes associated with an entity (e.g., a transaction) rather than the final state of the entity. Having all the changes from the very beginning provides tremendous opportunities for seeing an entity at any point in time, such as building any representation based on them, creating analyses that were not considered when the system was created, and time travel. The stream in this form might be the basis for creating other data products.

It is worth noting that a stream can also be used to implement a data product—to transport the data needed to build the data product. However, it's then considered an input interface.

VISUALIZATIONS

Our last example of a port is a visualization: various kinds of charts and dashboards representing data. They can be a good resource for nontechnical users, especially if they are combined with a filtering and data selection mechanism. This port provides visual representations of data in a relatively easy way. Such automatic visualizations can be supported by one of the platform capabilities.

Table 5.5 summarizes port applications for various situations.

Table 5.5 Characteristics of the data product ports

Type of data product port	Access type	Amount of data
Database-like storage	SQL-like interface Programmatically	Big amount of data
Files	Scripting Import to BI tools Open in simple tools like Excel and Google Sheets	Small to big
API	Programmatically	Small to moderate

Table 5.5   Characteristics of the data product ports *(continued)*

Type of data product port	Access type	Amount of data
Streams	Programmatically	Huge amount of data processing in real time
Visualizations	Dedicated tool/UI	Small to moderate

Having decided which kind of port representation to use, we can focus more on detailed design of a data product.

5.4.2   *Internal architecture view*

While the external architecture is fairly self-explanatory and easy to standardize, the internal architecture of a data product will depend significantly on the specifics of the data product, the way it is processed, and the technologies used.

Figure 5.12 shows how the internal architecture of the Cost Statement data product was designed. Based on it, we will extract the main components of the internal architecture of the data product.

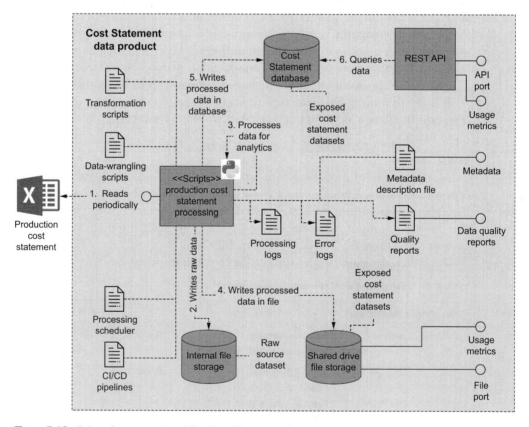

Figure 5.12   Internal components of the Cost Statement data product

The data related to production costs comes from spreadsheet files, which are constantly updated by the production team according to the established rules. To enable more complex analysis of this data, it is made available in the form of a REST API and files that will be used for financial analysis. The whole solution will be implemented as a set of Python scripts, run once a day by the scheduler.

These scripts read the current form of spreadsheet files, save them in their raw form, and then perform data cleaning and transformation to the target form, which is written to the database used by the REST API and files located on the shared drive. During data processing, processing logs, error logs, and a quality report are generated. The whole process is complemented by CI/CD pipelines and metadata describing the data product. All these elements constitute a data product—they are created and maintained by the data product development team.

The following sections describe the main elements of the data product's internal architecture.

DATASETS

One of the most obvious components of a data product is the dataset. Datasets are what ultimately constitute the essence of a data product. As described in an earlier section, a dataset can be one or more related tables, a file, data in a stream, or successive versions of processed data. In many cases, the dataset will not physically reside where the other elements of the data product reside.

For example, the dataset may be a remote file whose size or legal aspects prevent copying. In particular, the latter may be the case when, because of licensing, the file can physically reside only within the boundaries of a geographical region. Another example is a dataset that is part of a database running as a cloud service.

METADATA

In the data mesh approach, metadata plays a particularly important role that allows many processes to be automated. Much of the metadata, especially descriptive and configuration metadata, will be part of the internal implementation of the data product— that is, its name, business description, dataset schema, people responsible, data-quality metrics, and available ports. Metadata in its physical form can be described, for example, as a JSON file. We'll look at metadata in a little more detail in section 5.5.2.

CODE

An important part of data product implementation will be the parts of the code that enable creation of the final product, including, among other things, the following:

- *Cleansing and data wrangling*—Cleaning, repairing, and harmonizing data
- *Transformational pipelines*—ETL or ELT transformations, enrichment, and harmonization
- *Infrastructure as code*—Configuration of the container and orchestration infrastructure layers

- *CI/CD pipelines*—Processes that update the data product code after changes, verifying its correctness, and applying the changes to the production environment if the entire process went correctly
- *Scheduling processing code*—Configuration of systems that run regular data processing

In the previous sections, we looked at designing the data product; in the next section, we will discuss ensuring that it is prepared to be used in the data mesh ecosystem.

5.5 *Data product fundamental characteristics*

A data product should have the following characteristics:

- It can be found.
  - It must be described, named, and registered in the data product registry.
- It can be understood.
  - It has sufficient technical and domain descriptions for the user to interpret it.
  - It can be uniquely identified in terms of sources from which it originated to build a data lineage (understanding where the data comes from).
- It can be addressed.
  - It has a unique address that can be used to identify the data product.
- It is secured.
  - It can be accessed only by authorized entities.
- It can be used.
  - It has sufficient data to be used on its own (i.e., carries sufficient domain sense on its own).
  - You can combine it with other data; it has metadata and references that allow you to combine several data products into a larger whole.
  - It is accessible through publicly known and available protocols and tools.
- You can tell its availability and quality through metrics, user feedback, and quality reports.

The data product has to meet many criteria to be a full-fledged product. Metadata, which is described in the following paragraphs, plays an especially important role in this regard.

5.5.1 *Self-described data product*

The data product should contain all the information to understand and use it. This characteristic is achieved through an appropriate set of metadata.

In classical data management approaches, metadata is often separated from the dataset and tends to be scattered in many places. One of the fundamental properties of a data product is its autonomy. And autonomy means independence from specific solutions and that everything important about the data product will be found in one place, including metadata. While in data management in general "metadata is king," in the data mesh approach metadata becomes the fuel that drives the data product. Metadata is where all the key information for the data is defined.

5.5.2 Introduction to metadata

Metadata is data about data. It is mainly used to provide additional information about the data so that it is easier to understand and use with greater understanding. An ordinary data table may be a collection of insignificant values, but if we describe each column, and even better, link it to a standardized vocabulary or logical model, this data starts to become meaningful. As its user, I can consciously decide what is relevant to me and what is not, often without even necessarily contacting the original creators.

Of course, this is only an example of metadata related to semantics. However, there can be many more types of metadata.

The following is a list of some of the most relevant data product metadata types. In fact, this is not a closed list:

- *Business metadata*—Describing information about the owner (data product owner), describing the domain context (e.g., abstract, assumptions), domain affiliation, organizational unit, license type, and expiration date
- *Technical metadata*—About the technical team responsible for it, physical access method, links to the data product page (if any), and links to download examples
- *Operational metadata*—Description of ports, description of access policies, and how to obtain extended access
- *Physical schema*—Description of the data product, its attributes, data types, constraints, and relationships to other elements
- *Semantic metadata*—Links of the physical model to standardized vocabularies and logical models
- *Local lineage*—Information about the direct sources of the data from which the data product was created
- *Full lineage*—Information about the overall sequence of links that shows how data was created in a given data product
- *Quality metrics*—Metrics related to data quality, the amount of correctly and incorrectly defined data, information about missing data, incorrect formats, and compliance with data governance rules
- *Operational metrics*—Information about whether the data product is available, number of users, usage statistics, and SLA metrics

5.5.3 Metadata as code

In classical approaches to data management, metadata is gathered in dedicated tools, most often in a data catalog, where the submitted dataset needs to be enriched with additional information. In this way, metadata is separated from the dataset, which often leads to metadata descriptions that are not fully synchronized with the current form of data.

The data mesh approach assumes that the data product is autonomous and self-described, in a way that the self-serve platform and end users can use it for different purposes. Therefore, it is recommended to use the *metadata as code* approach, which results in data that will be easily interpreted by machines and validated and versioned using existing source code–oriented tools.

For example, a metadata description can be implemented using JSON notation. The data product's metadata description file contains sections dedicated to each of its aspects. An example file is in the following listing.

Listing 5.1   Sample data product metadata file outline

```
{
 "dataProduct": {
   // data product details
 },

 "domainDataSets": [
   // domain dataset details
 ],

 "schemas": [
   // dataset schema details
 ],

 "terminology": {
   // vocabularies
 },
 "security": {
   // security definition
 },
 "conceptualModel": {
   // conceptual domain model eg. OWL / RDFs
 },
 "lineage": {
   // lineage description
 },
 "dataQuality": {
   // data quality guarantees
 },
 "metrics": {
   // runtime generated metrics
 },
 "documentation": {
   // links to related documentation
 }
}
```

Let's take a look at examples of metadata related to a data product.

5.5.4 Data product metadata

Metadata about a data product is mainly descriptive so users can better understand its business sense and get information for further use. We can include data such as the following:

- *ID*—Unique identifier of the data product
- *Title*—Human-friendly name of the data product
- *Name*—Machine-friendly name of the data product
- *Business description*—Domain-specific description of the data product, introduction to the domain context
- *Terms of use*—Licensing type, and description of when, how, and by whom the data product can be used
- *Data product URL*—Data product–related site or project web page
- *Data product owner*—Information about the responsible person, such as name, surname, and position as well as contact details
- *Responsible data product developer team*—Information about the technical team maintaining the data product, including the technical support contact
- *Business unit*—Information about the company department that the data product is part of
- *Status*—Current status of the product (e.g., experimental, active, inactive, or temporarily off)
- *Since when collected*—The moment in time when data starts to be collected, not necessarily equal to the time when data starts to be exposed
- *Created date*—The moment of creating and exposing the data product
- *Last modified*—The last modification to the product (e.g., a changing data schema for underlying data)
- *Version*—The latest version of the product

Of course, these are just a dozen or so examples of elements that can be freely adapted, as well as adding others that are important in the context of a given organization. An example snippet of metadata defined in JSON format could look like the following listing.

> **Listing 5.2 Data product part description**

```json
{
  "dataProduct": {
    "dataProductId": "http://dp.meshflix.com/production/93384349834",
    "title": "Movie Production Cost Statement",
    "name": "movieProductionCostStatement",
    "businessDescription":
        "Cost breakdown of a production including … (much more text)",
    "termsOfUse": {
      "name":  "For internal financial related use only",
      "uri": "https://licences.meshflix.com/internal-use"
```

```
  },
  "dataProductUrl": "https://dp.meshflix.com/production/costStatement",
  "dataProductOwner": {
    "name": "Peter Meshlover",
    "uri": "https://emplyees.meshflix.com/320948234098234"
  },
  "dataProductOwnerContact": "peter.meshlover@meshflix.com",
  "responsibleTechnicalTeam": {
    "name": "Scrapers",
    "uri": "https://teams.meshflix.com/production/finances/scrapers"
  },
  "technicalSupportContact": "scrapers.team@meshflix.com",
  "businessUnit": {
    "name": "Movie Production",
    "uri": "https://businessunits.meshflix.com/production"
  },
  "status": "active",

  "sinceWhenCollected": "2016-03-06T12:14:53",
  "createdDate": "2020-03-06T12:14:53",
  "lastModified": "2020-03-06T12:14:53",
  "version": "13"
 }
}
```

As you can see, much of the data included is dictionary-like and should come from standardized dictionaries, especially if the organization wants to be FAIR compliant. A separate topic is human-friendly support for creating this type of metadata.

Many data product owners may not be comfortable working with a format like JSON. Even if it isn't a problem, it can be inconvenient. This topic is covered in later chapters. At this point, we can assume from a pragmatic standpoint that tools and mechanisms will be in place to make it easier for people to create these types of descriptions.

5.5.5 *Domain dataset metadata*

While the data product description is business oriented and different from technical details, the domain dataset part focuses on exactly that aspect, as shown in listing 5.3. This part of the metadata may include, among other things:

- *ID*—Domain dataset unique identifier
- *Ports*—Specification of available ports
- *Title*—Human-friendly name of the domain dataset
- *Name*—Machine-friendly name of the domain dataset
- *Description*—More detailed information about the data
- *Download URL*—Address to download sample of the data
- *Source datasets*—Links to other datasets that were the basis for the domain dataset
- *Version*—The latest version of the dataset

Listing 5.3 Domain dataset part description

```
{
  "domainDataSets": {
    "ports": [
      {
        "type": "file",
        "runtime": "sharepoint",
        "url": "https://internal.meshflix.com/sharpoint/files/3243223423"
      }
    ],
    "datasets": [
      {
        "domainDataSetId": "489345-4359834589-45383492-345",
        "name": "costStatement",
        "title": "Movie Production Cost Statements",
        "description": "More detailed description of the ",
        "downloadUrl":
      "https://internal.meshflix.com/sharpoint/files/3243223423",
        "sourceDataSets": [],
        "version": "13"
      }
    ]
  }
}
```

Having described the most important parts of a data product, let's focus on additional aspects that can be described.

5.5.6 Other kinds of metadata

The data product and domain dataset metadata are just the tip of the iceberg. According to listing 5.1, analogous metadata description sections should appear for terminology, lineage, conceptual model, security, and data quality. In these cases, it is useful to use existing standards.

One such source is a set of World Wide Web Consortium (W3C) standards that can be used directly or adapted to your needs. We do not describe these sections in more detail, because their specific use depends on the context of the organization. Nevertheless, table 5.6 presents examples for starting your search.

Table 5.6 Metadata description standards

Area	Standard	Description
Data catalog	Data Catalog Vocabulary (DCAT) Version 2 (W3C)	Defines a standardized vocabulary to describe the metadata of datasets stored in data catalogs.
Conceptual model	W3C Web Ontology Language (OWL) W3C Simple Knowledge Organization System (SKOS)	These formal languages allow the description of logical models of data along with semantic links between them.

Table 5.6 Metadata description standards *(continued)*

Area	Standard	Description
Lineage	W3C PROV (Provenance) OpenLineage (Marquez)	Specifies the language for describing the sources from which the dataset was created.
Data quality	W3C Data Quality Vocabulary (DQV)	A language for describing the quality attributes of a given dataset.
Security	W3C Security vocabulary	Language for describing the details involved in securing access to a given dataset.
General metadata description	OpenAPI Specification (OAS)	Targeted at the REST API language to describe application endpoints. Can be adapted to other purposes.

Although we've defined the main requirements for a data product, there are several additional characteristics to consider when making guidelines for creating data products in a particular organization. In the next section, we will look at five of these characteristics.

5.6 *Additional data product characteristics: FAIR and immutability*

We'll first focus on *FAIR* (an acronym for *findable, accessible, interoperable, reusable*). This set of principles was initially designed for scientific research data, to maximize its reusability and its ability to easily integrate with other data.

However, over time, it became clear that FAIR could be helpful in other situations. For example, government agencies in Australia, Sweden, and the European Union, among others, recommend its use for shared data. This section describes how FAIR can make data products even better, with a particular focus on linking related data to each other. In addition, we will touch on the topic of data immutability and its importance for creating data products.

5.6.1 *Findability*

Data should be easy to find, and its metadata should be easy to use by both humans and computers. In particular, the ability of machines to interpret metadata is crucial from the perspective of FAIR. Findability involves four specific principles:

1 (Meta)data is assigned a globally unique and persistent identifier.
2 Data is described with rich metadata.
3 Metadata clearly and explicitly includes the identifier of the data it describes.
4 (Meta)data is registered or indexed in a searchable resource.

As an example, take a look at the following listing to see a simple REST API returning Person data. (This example can be used to see how to apply FAIR to other interfaces in order to access data like databases, files, and messages.)

Listing 5.4 Person data returned by a REST API

```
{
 "dataProductId": "https://dp.meshflix.com/93384349834",
 "personId": "0173d228-ed2e-11eb-9a03-0242ac130003",
 "name": "David",
 "surname": "Datameshy",
 "gender": "male"
}
```

The data itself is nothing special. The more important part lies in metadata that could be like the following listing.

Listing 5.5 Person metadata describing the returned dataset

```
{
 "dataProduct": {
   "dataProductId": "https://dp.meshflix.com/93384349834",
   "title": "Person",
   "description": "Person data represents..."
   // .. other metadata
 },

 "schema": {
   "fields": [
     {
       "name": "id",
       "uri": "https://ref.meshflix.com/person/93384349835",
       "titles": "Id",
       "datatype": "string"
     },
     {
       "name": "name",
       "uri": "https://ref.meshflix.com/person/93384349836",
       "titles": "Name",
       "datatype": "string"
     },
     {
       "name": "surname",
       "uri": "https://ref.meshflix.com/person/93384349837",
       "titles": "Surname",
       "datatype": "string"
     },
     {
       "name": "gender",
       "uri": "https://ref.meshflix.com/generic/123393ed34",
       "titles": "Gender",
       "datatype": "enum"
     }
   ]
 }
}
```

As you can see, the data and metadata have their unique identifiers (principle 1):

- ID of the person instance in listing 5.4:

```
"personId": "0173d228-ed2e-11eb-9a03-0242ac130003"
```

- ID of the Persons data product in listing 5.5:

```
"dataProductId": "https://dp.meshflix.com/93384349834"
```

- Also fields from the schema have defined their unique identifiers in the form of URLs:

```
"name": "name"
"uri": "https://ref.meshflix.com/person/93384349837"
```

Data is described by rich metadata (principle 2) that we can see in listing 5.5. This information can include name, title, description, and schema details. This is only an excerpt, and a more detailed example is provided later in the chapter.

Metadata has an ID that references the original data product (principle 3):

- Referenced ID in listing 5.5:

```
"dataProductId": "https://dp.meshflix.com/93384349834"
```

Principle 4 tells us to put this (meta)data in some kind of searchable repository where data catalogs can be successfully used.

According to the characteristics described earlier, virtually all four principles are consistent with the essential attributes of the data product. Therefore, only the first principle imposes very strong conditions on the data product. Identifying *every* data element is certainly a desirable feature, but it can be challenging to achieve in practice and poses a significant obstacle for data product developers. Therefore, we suggest treating it as a recommendation or criteria for data product maturity.

5.6.2 *Accessibility*

For the data found, there should be clear rules for accessing the data. The metadata should clearly describe how to access the data, and the protocols used to access the data should be generally known standards:

1 (Meta)data is retrievable by its identifier using a standardized communications protocol:
   - The protocol is open, free, and universally implementable.
   - The protocol allows for an authentication and authorization procedure, where necessary.
2 Metadata is accessible, even when the data is no longer available.

As shown in the previous section, the data product has an ID in the form of the URL https://dp.meshflix.com/93384349834. According to principle 1, this should be a workable URL that can be used to retrieve information about the data product. For example, entering this URL into a browser should produce the final metadata file in the response. In this case, Hypertext Transfer Protocol (HTTP) is used, which supports authentication and authorization, so the whole principle 1 is fulfilled. Principle 2 says that this metadata link should be working, even when the data product is no longer available.

These accessibility principles can be seen as recommendations for creating a data product and its desirable features to facilitate its use. In particular, the permanent availability of metadata is essential if there is a need to refer to historical data (e.g., for legal reasons). Hence, at the implementation level, a registry of data product metadata that allows retrieving the data for any identifier can be helpful. Furthermore, standard protocols and formats should be chosen when creating infrastructure and platforms (e.g., HTTPS/JSON).

5.6.3 *Interoperable*

According to FAIR, data should be easy to integrate with other data, and therefore should be defined so that data in other data products, vocabularies, and ontologies can be referenced. In this case, FAIR proposes three principles:

1. (Meta)data uses a formal, accessible, shared, and broadly applicable language for knowledge representation.
2. (Meta)data uses vocabularies that follow FAIR principles.
3. (Meta)data includes qualified references to other (meta)data.

To make data interpretable by others, we have to describe the data model. We should use a well-recognized language, such as Resource Description Framework (RDF), OWL, JSON-LD, or Schema.org (principle 1). Also, we should use vocabularies that follow FAIR rules (principle 2). Listing 5.5 includes a reference to an enum defining a `gender` property:

```
{
      "name": "gender",
      "uri": "https://ref.meshflix.com/generic/123393ed34",
      "titles": "Gender",
      "datatype": "enum"
}
```

This is also an example for principle 3, as we refer to external definitions in the form of a fully qualified reference ("uri": "https://ref.meshflix.com/generic/123393ed34"). Beware that in the provided example the custom-created `gender` enum is used, but we could also use `https://schema.org/gender` alternatively for the same purpose.

If we want to go beyond a single data product to perform more complex analyses, we must have the appropriate means to do so. The previous FAIR principles are quite demanding because they significantly expand the amount of information that needs to be provided with metadata and data. Still, they are the only way we can get the advantage of using data by linking it. For example, relationships are not defined in external tools but are part of the data product description: its metadata. Thus, from a pragmatic perspective, these principles can be treated as recommendations when creating a data product and defining its maturity levels.

5.6.4 *Reusable*

The last point of FAIR focuses on data reusability, or the ability to apply the same data in different contexts. The principles associated with reusability are as follows:

1. Meta(data) is richly described with a plurality of accurate and relevant attributes:
   a. (Meta)data is released with a clear and accessible data usage license.
   b. (Meta)data is associated with detailed provenance.
   c. (Meta)data meets domain-relevant community standards.

Principles 1a and 1b could be achieved by having some additional entries in metadata, as in the following modified listing.

Listing 5.6   Extended Person metadata describing the returned dataset

```
{
  "dataProduct": {
    "dataProductId": "https://dp.meshflix.com/93384349834",
    // .. other metadata
    "termsOfUse": {
      "name":  "For internal use only",
      "uri": "https://licences.meshflix.com/internal-use"
    },
    "sourceDataProducts":  [
      "https://dp.meshflix.com/93384349834"
    ]
  }

  // .. schema
}
```

Here `termsOfUse` specifies a license for data usage, and `sourceDataProducts` specifies information about provenance (shortened for the sake of simplicity). The implementation of principle 1c would require using standardized domain-specific terminology and vocabulary—for example, `www.iso.org/standard/53798.html` for geographic information and services, and `http://cfconventions.org` for climate and forecast.

These principles focus on defining clear rules for using data (by providing licenses), provenance information, and recommending standards that apply to the domain. Subsections 1a and 1b are essential components of a well-structured data product. Subsection 1c can be seen as recommendations for creating a data product.

If you are interested in more details about FAIR implementation, see the initiative site at www.go-fair.org.

5.6.5 *Immutable*

FAIR can be an excellent addition to the essential criteria for creating a data product. Another critical aspect to consider is the mutability of the data provided by the data product. Mutability can be troublesome. Conclusions drawn from the source data may be hard to confirm later if the source data changes over time.

If, for example, decisions about ingredient proportions in a drug have been made based on the analysis of scientific studies, then getting to that unmodified source data may be necessary from a regulatory perspective. Therefore, data immutability should be a desirable characteristic of a data product.

DO DATA PRODUCTS ALWAYS HAVE TO BE IMMUTABLE?

One of the primary goals of introducing a data mesh is to democratize data by enabling access to the various data created within an organization. Not all data created in organizations is created with the same consumption patterns in mind (consumption of data from any point in the past). Yet, the value of making it available externally can be significant.

Despite the lack of immutability, data should be generally available as it is, especially in the context of data generated by transactional systems (e.g., read-only APIs based on command query responsibility segregation, or CQRS, architecture). Therefore, we treat immutability as a desirable feature of a data product. However, it is not a necessary condition that every data product must fulfill. A data product should explicitly declare whether its data is immutable and how past data can be accessed.

5.7 *Data contracts and sharing agreements inside the data mesh*

Let's recall the Cast data product we've seen on the data product canvas in this chapter. Take a look at figure 5.13. In particular, notice that this data product provides two datasets, one for actors and one for movie roles.

Imagine that John Doe builds this data product and that several teams start to consume it. A couple of months go by, and John Doe sees a decent amount of traffic on his data product.

One day, he takes extra time and calls up a few of the downstream consumers of the data product. They tell him they are making a lot out of the Actors part of the data product. To John's dismay, he is not able to find a single customer who's using the Movie Roles dataset. This is really confusing for John because he thought this is one of the most important pieces to accompany the Actors dataset.

So he asks the consumers. The answer is shockingly simple: "Yes, we would really like to use the Movie Roles dataset, but you're providing them in a custom format we're not able to process further."

A frustrated John goes on to iterate on his product, to incorporate a format the consumers can use. That's how product thinking works, right? Except, in a company,

Name	Description	
Cast	Contains information about actors and roles they play in the specific movie	
Data Product Owner	Business Capability/ Domain /Bounded Context	System
John Doe	Produce Content	Hitchcock Movie Maker
Classification (source aligned/consumer aligned/shared core)	Classification (virtual/materialized)	Life-Cycle Classification (experimental/stable)
Source aligned	Virtual	Stable
Input Interface	Output Ports	Security
Cast relational DB	REST API	Public
Inbound Flow	Outbound Flow	Volume
Actors Movie roles	Actors Movie roles	10 GB
Datasets		
Actors Movie roles		

Figure 5.13   The Cast data product canvas

it should not. Outside a company, it usually doesn't work that way either. In the outside world, the producing API would get dozens of "bug reports" or "feature requests" if this situation plays out.

The reason is that consumers and producers of products enter into a *mutual relationship*. Company-internal product consumers, especially in the data realm, sometimes forget that. A mutual relationship means the following:

- *The product producer has responsibilities.* The producer must properly care for the product and make decisions in the best interest of the product. The producer is responsible for informing consumers of updates and for telling them of any plans to drop a column, to change the schema, or vary the meaning of the data.
- *The product consumer has responsibilities.* The consumer must tell the producer what's wrong, what's good, and what's missing. The consumer is also responsible for telling the producer how the data is being used, and which transformations must be applied to the data to make it work for a particular use case.

This mutual relationship sometimes gets lost inside the company context even though it is natural outside of it.

> **KEY POINT**   Product thinking works both ways. Products are two-way relationships. Outside the company context, this usually works. But inside a company, this two-way relationship often turns into a one-way relationship in either direction. It's important to ensure a mutual relationship. In the data mesh context, data contracts and data sharing agreements are there to help accomplish just that.

Data contracts and data-sharing agreements are still largely topics of ongoing discussion, but they seem to emerge as one possible tool to foster this mutual consumer-producer relationship. We discuss these options next and then outline how to get started with them.

5.7.1   *Data contracts and sharing agreements*

Piethein Strengholt describes *data contracts* as delivery or service contracts (see "Data Contracts—Ensure Robustness in Your Data Mesh Architecture," http://mng.bz/gwnE). If we look at the preceding Cast data product, a data contract could include information like this:

- This is a production-level dataset.
- The dataset is checked for broken records and does not contain test data.
- The interface delivers the data within one second inside the company network.
- We guarantee 95% uptime.
- The roadmap includes a couple of new datasets to be released over the next few months.
- The data product is currently in version 1.0.10.
- We use semantic versioning. That means a bump to 1.0.X means bug fixes, and a bump to 1.X.0 means we added data but did not break or remove anything. Both of these types of changes are downward compatible.
- The schema of the data and any additional metadata.

A *data-sharing agreement* extends on this data contract. While the data contract is still heavy on the data-producer side, the data-sharing agreement specifically targets consumers. It is there to answer the questions of how a dataset is planned to be used and the needed level of security. Data-sharing agreements, therefore, involve the collaboration of producers and consumers. For this dataset, the consumers and producers might reach an agreement like this:

- The goal of sharing this dataset is to enable consumers to inject insights from the actor and role combination into other services. These might be other data products or not.
- The datasets are intended to be used together, using the standard combination mechanism of the common actor identifier to join, as is common at Messflix.

- Since the data is to be used across a wide variety of services, the goal is to have it available publicly, including the actor names, which should be fine with the security level.
- Since a lot of consumers want to analyze data historically, the data will be available with a backfill of three years.

In this agreement, we can spot a lot of collaboration and intention of usage by the consumers. This agreement helps the data product owner John Doe design the data products well from the start. It also prevents him from including unnecessary datasets. The only way to create such an agreement is for John and his consumer to get into a room and talk, before or while he creates the data product, not after.

Let's now take a look at how Messflix as a company could help to implement such data contracts and sharing agreements across the data mesh.

5.7.2   *Implementing data contracts and sharing agreements*

Data contracts and sharing agreements, like the two outlined in the preceding section, can seem daunting to implement. They need to be stored somewhere, possibly have an automatic way of checking them, and must be up-to-date.

Therefore, we recommend a practical step-by-step approach. In our eyes, the most important part to get started is to kick off the discussions between data producers and consumers. On the other side, we warn you to not let a contract-like agreement kill your early data mesh seeds.

> **KEY POINT** We recommend not focusing too much on the contract-like nature of these two artifacts but rather on the mutual discussion of data consumers and producers. In particular, never let the development of a data product be slowed by a not-yet-perfect data contract. It's the discussion that's important, not the final artifact.

Messflix already has an MVP of a self-serve data platform and a few data products, including a basic data catalog. The base work is there, and some data products are as well. So at this point, it's fair to introduce data contracts and sharing agreements in a basic form to make the work of John and his consumers easier. Here are the three main steps:

1. Inspired by the article by Strengholt, the Messflix federated governance body decides to use of a simple web form that can be filled out. This basic data contract is filled out by the data producer of the product. A second web form is used for a joint data-sharing agreement between the producer and consumer. The output of these web forms is stored next to the data catalog. The data catalog contains links to this data contract and agreement.

   The output of step 1 should be that data producers get into the habit of collecting requirements, as discussed at length in this chapter. Data consumers also are getting used to talking to producers. It's about the cultural shift, not about the documents per se.

2 Once your data mesh grows and people get into the habit of communicating, it's time to integrate the data contracts and agreements with all the metadata in your data catalog. Messflix can take this step, after it has a GUI available for data producers and consumers to use. The GUI might be one for data product registration or might be a good data catalog. In any case, after the company has this ready, it integrates the web forms into the GUI and makes sure the agreements and contracts display together with the metadata of the data products.

The output of step 2 should be an integration of the contracts and agreements into the daily work of every participant.

3 Start to automate parts of the contract and agreement processes. This might mean that Messflix has a simple way of providing access policies via the GUI or that Messflix calculates standard metrics for the data products that can be compared to SLAs.

The output of step 3 should be that the contracts and agreements feel easy to use and add a benefit to the participating parties.

As you can see, with step 3, the implementation and automation blend together with the data catalog. Once the cultural shift is in place, mutual collaboration kicks in and becomes a natural part of the self-serve platform and its roadmap.

In this section, we presented tools and techniques to describe a data product so that it can be understood by others (metadata) and used to connect to other data products (FAIR principles). As you can see, creating a useful data product requires a well-thought-out design, established rules, and a set of tools to create them efficiently.

Although we've showed how to design and craft a data product, creating an ecosystem of data products will require standardization of rules for creating and describing those data products, which will be the responsibility of the data governance team. It will also be required to provide a whole set of tools to support teams creating new data products, which will be enabled by the self-serve platform. We will also need strategies for transforming the architecture of existing systems and data into data products. These topics are addressed in subsequent chapters.

Summary

- To make data valuable, we should treat it as more than just an asset.
- To treat data as a product, we apply product thinking to it.
- Data products should be created with users in mind.
- A data product should address clearly defined user needs.
- A data product is an autonomous, read-optimized, standardized data unit, a node in the data mesh architecture, containing at least one dataset (the domain dataset), created for satisfying user needs.
- The data product owner, with the data product development team, is responsible for creating and maintaining the data product, optimizing its usefulness for users.

- Data product data is accessible through one or more ports.
- A data product exposes information interfaces to make it findable and understandable outside the context of its creation.
- A rich metadata description enables data discovery and reusability.
- FAIR principles can be a well-defined base for standardizing data product descriptions.

Federated computational governance

This chapter covers

- Understanding our definition of data governance
- Learning the key benefits of data governance
- Defining the expected deliverables of data governance
- Structuring data-related policies
- Federating data governance
- Making data governance computational

In chapter 4, we kick-started our data mesh and included a lot of governance work right from the start. This chapter dives deeper into how to perform this crucial step.

NOTE While we understand that you may want to get straight to the implementation of data governance, this would be counterproductive. This topic can be approached in too many ways. Governance centralization and automation may be implemented at many levels, creating a vast matrix, impossible to describe in a single chapter. Instead, we show you options and give you pointers on starting the governance design and implementation processes. Still, you need to envision how to utilize governance best to derive value in your organization.

First, we will discuss what data governance is and paint a broad picture of what it means to federate it and make it computational.

Second, we will explain why implementing data governance is a good idea. At the beginning of this book, we indicated that you could implement the principles we describe with varying levels of detail. The second section explains why this nontechnical activity may add value to your business.

Third, we present multiple data governance models. We will show you the extremes of the responsibility distribution—the centralized data governance model and the decentralized data governance model—and follow with the federated Governance model, which takes the best from both approaches and minimizes the downsides of each.

We finish this chapter by showing you the range of possible data governance automation levels. After reading this chapter, you will be able to do the following:

- Design the structure of data governance and define expected deliverables
- Split responsibilities among data governance actors
- Design automation of policy enforcement

Let's start by presenting a general overview of data governance.

6.1   *Data governance in a nutshell*

Before continuing, we must warn you that data governance is a vast concept, with many often incompatible implementations and interpretations. We describe some of these extremes in section 6.4.1. Here is the general definition we compiled for this book.

> **DEFINITION**   *Data governance* is a collection of information-related processes, roles (with a strong emphasis on decision rights and accountabilities), policies, standards, and metrics oriented to maximize the effectiveness of deriving business value from data.

As you can see, data governance describes an environment in which data can be transformed into information, information to knowledge, and so on, up to the business value.

The first and most important point to understand about data governance is that it's a continuous process, not a state. Putting it in motion may be a project, but it needs to become the modus operandi of the company data environment to be effective.

> **DEFINITION**   According to the *Data Management Body of Knowledge* (www.dama .org/cpages/body-of-knowledge), data governance is one of 11 data management knowledge areas. *Data management* deals with all aspects of data handling, from acquisition to architectures to policies. We need to be careful not to expect data governance results belonging to other areas of data management.

DEFINITION *Architecture governance* processes identify, manage, audit, and disseminate all information related to architecture management, contracts, and implementation. For companies dealing with a smaller diversity of data sources and a limited number of systems, the two topics may be overlapping so much that it wouldn't make sense to increase the bureaucracy by duplicating the governance structure to tackle architectural problems. However, in the behemoth of a corporation, you may need to create architecture governance as an equal partner to your data governance. This requires an additional effort but may be well worth it.

Remember Candace and her snow-shoveling business? After reading *Data Mesh in Action*, Candace realized the value of being data driven. She also realized that decentralization was critical to extracting value from her data.

In year 4, Candace extends Adam's and Eve's teams. They now head a small group of 5–10 snow shovelers. Candace realizes that the company needs to be more data driven with this number of people. She knows she has to communicate one message to Adam and Eve: "Collect and use more data!" So in year 4, she makes the central decision to tell the team leaders to keep time on all shovelers and collect all the metrics that work well (figure 6.1).

Figure 6.1 Candace and her newly expanded snow-shoveling squads

But the year doesn't end as expected, little has improved, and Adam and Eve seem unhappy. They can't make sense of the data Candace prescribed them to use. Again, Candace forgot how different the two domains of Adam and Eve are. Candace made a central decision but is really lacking the specific knowledge to make a good central decision on this topic at all.

Adam and Eve are probably the best people to decide which data to use. So before year 5, Candace sits down with Adam and Eve and they decide the following together:

- They want to use more data to inform their decisions; they all agree it's necessary at this size.
- Adam and Eve decide for themselves which data pieces they collect.

Year 5 ends with another nice profit. The two decisions here display why that is. Adam, Eve, and Candace have formed a federated governance body, decided one fundamental rule together, and realized which data to use should be left up to the very heterogeneous domains.

> **DEFINITION** *Federated data governance* is a data governance model. Enterprise-scale decisions are made by the central governing body, and decentralized units are autonomous decision-makers within their domains for all other affairs.

This is *federated governance in action*—a balance between central decisions and local freedom to maximize the local value. But it's not enough for Candace. With the profits from year 5, Candace goes into a spending spree and expands to 20 teams for year 6. The new governance body adds a rule:

> *Local teams can collect data and put the Excel files onto Candace's Dropbox for sharing and to extract some value together.*

For Adam and Eve, this turns out well. They've been working together for a long time, and Eve collects her metrics on driveway lengths and shovel breakdowns that Adam uses to optimize his prices. Eve has put them into a nice Excel sheet with the naming she and Adam have been using over the last few years.

But the other 18 team leads aren't so happy. They have no idea how to read Eve's Excel sheet. So in the next meeting of the governance round, they put up another rule:

> *Shared data pieces have to carry a description explaining the columns and the data.*

It turns out this also enables the other 18 teams to share more data, such as data on the performance of their employees, pricing information for certain city parts, and the like. Unfortunately, sometimes people forget to put up the description with the flood of data. But luckily, Adam, a self-proclaimed hobbyist programmer, writes a little script that goes through every Excel file and emails the owner if the description is missing.

Because the data is sharable and each team can combine it with their data now, profits soar, and Candace ends year 6 swimming in money, surrounded by dozens of happy employees.

In year 6, a lot has happened. First, the business stakeholders realize the value of sharing and combining data. Still, they also realize this is possible only with additional rules set by the governance body and automated checks. The automatic execution of the federated governance rules adds a final word to the topic of this chapter—*computational*—

which makes it *federated computational governance*. The following is our definition; again, we consciously try to be as inclusive as possible.

> **DEFINITION**   *Federated computational data governance* is a data governance model in which policies are translated into algorithms and enforced automatically by the IT infrastructure wherever feasible.

Let's now try to convince you why you should consider data governance a good investment rather than the collateral cost of data mesh development.

6.2   *Benefits of data governance*

The problem with describing the benefits of any high-level solution is that they tend to reflect an ideal world. Let's look at some of the data governance benefit categories and discuss the underlying assumptions required for the benefit to occur.

This should help you form your own opinion about the amount of effort you'll want to invest in this topic. Also, it will help facilitate discussions with the stakeholders you decide to involve.

6.2.1   *Business value perspective*

Let's think about the significance of data governance on decision-making processes in your company. There is a common belief that a decision-maker who has access to a relatively large volume of data should feel well equipped to make decisions. However, such a volume of data comes with its challenges.

First, it's easy to get to the point of information overload. A high volume of data may lead someone to the conclusion that they have "more than enough" data. But, sometimes the volume may be misleading, as all the accessible data may come from, for example, just a few, unrepresentative sources which happen to be easiest to access or digest.

Second, the data may not be adequate regarding the time it represents. Let's imagine someone making budgeting decisions based on the quarterly results of their team, and they usually do it after the data for the previous quarter is provided to them. If this person is required to make their decision earlier, their accuracy may suffer. They will base their decision on inadequate data related to previous quarters.

Finally, the data may be inconclusive. If the analysis is appropriately designed, one of the expected and valid outcomes should be the answer "based on the collected data, we cannot distinguish between two options." Without access to additional data, the usual approach, summarized with "get me some type of answer," is as reliable as the good old coin toss.

It all comes down to the known truth: having the data is not equal to having insight. The data governance in this situation may help by ensuring that users have access to well-described metadata, revealing the actual information content of the data used. But that is not all data governance offers to people looking to increase the business value of collected data.

Data governance also enables the effective use of data to derive business value, ensuring that users have a deeper comprehension of the meaning behind numbers stored in tables. It is made possible thanks to the governed terminology directories, master data management, cooperation between the business people and data crowd on, for example, naming conventions, data quality measures, and data processing.

It is easy to find a straight path to a declaration that data governance, via the improved understanding of the organization's business models and data-driven decision-making, leads to enhanced business planning and increased operational efficiency.

6.2.2 *Data usability perspective*

Data governance can also add value to the business from the data usability perspective. Working with data in a large organizations often comes with four main questions that quickly turn into full-blown problems:

1 What data do we have available?
2 Where is this data?
3 How can I access this data?
4 What is the quality of this data?

Data governance helps answer these questions by assigning responsibilities and metrics related to data findability, availability, and usability. Well-designed data governance will ensure that a known and accountable entity, responsible for the development and maintenance of a continuously updated data catalog, offers insight into what data is available and its access requirements. That data catalog provides a straight answer to the first two previously listed questions.

Data governance also covers concerns related to data security and safety, including access rights and permissions. Again, data governance clearly indicates who is responsible for each bit of data, who can by default use it, and the allowed access protocols. With such a structure in place, the answer to question 3 is easy for data consumers to find.

Similarly, data governance means assigning responsibility for metadata management. It means there should be a clear definition of data quality metrics, and a clear indication of parties and tools ensuring availability of accurate metadata for each data asset.

The conclusion is obvious: data governance done right offers all means for data to become FAIR, a cornerstone of wide usability.

6.2.3 *Data control perspective*

We operate in an era of a constant struggle, as companies and parties are willing to go to great lengths to profit from illegal acquisition of company data or to prove in court that data was mishandled or misused by the company. As a result, the data environment's security, safety, and legal compliance is not a mere luxury, but a necessity. One of the outcomes of data governance is clear ownership of data at each stage of its life cycle.

However, data governance does not stop at pointing fingers. Instead, it helps data owners become or stay compliant with internal and external regulations by doing the following:

- Clearly stating the demands imposed by regulations such as the GDPR, California Consumer Privacy Act (CCPA), or HIPAA
- Providing frameworks enabling meeting these demands

The difference between people doing what they might and data governance offering a coherent way of addressing all questions related to data oversight may equal tens of millions of dollars saved.

Yet again, as a process, data governance is not about creating a glossary of terms or a repository of regulations. Instead, it's supposed to evolve its policies, add codes of conduct, and review best practices. We hope we managed to convince you that data governance is all of the following:

- An essential element of increasing business value derived from data (or preventing the losses), by enforcing transparency of data assets' contents
- A way to maximize usability of data assets, by developing clearly defined roles of responsibility and accountability for data, as well as ensuring that data assets and their access points are mapped and available to data users
- Critical for control over data assets and compliance with internal and external regulations, by having the authority and access to expertise allowing development of actionable policies

To achieve all that, you need to take these steps:

1 Define the deliverables you expect from your data governance bodies.
2 Decide how you will distribute responsibilities and accountability for various governance aspects.
3 Ensure that your governance protocols don't introduce bottlenecks and that the administrative overhead won't slow development.

We will guide you through a possible solution in the following sections, starting with helping you manage the expectations and setting proper governance outcomes.

6.3   Planning data governance outcomes

Data governance is a process involving multiple people across the organization. If you wish to create a data governance framework, you need to ensure that the people you engage are well informed about what is expected of them. Even though data governance is a continuous process, it is expected to deliver explicit outcomes. Defining these outcomes will help you in two ways:

- It will provide a clear vision of what's to be achieved to all the stakeholders and will manage their expectations.
- It will focus on goals rather than processes and make it easier for you to design a framework fitting your organization's needs.

To understand this better, let's get back to your adventure at Messflix.

Chapter 3 showed you how to set up an initial data governance body for your MVP. To better understand the flow of the data governance process, you ask the participants to model steps they would take to transition the general strategic direction into actionable pieces of work.

The exercise starts with two strategic goals. One is sales improvement, and the other is ensuring security of Messflix data. You don't expect the solution to cover all the tasks required to achieve this goal, but are looking for an example of how they would divide and narrow the scope of work before getting to the implementation details. Figure 6.2 presents the result.

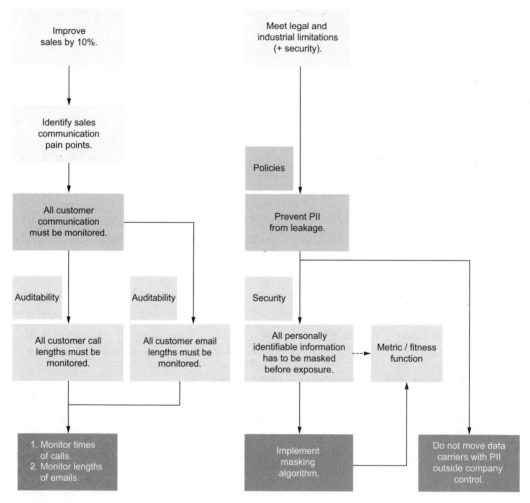

Figure 6.2   Breaking down governance decisions

As you can see, one goal requires six steps, and the other requires five. Let's see how such a breakdown can be generalized and how you can assign responsibilities to the levels to ensure control over and the governance of the whole process.

6.3.1 Hierarchy of data governance outcomes

The data governance process can be efficiently designed if we understand its deliverables. These can be split into three general strata, related to three levels of data governance operations:

- *Strategic*—Outcomes bidirectionally related to the company's strategic direction and environment. Outcomes should reflect a clear translation of strategic goals into data-related actions, usually through policy development.
- *Tactical*—Dealing with practicalities of policies' requirements, thereby aligning expectations with the company's technical and organizational environment.
- *Implementation*—The shop floor actions ensuring that the policies are not just on-paper solutions.

Setting up a complete system that allows end-to-end data governance ensures that your design follows a hierarchy of more and more detailed guidelines.

This process all starts with the business strategy. The business strategy may result in a set of strategic objectives, each of which can be described with its expected key results. *Objectives and key results* is abbreviated as *OKRs* (as noted previously in chapter 2). Policies may be aimed to fulfill OKRs or implicit business requirements. In addition, policies can define elements guiding the development process, such as nonfunctional requirements, principles, standards, constraints, or conventions.

Figure 6.3 presents the general structure of data governance layers. In yellow, a business layer feeds requirements into data governance. This is primarily one-dimensional communication. In green are indicated policies we spoke of earlier. In gold are nonfunctional requirements (*quality attributes*, but we avoid this term so as not to induce confusion with attributes describing the quality of the data itself), principles, constraints, standards, and conventions. Finally, orange indicates the implementation layer.

In the following section, we describe how the responsibility for each layer can be distributed among parties, depending on the assumed governance structure.

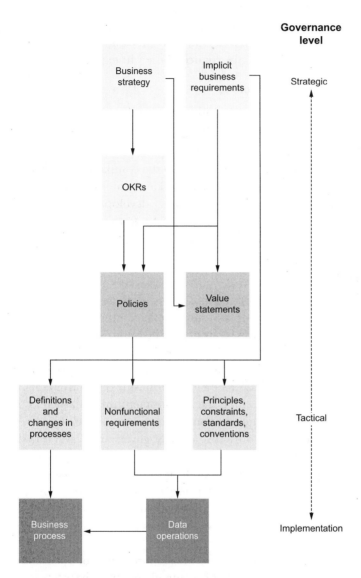

Figure 6.3 Hierarchical structure of data governance layers

6.3.2 *Strategic-level outcomes*

Data governance at the strategic level needs to provide links between company strategy and expectations derived from industry standards and internal workings of data operations. The two main tools we propose here are value statements and policies.

You should expect your governance team working at this level to provide the rest of the company with information on the right things to do.

DEFINING VALUE STATEMENTS

We touched upon the value statement in chapter 3. We explained it's an assertion of causality between a business action and the resulting business value.

A value statement is an important link between business strategy and business actions. These statements do not translate directly into policies or implementation, but serve as a reference point for them. All business actions are performed in the broader business context (and make no mistake, IT and data operations *are* business actions!). Now, actions bring consequences. The question is, in what light do we evaluate the expected outcomes?

> **On the consequences of the lack of value statement**
>
> Let's look at a real-life example. A data scientist proposes a communication test to improve customer understanding: nothing fancy, just A/B testing composed of two messages. The business manager responsible for this communication channel shoots the idea down, asking, "Will performing this test immediately improve my direct KPIs?"
>
> The data scientist cannot convince that manager to send two types of messages, with one likely to perform worse than the other. He is instead expected to come back with just the better ones, but with no testing!
>
> A clear data-related value statement justifying a locally suboptimal action that promises better future performance would be of great help.

You may find a definition indicating that a value statement is supposed to show what the company "believes in." However, it is hard to imagine what "the company" believes. So instead, think of a value statement as a list of the company's highest priorities.

In chapter 3, we presented a general value statement structure, as provided by Robert S. Seiner in *Non-Invasive Data Governance*:

Organizations that [take some action], demonstrate [business value improvement].

In practice, this means that if you plan to take an action directly related to a value statement, you should be able to end any discussion undermining the necessity of this action by using the following argument:

We should take this action, because according to our value statement, it will bring this benefit.

This is, of course, the ultimate argument for the need to take an action. It cannot end the discussion on, for example, a timeline or a budget for such an action.

It is worth remembering that data value statements will be based on the company strategy. So, for example, the statement "Organizations transparently sharing data with the world are perceived as trustworthy" may be true in some cases. Still, we wouldn't be prepared to propose it in the environment of, say, corporate banking.

Don't aim to create overly sophisticated or vague statements. Instead, use them as a codification of common sense.

The statement "Organizations that put effort into proper data documentation demonstrate a lower cost of deploying new machine learning models" may be used as an argument in a discussion with the data owner, who considers its documentation a waste of time. However, the data owner's time can be weighed against the time of people trying to use that data in the future in the context of company priorities.

Overly vague or unclear statements like "Organizations that make a brouhaha about data demonstrate high income" are not nearly as helpful.

CREATING DATA POLICIES

Policies are the primary tool in the central governance body's toolbox. They enable consistency of data solutions across the organization and ensure interoperability of data products.

In appendix B, we present as an example the metadata management policy developed at Messflix. (This policy is based on a metadata policy prepared by the UK Office for National Statistics, http://mng.bz/e76v, and published under Open Government License 3.0, http://mng.bz/pOe8.)

This particular example of a policy is specific in terms of accountability of the metadata, but from the technical perspective, it specifies only the location of the central metadata repository. It also links to the retention policy as a source of additional information. Therefore, it leaves data product owners a lot of operational freedom regarding implementing necessary measures.

The following list presents some policy elements that you may use to create a policy frame:

- *Information card*—Metadata of the policy, presenting information such as the owner of the policy, contact details, and version info.
- *Purpose*—A short explanation of the expected outcome of setting up this policy. It can be clarification of procedures, consistency of behaviors, outlining standards, etc.
- *Scope*—The definition of context in which a given policy will be used. It may relate to groups, locations, project types, periods, etc.
- *Goals*—Identification of expected effects on the organization. The related KPIs may accompany it.
- *Responsibilities*—Clearly defined persons with assigned responsibilities outlined in the policy.
- *Technical guidelines*—If applicable, the required/promoted technology stack will be identified and listed.
- *Reporting requirements*—If the actions driven by the given policy require reporting, the reporting schedule should be clearly stated. If the reporting parties were not defined in the Responsibilities section, they should also be identified here.

When preparing consistent data governance policies in your organization, you need to think about legal and industry-specific requirements for the data you work with. However, to give you a starting point, let's look at key policy types your data governance body will have to deal with:

- *Data collection*—Specifying, for example, the purpose of data collection, related data acquisition processes, and routines
- *Data inventory*—Specifying timelines and life cycles of data, security and safety technologies, and rules for destroying the data
- *Data access*—Specifying data sensitivity and access levels, to ensure that data users will be given appropriate access to the data
- *Data quality*—Specifying roles responsible for ensuring data quality, and tools and processes allowing them to serve this purpose
- *Data usage*—Specifying data use limitations resulting from laws, standards, and ethics
- *Data integrity*—Specifying ways to ensure the consistency, reliability, and trustworthiness of the company's data at each access point
- *Data security*—Specifying all the measures your company implements to prevent data loss and misuse

Each of these topics may require more than one policy. To get a bit more specific, let's look at a few policies related to data security:

- *Employee requirements policy*—Clarifying employee behaviors associated with dealing with data
- *Data leakage prevention policy*—Describing ways of monitoring sensitive data transfers
- *Encryption policy*—Defining recommended encryption technologies used to secure the data

We realize that data governance seems a daunting task. However, you should remember that, like the rest of data mesh, it's not a task you're expected to do yourself.

TECHNOLOGY STACK–RELATED POLICIES

The topic, which should be approached at the policy level with extreme caution, relates to the technology stack. There is a fine line between your central data governance body having a say in choosing the strategic direction of the technology stack and being overburdened with a selection of tools for each possible data task in the company. Therefore, your central data governance body may be inclined to participate in the development of a toolbox by enabling the following:

- Development of policies
- Documentation
- Data catalogs
- Metadata management
- Master data management

All these tools aim to standardize elements of operations shared by all development teams, not affecting the details of product development itself.

The central governance body needs to clearly distinguish what tools it wants to support centrally, using, for example, the economy of scale, to ensure cost-effectiveness, or to avoid problems with compatibility. Within this category, the body should again distinguish what tool will be mandatory to use by all development teams (and limit this list to a required minimum) and what sets of tools serving similar purposes could be offered as a selection list.

The central governance body could decide on a cloud infrastructure provider (if the governance body negotiated preferential prices), or on a logging solution (to simplify maintenance of a critical functionality). For codebase maintainability, central governance could also decide to limit a list of tools for, for example, event processing.

The tools not requiring central support nor affecting the interoperability of the teams should be left at the discretion of data product owners.

6.3.3   *Tactical-level outcomes*

Tactical-level governance means ensuring the feasibility of the proposed solutions. The strategic level of data governance focuses on doing the right things, whereas tactical-level governance focuses on doing things right. To ensure that your data governance does not end with the publication of policies, you need to discuss at least two critical topics: nonfunctional requirements of policies and data responsibilities.

DETAILING POLICIES

Designing a policy that can be implemented requires a good knowledge of the environment. Let's take as an example a policy related to data security.

We could think that a policy requiring biometric scanning as an authentication method for access to the company's laptops would increase the safety of data. Let's assume that such a solution would indeed increase security, but what if most of the company's equipment is not equipped with the required scanners? Maybe updating the personnel's equipment would be a good idea anyway (if it's obsolete and slows all company's operations), or maybe the difference between biometric and two-factor authentication does not justify the costs.

A data security policy could also define other implementation-driving factors. The principles may define which types of data have to always be encrypted, such as PII or the company's financial data. The constraints may define the lifespan of this data. The standards may define encryption algorithms used. Preparation of the policy details requires a good understanding of the data that's in the possession of the company and its level of sensitivity; the timeline of each data type's business usage and related legal constraints; and finally, the currently implemented standards and how they compare to industry standards.

Discussing the feasibility of proposed policies is a good measure, preventing actors at a high level of governance from operating from an ivory tower. To implement this discussion in your company, you'll need to develop robust mechanisms for a bilateral communication of policymakers with subject-matter experts that include, for example, a transparent and searchable feedback cycle. In addition, to ensure that your governance body can find a balance between policy direction and applicability, you need to include processes of utilizing internal resources or acquiring outside help in your governance setup.

ASSIGNING ACCOUNTABILITY AND RESPONSIBILITY FOR DATA

The primary goal of the data governance process is to ensure *accountability* for each bit of the company's data. Therefore, it is the most critical element to keep in mind, independently of which path to data governance you may take.

Similar to nonfunctional requirements, this part of governance requires the know-how of a company's operations and needs to reflect the realities of data use. To achieve clarity in terms of data accountability, you should ask your governance body to answer a set of questions concerning each data asset:

- *Who?* To properly execute accountability, make sure your organization always knows the following:
  - Who owns the given bit of data?
  - Who approves the given bit of data to use, and who decides its access rights?
  - Who sets up security measures to protect the given data, and what are they?
  - Who is responsible for compliance with data regulations?
  - Who is using the data?
- *What?* This indicates the precise definition of the kinds of data your organization processes, and *who* should have access to each type of data.
- *When?* If time constraints are placed on data availability (e.g., imposed by regulations), they should be taken into consideration by the data governance and clearly defined as to *what* kind of data access is time dependent for *whom.*
- *Where?* This question is critical from a data security point of view. Ensuring clear data storage for sensitive data makes it much easier to detect *who* accessed *what* and *when.*
- *Why?* Multiple constraints exist on data usage, whether legal or ethical. Ensuring that the data is used with a clear and proper purpose is one of the reasons behind setting up the whole data governance process.

Knowing all that will give your company a good understanding of the responsibilities of each person who has access to any bit of the company's data.

One thing to remember: as with most other data governance activities, answering these questions is not a one-off exercise. The data governance team needs to ensure that data assets are reviewed periodically (with the period depending on the nature of the data contained in each asset).

6.3.4 *Implementation-level outcomes*

The implementation level is where the hard work occurs, where data is generated, maintained, processed, and accessed. Without ensuring that all the policies are actually taken into account when implementation decisions are being made, the whole governance process is just a massive waste of time and effort.

What can you do to help your development teams go beyond the apparent expectation that each employee will stick to the rules defined in policies? We propose you think of implementation-level governance in two categories. One is the governance of domain data, and the other is the governance of the central software platform.

DOMAIN GOVERNANCE

Domains are the default granularity of data ownership in a data mesh. What should you expect data product owners to provide in the context of data governance?

The essential role of data owners in data governance is their input into metadata management. They need to design, deploy, and manage data models for their internal use and connect them to centrally governed metamodels and ontologies of the company's data.

Responsibility for the development of data models implies understanding the definitions of data and providing data users with a point of contact for their questions and requests. If data is generated and managed at the domain level, the first line of data quality control will also be implemented there. You should expect domain governance to provide processes for monitoring the quality of data presented to the outside world and used internally.

With the domain level as the main access point to data, as in the case of domain-oriented data products, the domain governance body has the responsibility for implementing data access policies.

CENTRAL PLATFORM GOVERNANCE

In chapter 3, when describing the implementation of the Messflix MVP, we mentioned the principle of self-serve infrastructure as a platform, defined as the central platform. We expand on this topic in chapters 7 and 8. From a data governance perspective, we could generalize it to the IT solution connecting data products and data producers with data consumers, whether they're humans, other services, or other data products themselves.

What would be expected from the team responsible for implementing such a platform from the data governance perspective? First and foremost, the team members should help formulate technical details of data access policies. Any solution deeply incompatible with existing infrastructure would mean the creation of a bottleneck until the platform team could restore the alignment.

Second, they should develop a clear set of quality metrics used for data product evaluation. And third, they should provide standards of data documentation. They should ensure that each data product owner can easily find information about what the metadata of their data product should look like. Finally, they need to collect and communicate all the data product requirements.

Now that we know the outcomes you should expect from data governance, let's look at how data governance can be structured.

6.4 Federating data governance

Data governance spans a company's entire structure, starting with C-level executives and ending with intern developers who write code for software solutions. However, as much as each level of personnel needs to have a role in the governance process, we generally distinguish two primary levels: central and local.

Depending on your organizational structure, the details may differ. Still, a rule of thumb is that *central governance* is responsible for decisions spanning the entire organization. On the other hand, *local governance* means control over a single system or set of systems.

In the case described in chapter 3, the central governance setup at Messflix is embodied by the data governance team. Depending on the data governance's maturity level, you may encounter a data governance council, data governance partners, data governance office, etc.

On the other hand, there are people responsible for day-to-day data operations. In some cases, they may be called data stewards (or domain data stewards); sometimes this role will be performed by product owners who are responsible for developing IT systems. For example, in a data mesh, this function is carried out by data product owners.

This chapter describes how responsibilities for various layers of data governance can be distributed.

6.4.1 Thinking of data governance in terms of "sliders"

The two extremes of data governance are the centralized operating model and decentralized operating model. The former assumes full decision-making capability in the hands of a central governing body, with respective teams left with just the implementation of decided solutions. On the other hand, the latter often does not even allow the existence of a central governing body, shifting the full responsibility for data operations aspects to developers.

The *federated model* aims to find a balance between the long-term perspective and big-picture view offered by the central governance body, and the dynamics and flexibility of development ensured by a high level of autonomy of empowered product owners.

There is no one-size-fits-all solution. Depending on the specifics of your organization, different centralization levels may be optimal. However, there is no need to overcomplicate things by trying to split responsibilities case by case for each product owner. Previously, figure 6.3 presented the hierarchical structure of data governance layers. Figure 6.4 represents further generalization of this idea, with vertical "sliders" dividing the responsibilities for different levels of governance.

Are your data product owners capable of defining nonfunctional requirements for policies? Let them do it. Would they prefer to get them from upstairs, trusting that the data governance team will consider the view of multiple teams? Shift the responsibility there. You may need to modify the proposed tree and add intermediary levels. We suggest identifying the split point on the general structure. This approach is much more

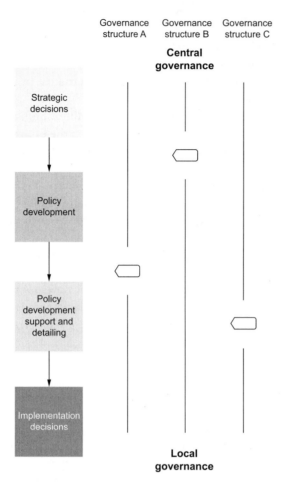

Figure 6.4   **Various governance structures, with responsibilities split at different points within the data governance layers**

robust than allowing some, maybe even more experienced, product owners to make their own rules, different from those adhered to by others.

6.4.2   *Extreme ends of data governance models*

As we previously mentioned, depending on your organization's needs, your governance model could be positioned on a scale between centralized data governance and decentralized data governance. Let's look at these models in a bit more detail, because to design any hybrid solution, you will need to select and combine elements from both.

CENTRALIZED DATA GOVERNANCE MODEL: TOP-DOWN DECISION FLOW

As we mentioned previously, a top-down management model is at one extreme of data governance. In this case, a single governance body or even a single person makes decisions and shapes all data governance.

This approach has some benefits. For example, decision-making in smaller environments may be highly time-effective. Usually, the centralized governance model also assumes central control over the costs of data-related operations—it implies a much higher level of control and ease of financial planning. The other benefit may be clarity of reporting structure. Because all the reports are directed to a central governance body, there isn't much space for misinterpretations and oversimplifications, which are common at report collation by middle management. Also, the central governance team should have access to the expertise required to fulfill legal obligations, whereas expecting every product owner to have such capability may be too optimistic. Finally, a centralized approach makes ensuring master and metadata cohesiveness easier from a pure data perspective. A single body owning its setting can ensure that data consumers' requests are introduced in a way that does not disrupt any data areas.

The most obvious cons of this approach are the rigidity of the whole setup and stripping freedom of choice from the development level. While this approach may be a viable option for a smaller organization, but with an increased number of data sources and teams, the central governance team becomes a bottleneck. Furthermore, too many complex problems requiring the attention of a group often lead to the loss of the bigger picture. Finally, a centralized model, requiring formal communication, leads to overgrown bureaucratic overhead on even the simplest operations and modifications needed at the local level, aggressively slowing development.

DECENTRALIZED DATA GOVERNANCE MODEL: BOTTOM-UP DECISION FLOW

We can implement decentralized governance in two ways. One is leaving data ownership to software system product owners, and the other is regulating data governance with all kinds of data committees, guilds, or councils.

Such empowerment of product owners has some benefits. For one, each system can be quickly changed and adapted. Also, such a setup often leads to open development platforms, where anyone can experiment and provide business with new tools, products, and services. Furthermore, decentralized structures are believed to be more meritocratic. Last but not least, the independence of systems leaves the whole setup less likely to contain a single point of failure.

However, this garden of roses does not come without a thorn or three. First, each system team working independently on its infrastructure protocols may cause major disconnections, and the big picture of owned data may be lost. Second, maintaining the expertise required to fulfill legal obligations, for example, becomes multiplied or missing, at the same time increasing the cost and lowering chances of covering the entirety of data operations. Third, data infrastructure initiatives lack the power of the scale, and differences in technology stacks and formats lead to an increased difficulty of cross-domain analysis.

6.4.3 *Federated data governance model*

As this chapter title suggests, a federated data governance model is the one that the data mesh proposes as a way to combine the strengths of two extreme models and eliminate their weaknesses. If this model is well executed, its main benefit results from combined strengths of the central governance body offering long-term vision and the cohesiveness of strategic initiatives and far-reaching autonomy of product owners, who are capable of flexible management of their domain.

How do you do a federated data governance right? In an October 2019 Gartner report, Saul Judah lists seven foundations for good data governance (see "Best Practices for a Modern Data and Analytics Governance," http://mng.bz/Oo0R). We have divided these foundations into three main focus areas:

- Decision space
- Governance structure
- People

Let's see how federated data governance can help you lay them.

DECISION SPACE FOCUS

The *decision space* in this context is the decision-making environment, including decision points, supporting data, possible decisions, and their quantified outcomes (e.g., within a risk management framework). If well designed, this focus ensures that decisions are consciously made and well informed. The following critical elements ensure that the decision space is built in a way that enables the decision-makers:

- *A focus on business value and organizational outcomes*—You need to ensure that your data product owners indeed work closely with their business domains. This focus will offer them a deep understanding of the immediate business needs of business units. On the other end, your central governance body should provide alignment for strategic initiatives with enterprise priorities.
- *Transparent decision-making that hews to a set of ethical principles*—The ultimate acid test for each decision is its adherence to value statements, described in section 6.3.1. Ensure that the value statement developed by the central governance body agrees with your company's ethics. It will offer data product owners clear guidance and boundaries for their decision-making processes.
- *Internal agreement on data accountability and decision rights*—You should design your federated data governance with a good understanding of various levels of responsibility and accountability and their distribution. As mentioned in section 6.3.3, the split of responsibilities between the central governance body and data product owners should be clearly defined at the hierarchy of governance layers, not case by case.

GOVERNANCE STRUCTURE FOCUS

In this context, the *governance structure* is the design framework and implementation of rules and policies aimed at ensuring proper handling of the company's data. On the one hand, it should be as transparent as possible, not imposing any unnecessary work related to maintenance of the framework itself. On the other hand, the governance structure needs to be all-encompassing; there should be no way to handle company's data outside of this framework. Ensuring that the following elements are deeply embedded in the governance structure will increase its resilience and purposefulness:

- *A trust-based governance model that relies on data lineage and curation*—Ensure that the complete log of data lineage is among the responsibilities of the central governance team and is automatically executed within the central platform. You then need to trust your data product owners to use the offered environment, not try to circumvent it.
- *Risk management and data security included as core governance components*—Such problems require broad, expensive-to-acquire expertise and careful local implementation. Ensuring proper resourcing of the central governance body can allow them cost-effective acquisition of said expertise. Furthermore, offering data product owners sufficient access to expert knowledge may ensure that risk and safety concerns are addressed in actual existing systems, not only on paper.

PEOPLE FOCUS

The effectiveness of any system is dependent on its the adoption by intended users. In this context, it's the people who make governance efficient and fit for purpose. The following elements facilitate the wide adoption and deep understanding of governance, its role, and related expectations:

- *Ongoing education and training, with mechanisms to monitor their effectiveness*—As in the case of risk management and security, well-provided central governance may develop a second line of control by, for example, monitoring data product owners' training and skills, and supporting their learning wherever necessary. This focus also ensures a higher quality of education by utilizing the economy of scale to cost-effectively purchase training.
- *Collaborative culture and governance process that encourages broad participation*—If you ensure clear communication channels connecting the central governance body with data product owners, the dynamic nature of federated governance will manifest itself. The empowered position of data product owners has collaboration and participation embodied in its structure.

At Messflix, you opt for three separate central governance bodies and a far-reaching autonomy of data product owners.

MESSFLIX DATA GOVERNANCE COUNCIL

As pictured in figure 6.5, the primary role of the data governance council at Messflix is to monitor the business strategy and make sure that data initiatives are aligned with it. The tools at the data governance council's disposal are at the policy level.

It is also worth mentioning that the data governance council's responsibility is to ensure that the data mesh meets the business needs and requirements.

> **NOTE** The data governance council in this setup could be compared to the legislative arm of the government. It decides what should happen, but not necessarily how it should happen. However, to avoid bureaucracy and document duplication, some policies should be very detailed and not require additional reading, such as documents prepared by other bodies. In such a case, appropriate experts should pass the parts of policy related to implementation to the data governance council.

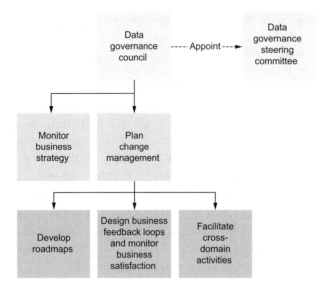

Figure 6.5   Responsibilities of the Messflix data governance council

Another prerogative of the data governance council is appointing and dismissing the data governance steering committee members.

The data governance council is composed of people not directly involved in software development. This measure distances central governance from the operations.

Such strict disconnection is not necessary. However, it may prevent the imbalance introduced by strong-willed data product owners who could effectively turn such a setup into centralized governance under their rule.

MESSFLIX DATA GOVERNANCE STEERING COMMITTEE

The Messflix data governance steering committee is set up to work closer to governance execution than the data governance council. Its members, appointed by the data governance council, are subject-matter experts either recruited from existing development teams or hired from the outside to fill gaps in required competencies.

The team's role in the Messflix governance structure is two-fold (figure 6.6). One task is to monitor legal and industrial environments, and translate the observed changes into standards and requirements presented in policies. The other task is the development of nonfunctional requirements for policies, both developed by themselves and by the data governance council.

This body works on the details of master and metadata management, security, and solutions, allowing communication between data products and automation of technology-based policies. They are also responsible for oversight of the work of the central platform team.

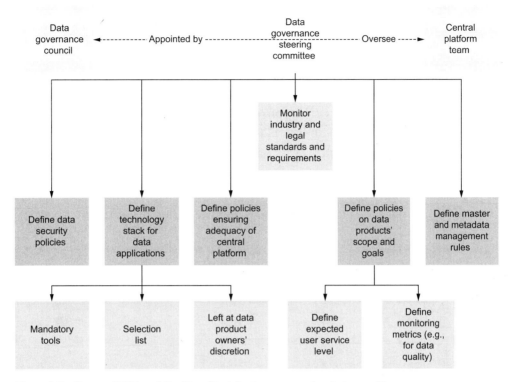

Figure 6.6   Responsibilities of the Messflix data governance steering committee

Figure 6.7 presents the structure of the data governance steering committee. It's worth mentioning that some committee members have more than one of the identified positions. This is because the developed structure is created to reflect responsibilities and expertise required for the company's functioning, not the knowledge of available individuals.

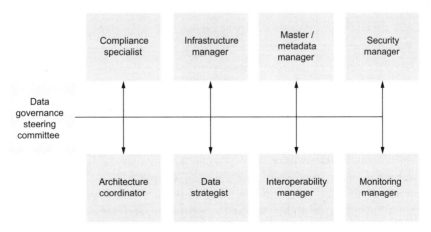

Figure 6.7   Composition of the Messflix data governance steering committee

MESSFLIX CENTRAL PLATFORM TEAM

The central platform team is tasked with developing the self-serve data infrastructure as a platform for Messflix. This development team is built around the former Data team.

On the one hand, The team's responsibility is to monitor policies related to operations of the central platform and to make sure the implementation meets the requirements. On the other hand, team members are to be actively engaged in policy development and tasked with providing feedback and specific advice on implementation. It is also the team's job to support groups deploying data products and connecting them to the mesh (figure 6.8).

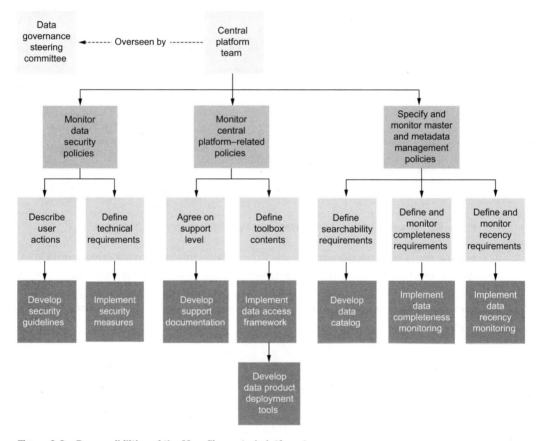

Figure 6.8   Responsibilities of the Messflix central platform team

MESSFLIX DATA PRODUCT OWNER

Messflix data product owners have complete control over the operations of their team. However, their freedom of operations is restricted by the principles, constraints, and standards described in the nonfunctional requirements. Still, within these boundaries, it is their responsibility to take appropriate actions to implement solutions needed to meet the expectations of businesses they work with.

However, a substantial change, a data ownership element, distinguishes their new data product owner position from a previous product owner's. They now have complete control over data models and schema used within their domains but have to meet precise criteria for all the data they present outside in the form of the data product (figure 6.9).

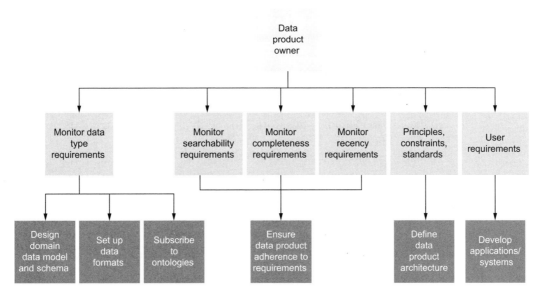

Figure 6.9   Data governance–related responsibilities of Messflix data product owners

Knowing *what* needs to happen is a necessity. However, to put this knowledge *into action*, it's good to have a process turning a group of concerned stakeholders into a well-functioning team. In the next section, we'll show you how you can approach this problem.

6.4.4   Setting-up governance team operations

Here we present steps for governance implementation, as presented by the Business Application Research Center (BARC):

1   *Define goals and understand the benefits.* This step is critical from the perspective of being able to convince the appropriate stakeholders. The alignment of project and enterprise strategic goals is key to successfully implementing data governance in the enterprise.

2   *Analyze the current state and delta analysis.* This is another critical element of communication. The viability of the benefits resulting from governance solutions results from comparing the expected and current situations.

3   *Derive a roadmap.* This is another method of building the proposed solution's viability and a prerequisite of expectation management.

4   *Convince stakeholders and plan the project budget.* This is a must-have. Focusing on the benefits and viability of the solution usually works best. From the business perspective, the properties of the solution are not necessary. As we mentioned, sometimes iron-fisted single-person governance may be the optimal solution for the company. Neither decentralization, not achieving FAIR, nor even increased data connectivity may be convincing enough. The choice should become evident if you connect these effects to business value.

5   *Develop and plan the data governance program.* This is what we're helping you with in this chapter. First, you need to have a clear vision of how things should look before putting things into motion, from the organizational structure to the division of responsibilities.

6   *Implement the data governance program.* This is the hard work. Fortunately, as with all data mesh elements, this work is not only yours. Federated data governance is a team effort.

7   *Monitor and control.* In this critical yet often overlooked element, the data governance council, or its equivalent, should decide on quality metrics early and ensure their implementation. Business feedback is vital as an element of the second line of progress control.

At this stage, you will have clearly defined responsibilities and accountability for different aspects of your data assets, from adherence to regulatory requirements, to data ownership, to monitoring of data-quality metrics. When describing the central governance model, we warned about bottlenecks and overhead resulting from the communication requirements. Federated governance may remove some of this burden, but if done manually, the number of repetitive tasks laid on the central governance body may still result in a significant slowdown of operations. The next step in unclogging the development pipeline is automating repetitive governance tasks, making data governance computational.

6.5   *Making data governance computational*

This section explains what *computational* means and why making data governance computational is necessary from the very beginning of your journey.

Making governance policies entirely computational requires two steps. Step 1 is to convert the policy into a form that can be automated, and step 2 is to automate the execution. In step 2, it is not necessary to automate everything. Instead, you can choose a level of automation that fits your current level of data maturity and slowly increase that by repeating these two steps from time to time. By *computational,* the data mesh paradigm describes the automatic testing or execution of data governance rules.

Our starting point is an understanding of our policies, which we should now have in a written form. They could read, for instance, as follows:

- No personalized information is allowed to be shared without strict access control.
- All data should contain metadata that identifies its business domain.

The first policy is meant to help implement privacy regulations. In contrast, the second one aims to make data more FAIR by using the company's pool of ubiquitous language for business domains.

Neither example is a must-have policy. Indeed, the second one might be too tight for the average company, but for Messflix, both do fit.

Computational data governance is necessary from the very beginning of the data mesh to utilize the mesh character itself. Without governance, it is not possible to consume or combine nodes of the data mesh in a self-serve manner. If this is not possible, human intervention is needed, which doesn't scale and thus stops the data mesh at its beginning.

6.5.1 *Making policies computational*

Making a policy *computational* means turning it into an algorithm.

> **DEFINITION**   We can loosely define an *algorithm* as a set of steps that can be automatically followed, possibly having an input and an output.

Turning a policy into an algorithm sounds like something a developer would do. But that's not recommended at all. Instead, the governance team should do it because turning a policy into an algorithm will always put a particular interpretation into the words, which means the policy will get modified or clarified by this process.

At the same time, the governance team will also have to think about how deep it wants to go by enforcing a particular policy. Let's look at two examples to understand this.

EXAMPLE 1: BUSINESS DOMAIN INFORMATION

The policy for this example is as follows:

- All data should contain metadata that identifies its business domain.

From our MVP, the governance team can turn this policy into an algorithm pretty easily, as shown here

- Input—Metadata for a domain data product from the central registry.
- Retrieve the business unit key in the metadata.
- Compare it to the list of business units.
- Output—`True` if the business unit is contained in the list, `False` otherwise.

The governance team members will quickly realize that at this point, they will have to actually define the list of business units someplace. They might choose to ignore specific units, choose a standardized spelling, or simply refer to an already existing source of truth.

Whatever they do will affect the actual policy and slightly change it. The second example is a bit deeper.

EXAMPLE 2: PERSONALIZED INFORMATION

Here's the policy for example 2:

- No personalized information is allowed to be shared without strict access control.

The governance team will likely have a hard time putting this policy into an algorithm, and so would we. The last policy applied to only one specific metadata field, whereas this policy regards all of the data contents.

In this case, we can develop a simpler good-enough version of this policy, as follows:

- Input—Data of one actual domain data product.
- Check whether the data is in the form of First Name Last Name or X@Y.Z or typical IP addresses.
- If that is not the case, return `True`; otherwise, return `False`.

The key takeaway is that the algorithmic policies will differ from the actual policies we want to enforce. That is fine as long as we keep that in mind and update the algorithmic policies whenever needed.

6.5.2 *Automating policy checks*

To make the rule automatic, we have a lot of freedom. The six levels of vehicle autonomy (http://mng.bz/YGBB) can serve as a good guideline for slowly iterating through *stages of automation.*

For Messflix and these two examples, we don't think it's necessary to turn them into wholly automated policies. As you saw in the previous section, doing so is pretty hard. And if we are just starting with our data mesh MVP, it might not even be necessary to turn the business unit policy into something fully automated.

The six levels of autonomous driving can be roughly summarized as follows:

- *Level 0*—No automation at all. Someone operates *everything.* That is your starting point. You drive yourself.
- *Level 1*—Assistance system, providing some kind of help, such as monitoring/alerting, like a speed monitor or a distance monitor.
- *Level 2*—This level describes partial automation of a part of the system you want to automate. But the operator still has to do other things. For example, the "keep distance" function or a "lane assist" function in a car fits into this category.
- *Levels 3 to 5*—Fully autonomous operation, although in steps. We won't need the details; we'll just call it *autonomous.* This means you can let go of the driving wheel.

Let's apply these levels to our policy-checking system. If we keep our system at level 0, we don't get any automatically enforced policies. If we start with our business unit policy, that might be fine, but once many data products get added every week, we will want some degree of automation.

However, we will need some kind of automation from the beginning for the personalized information policy if we consider this policy truly important. Our human resources will not be able to go through vast amounts of data.

If we keep the first policy at level 0, a person from the Yellow team will need to go through the JSON files and validate them. So let's keep that for now.

What would a level-1 system for the personalized information policy look like? Every time new data is pushed into the corresponding Git repository, a script launches and goes through the data, searching for a couple of predefined patterns. As a monitor, the only thing it should do is return the corresponding rows and the found pattern to the team members that pushed the data. They can then decide for themselves whether they just broke the policy.

Once the Yellow team feels confident with its script, the team members could decide to turn it into a level 2 system by advancing with partial automation. That means they would install it, for instance, as a pre-commit Git hook inside the repositories where the data lives. Then, every time a person pushes new data into the repository, the checks will automatically run before the data flows into the system. The Yellow team might even decide to stop the commit by returning an error if the policy is not met.

Of course, because checking for personalized data isn't easy, this automated script could still be faulty. So the Yellow team would provide an override option on its first try.

A level 3+ autonomous *system* for this part would have an improved policy-checking script and no override option, possibly applying automated transformations to the personalized data to not stop the flow of the emitting team. This could include a pseudonymizer or a white-out function.

As you can see, it's easily possible to iterate through the stages quickly, have various checks at different levels depending on where the human bottleneck is, and consider the severity of governance rule breaks.

Summary

- Data governance aims to clarify processes, roles, policies, standards, and metrics, enabling effective derivation of business value from data.
- Data governance outcomes can be organized into a hierarchical structure, from strategic outcomes influencing the enterprise as a whole, to outcomes affecting local decisions.
- Data governance outcomes can be decided on centrally or locally, or the responsibility can be divided between central and local authorities. Moving the bulk of responsibilities toward either end of the spectrum has pros and cons.
- A data mesh assumes that the responsibilities for data governance will be split between central and local authorities. One method to divide these responsibilities is to use the hierarchical structure of outcomes, and choose a threshold dividing central and local governance authorities' areas of control.
- The model most often fitting the data mesh is one where policies are decided on the central level, but data product owners have operational freedom and independence of their implementation.
- In many cases, policy enforcement can be embedded into the central platform.

7

The self-serve
data platform

This chapter covers

- Understanding how our MVP fits into a self-serve data platform
- Building a self-serve data platform in three iterations
- Applying platform thinking
- Exploring X as a service
- Working with the modular plane architecture

In the first part of this book, you learned all the basics of the data mesh. That included building a data mesh MVP for Messflix within a month in chapter 3. The data mesh MVP contains a minimal self-serve platform.

After Messflix starts to build data product after data product, a lot of duplication of efforts happens in terms of ingestion tooling and other data-related technologies. These data-related skills are specialized. Thus, once we start to grow the number of data products, it is time to recall an already known idea: self-serve platforms.

The purpose of a self-serve platform is to take the duplicated and specialized skills out of the many development teams and put them into one platform. Because the platform will be used by many teams, we usually strive to make it *self-serve*, meaning it retains as much of the development teams' autonomy as possible.

> **KEY POINT**   *Platforms reduce duplicate effort.* A self-serve platform is a key to the data mesh, because a lot of data mesh skills are quite specialized. Thus, a lot of duplicate effort will take place across data-producing and -consuming teams. A platform reduces these efforts, enabling them to be done once and providing them as a capability in a self-serve manner to the data-producing and -consuming teams.

This chapter focuses on exactly that: how to build a proper self-serve data platform and a handful of concepts that come in handy for doing it right the first time around. We will do so by first recalling our minimal platform from chapter 3. And then we'll improve it in three separate iterations.

In the first section, you'll learn a definition of *platform*. We'll also dive into *platform thinking*. We'll apply these two concepts so you can understand first and foremost why we are building a platform (product), and then we'll quickly group the target user groups of our platform.

In the second section, you'll learn about *X as a service* and apply this collaboration mode to make the data consumers' work easier.

In the third section, you'll learn about modular plane architectures in the context of platforms, as well as the architecture of a generic platform. We'll apply that to make the data producers' life easier.

In the last section, we will take another round of inspiration from the previously learned concepts and apply them to increase the value for the data producers by a lot.

To make life easier for you, table 7.1 shows the concepts you'll learn in this chapter as well as an overview of the three iterations of our self-serve platform.

Table 7.1   Concepts explained in this chapter

Concepts	Section
Definition of platform and platform thinking	7.1
X as a service	7.2
The architecture of a platform	7.3

The topic of *federated computational governance*, with an emphasis on *computational* (which you discovered in the preceding chapter), is of particular importance. We will highlight it again in each iteration. Let's take a look at our already existing platform.

7.1   *The MVP platform*

In chapter 3, we built an MVP for our data mesh. It consists of the following:

- A central CSV store in the form of a Git repository
- A simple scripted mechanism that allows for checking in a configuration JSON file containing a data product definition
- A simple governance rule check
- A wiki page explaining how to use this Git repository from both a data consumer and a data producer perspective

Figure 7.1 shows the technical architecture of our minimal platform. You might recall it from chapter 2. You can see the central Git repository for data products that live inside the self-serve data platform, maintained by the Yellow team. Also, both team Yellow and team Green are data producers. Finally, we have an analyst who is consuming data by using the self-serve data platform.

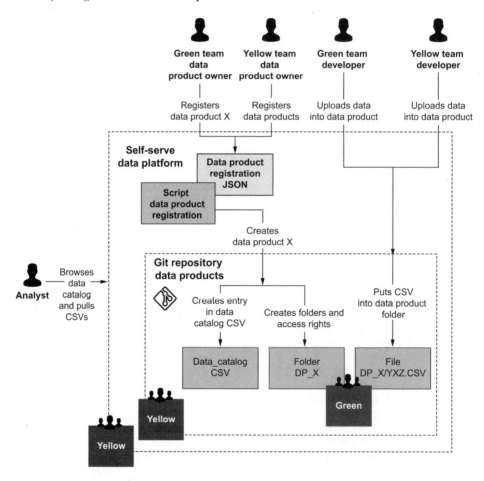

Figure 7.1   The basic interactions of users with the first version of the platform

In our MVP, we deploy a registration script. This registration script validates the provided JSON and checks for simple governance policies. At the beginning of the data mesh, Messflix decided to focus on findability and accessibility, so the first computational checks test for completeness of the metadata that is checked in, particularly fields such as description, business unit, owner, and the like.

The result of the computational check is then played back to the data product owner who registers the product so they have a chance to correct possible mistakes. This is a simple version of federated computational governance.

But what exactly is a platform in general, and why did this one emerge as our first solution?

7.1.1 Platform definition

We will use a generic definition of *platform* that unifies many current definitions. Economists tend to define platforms this way.

> **DEFINITION** A *platform* mediates between different parties. Its purpose is to make interaction faster, easier, better, more valuable, and more frictionless.

For every platform, we need to identify at least three things:

- Which *parties* are mediated between?
- Which *interactions* are taking place through the platform?
- How does each party *interact with the platform*? How does the "mediation" work?

Let's answer these questions for our MVP platform.

APPLICATION TO OUR PLATFORM

If we look at our platform MVP in our architecture diagrams, we can quickly see interactions. However, the platform already abstracts a few things away. So let's take a close look at figure 7.2.

Which parties are interacting with the platform? We have data product owners and developer teams, which we can group into *data producers*, albeit the two subgroups will have different requirements that you should consider separately.

We have analysts and other development teams as our *data consumers*. Again, we have two very different kinds of consumers with different requirements.

Finally, we have a lot of *data products*. Considering data products as a party is a big advantage. First of all, it displays the true nature of the interaction. Data consumers' prime interests are the pieces of data, not the people producing them. Ideally, that's all they would need, but of course, that is never enough because data consumers need context to work with data.

So the second interest of data consumers is to communicate with the data producers. In the data mesh, we aim to have that communication automatic because any personal communication does not scale into the mesh. Automatic communication happens primarily through the data catalog or the discovery endpoints of the data products or any other automatic mechanism we build into the self-serve data platform.

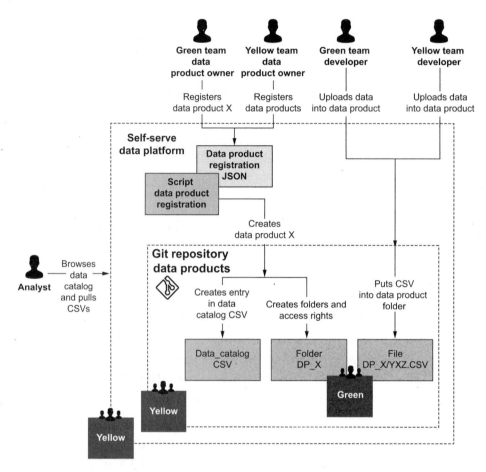

Figure 7.2   Data producers, data consumers, data products, and their interactions

Communication through the data catalog is simple: data producers provide metadata, lots of it, and it's well maintained. Data consumers read and consume the metadata. That's it. That's all that should be needed. If that is not enough, the data products are likely not described well enough. This highlights that another goal of the self-serve data platform is to facilitate communication between data producers and data consumers.

Figure 7.3 depicts these three major parties—data producers, consumers, and products—and their respective interactions.

NOTE   Including "things" like data products as parties in a platform's description might seem weird. But it enables us to fit almost all kinds of platforms into the platform definition: developer platforms, deployment platforms, and basically all platforms where the main interaction is between the developer and a set of tools. So far, we have found this to be very useful. It allows applying all other platform frameworks to these platforms as well.

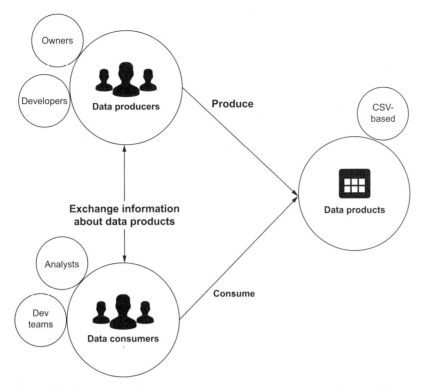

Figure 7.3   The three platform parties and their interactions in detail

Whether you want to consider data products as a platform feature as well is your choice. There is no right or wrong answer to this question, but you should at least have one answer that you base your work on. So now let's see why we are choosing to consider data products as part of the platform for our MVP.

7.1.2   Platform thinking

To understand the idea behind platform thinking, we find it easier to use a nonsoftware example. Imagine a woodworking shop. A bunch of woodworkers share the space. It also has an owner who provisions everything. Multiple people are using saws, hammers, chisels, and various power tools to make furniture.

What usually happens in woodworking is that people start to make a few customized tools. That could be a simple dovetail guardrail; it could be a special chisel or a carving tool. The woodworkers need these in their development process because the alternative is to make a piece less perfect and spend a lot of time doing harder work.

Now, the workshop owner could just buy a bunch of special-purpose tools. But to truly make this useful, he would need a huge inventory of them and a decent catalog to find the right tool.

Instead, he could provide something else: a special station for making special-purpose tools, including a few measurement instruments, a drawing board, possibly some metalworking instruments, and the like. Additionally, he could organize a short meetup on Wednesday evenings to let people showcase their special-purpose tools.

What the workshop owner would be utilizing as an alternative to stocking a lot of specialist tools is *product thinking*—providing people with the tools they need. In the second alternative, however, he is leveraging another idea called *platform thinking*.

The workshop owner is providing a platform: the special-purpose tool station that enables others via self-service to easily increase their output flow of high-quality furniture. He is utilizing the analysis of the flow of work, the sequence of steps the individual woodworkers are taking, and the analysis of duplication of abstract steps involved.

Figure 7.4 depicts this flow for the construction of three chairs. The first chair is produced in four steps. Step 3 is building a custom tool and then using it; this workflow requires a long time but results in a high-quality chair. The second chair is built without a custom tool, resulting in a shorter build time but a lower-quality chair. Finally, the third workflow uses the platform, which produces a high-quality chair in a shorter time frame than even chair 2.

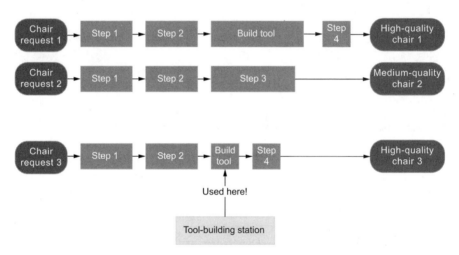

Figure 7.4   The workshop workflow speeds up, thanks to the platform.

Platform thinking is not an *alternative* to product thinking. We consider it simply a second lens through which to view things. The output-oriented lens still keeps an eye on the organizational perspective.

We recommend focusing on delivering foundational services that do the following:

- Can be used in self-service, to keep the unit's autonomy and ability to react to change
- Enable units to experiment with variations, to help them react to change

In our woodworking example, this is exactly what we have. Every woodworker can go on as desired. No one is forcing the woodworkers to do anything different, but they have the option of using the tool-making station. The station has enabling tools such as measurement instruments, pencils, and drawing boards—everything needed to design, prototype, and build special-purpose tools. Wednesdays help the woodworkers widen their horizons and provide ideas to experiment with, in effect, helping the woodworkers to come up with good experiments to run.

Traditional platforms

The word *platform* makes some CIO/CTOs shiver because a lot of platforms do not support the idea of platform thinking. If your "platform" is a fancy deployment machine that requires every development team to have an expert who can use that fancy deployment machine, no team is actually "free to choose to use the platform." Hence, there is a boundary in adopting the platform. Such a platform will likely restrict the team because it locks them in. After all, if you have a Jenkins expert on every team, there is next to no incentive to switch to a 20% better platform that is not Jenkins.

The platforms that emerge out of platform thinking are lean and thin. These platforms are never launched as big and comprehensive pieces. Instead, they are built iteratively and carefully to enable teams and not limit their autonomy.

In fact, the larger the participant base becomes, the leaner the platform should become, in a sense. With more participants, the friction points grow, and we need to avoid friction at all costs; otherwise, we slow the flow, instead of enhancing it.

Next, let's apply platform thinking to our MVP platform.

APPLICATION TO OUR PLATFORM

Initially, Messflix has analysts and development teams. The development teams are data producers, while the analysts and possibly other teams in our example are data consumers.

Our initial MVP platform focuses mostly on the data consumers in applying platform thinking. Let's explore the workflows to understand why. If we take a look at the data analyst workflow, it typically consists of steps such as these:

1. Browsing datasets
2. Finding the right dataset
3. Exploring and understanding it
4. Possibly combining it with others

The MVP platform allows a data analyst to combine almost all of these steps into one or two. Browsing and finding the right dataset as well as understanding it can all be done by reading the data catalog. Combining datasets, at least from the technical perspective, is easy because they all come in CSV format. Figure 7.5 depicts the comparison of these two workflows.

The MVP platform thus saves a substantial amount of time for data analysts each time they go through their Problem > Solution cycle.

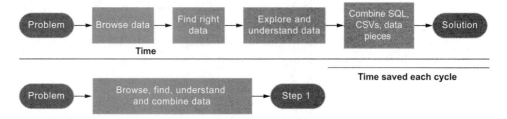

Figure 7.5   The analyst workflow speeds up, thanks to the platform.

For data producers, not much has changed. The data producer workflow usually involves capturing the data, then moving it to a storage location and exposing it to data producers. The creation of a new dataset also involves describing the dataset with metadata.

The MVP platform produces a common set of tools for describing, storing, and exposing data, but doesn't make it much easier than what the data producers did before in most cases.

> **NOTE**   Platforms have one problem: their value is intrinsic, meaning it applies only to parts already connected to the platform. In our example, the data analyst has an easier time browsing and exploring datasets only after at least two datasets are on the platform. And of course, the value increases a lot by putting more datasets on the platform because the data analyst will eventually have to look only into the platform to find the datasets.

We picked the analyst's workflow because browsing and exploring datasets are also common tasks for development teams that want to use other teams' data, for data scientists, and for ML engineers. As you can see, though, the workflow for data consumers still takes a pretty long time and still involves manually browsing through long CSV files. In our first iteration (described in the following section), we'll try to speed up their processes by leveraging the X-as-a-service idea.

7.2   *Improvements with X as a service*

Messflix decides to form a small team to take care of the platform for now. Two veteran data engineers start to maintain and develop the platform.

The data analysts responsible for reporting really enjoy the new data mesh and are excited about the new datasets that the Green and Yellow teams provide. Both teams keep on growing their number of datasets and products.

However, a couple of data scientists and machine learners who look at the data only from time to time to identify necessary datasets are having trouble with it. They are having a hard time digging through the CSV-based metadata catalog. In particular, some of the domain data products depend on each other, and it is essential for the data scientists and machine learners to understand the lineage in order to see which data is derived from where.

DEFINITION When referring to *lineage* or *data lineage*, we typically mean a representation of where the individual pieces of data came from. If you have a dataset that consists of revenues per customer, two base sources will likely be involved: the payments of some customer IDs, and then the customer dataset that maps IDs to other properties like name or gender. *Lineage* simply means making exactly this part of the information visible in any way. It means listing the two sources, the customer dataset, and the customer IDs—maybe with a tree-like representation, maybe with more metadata. It also means we need some kind of manual or, hopefully, automated way of recording this information.

So people do what they usually do and call up the two engineers on the data team and ask them to help them dig through the catalog. If the platform is successful and has lots of data, the central team will end up doing nothing else but answering calls all day long.

But that leaves them with no time to work on the platform, and it won't scale. So let's look at X as a service to understand how platform teams can improve their communication with others.

7.2.1 X as a service explained

Team Topologies is a framework created by Matthew Skelton and Manuel Pais for modern technology organizations. Described in their book *Team Topologies: Organizing Business and Technology Teams for Fast Flow* (IT Revolution, 2019), this framework helps to design teams and their interactions in a way that optimizes the flow of produced value.

As such, it is a great example of socio-technical architecture. In the framework, we're considering only three ways teams can interact, and one of them is X as a service.

We will give you a better definition of this in a minute, but we would like to return to the wood workshop example once more.

WORKSHOP TOOL-BUILDING AS A SERVICE

Our tool-building station is becoming well adopted by a wide variety of woodworkers. But Bill, the owner of the workshop and the maintainer of the station, would like to drive up its adoption because he thinks it's a great thing!

So the next day, he's at the station and simply starts to talk to everyone who walks by. He's giving a hand to people, helping them build a few new tools. He's working together with them; you could say, he's *collaborating* with them.

However, the next day he realizes that all these different kinds of woodworkers still aren't able to build the tools themselves, so he changes his approach. On the second day, he's merely assisting, teaching, and educating people about how to build tools and how to use the tool-building station. He explains where they should draw their first sketches, and where the measurement instruments are located. You could say he's *facilitating*.

Quite pleased with himself, Bill continues like this for a while. After a week, he starts to add a few things to the station. He also reorganizes a few of the boxes located by the station to make them more accessible. He's about to leave when a bunch of the woodworkers approach him and ask him to facilitate again. It appears that a lot of them still are not able to use the tool-building station, because things changed since the last time.

The next day, Bob decides to use yet another strategy: he starts to redesign the complete station. This time, he tries to make it as self-explanatory as possible. He puts up a large sign that describes the process of tool-building:

1 Sketch out your tool on the left side by using the paper and pencils beneath the station.
2 Use the saws and other tools located to the left to make your tool.
3 Try out your tool on the sample wood located to the right.

He also puts up labels and reorganizes things again.

The next week something incredible happens. Nothing. No one reaches out to Bob, and yet, when he visits the workshop again, a lot of people, even new people, are using the tool-building station. He thinks to himself, he's done it, the tool-building station, or tool building in general, has become a *service*. We might even say he's created *tool building as a service.*

X AS A SERVICE CONTINUED

As you can see from this tool-building example, this collaboration model of X as a service fits quite well with a product like a platform. The other interaction modes in the Team Topologies framework are called *collaboration* and *facilitation*. They work a lot like what Bob did on his first two days.

In their book, Skelton and Pais define *X as a service* as "consuming or providing something with minimal collaboration." X as a service should be the default operation mode when a platform team interacts with other teams through their platform.

The idea behind a platform team is that it provides an internal product to the other teams that are producing value. The analysts who, for example, help the product people make important decisions are producing value, together with the product managers, and the development teams are improving the product and also providing value.

The key point is that many such value-producing teams exist. Almost all teams (or units) should produce value. But at a certain scale, it becomes necessary to provide internal products to speed up the rest of the teams.

If each team runs its own CI system, that is totally fine for one dev team, for two dev teams, and maybe for three dev teams. But beyond a certain number, the costs of duplication simply are much larger than creating a team to take care of this.

But note that a platform team cannot operate well if it has any kind of friction. It has to provide the service without becoming a bottleneck. X as a service is just that; it means the interaction is as seamless as an API. And that means both the platform and the interaction with the platform should work seamlessly. Basically, almost no verbal, nonstandardized communication should occur between other teams and the platform team.

In our previous example, you should see right away that human communication simply won't scale and thus becomes a bottleneck. If the data engineers spend their days understanding lineage, they won't have time to speed up the platform. And every minute they spend on speeding up the platform becomes 10 times that speedup because the platform is used by multiple teams, up to a certain point.

X AS A SERVICE OBSERVED

The difference between collaboration/facilitation and X as a service might be quite familiar to you. We have seen a lot of data organizations try to switch to an X as a service collaboration model lately.

These data organizations have data teams that are centralized and tasked with both ingesting data sources as well as modeling them out and providing reports and dashboards on top of them. Usually, the collaboration between report requesters and the central data team is one of *collaboration*: the requester asks for a report, the central data team creates it, and then the requester asks for additional changes.

However, reporting and dashboarding simply don't scale for some of these organizations. They then try to make the data team into a platform team with a bunch of analysts and analytics engineers spread out across the company.

The central data team becomes a "platform team" by focusing on just the data ingestion part and possibly on modeling a few key data pieces. On the other side, then, analysts and analytics engineers will pick up this data and produce reports and dashboards on top of it.

The interaction model here changes substantially. The central data team will have to do some serious product management by ingesting and providing datasets that are commonly used across the user base and align with the future direction of the company. If they are doing this well, they manage the transition to a *data-as-a-service model* in their interaction with other parts of the company.

However, as you might've guessed, this collaboration mode, which is typical for a platform team, also requires a certain level of matureness, especially in terms of product management. So take this as a caveat when approaching the creation of your platform team.

Now it's our turn to remove this communication bottleneck and turn the collaboration mode into X as a service for our company, Messflix.

7.2.2 X as a service applied

To make the platform scalable, we need to remove the people's need for calling up the Data team. In our example, they are having problems in the discovery phase. So a good option would be to substitute the CSV-based, hard-to-read data catalog with an easy-to-read, easy-to-deploy data catalog with advanced features. It should, for instance, include a visual lineage and proper search functionality.

Figure 7.6 depicts the new architecture. The data catalog is pulled out of the Git repository and replaced by a proper data catalog called DataHub.

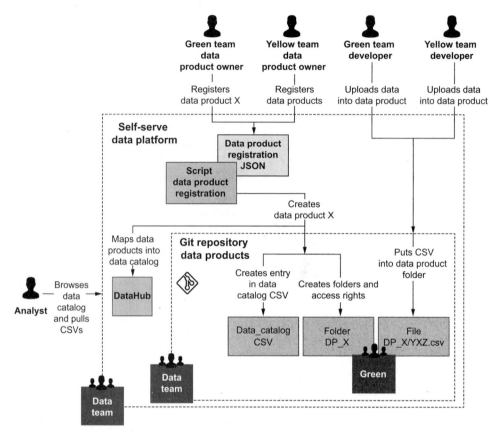

Figure 7.6   The new platform, with a central DataHub as data catalog, removes the central data team as a knowledge bottleneck.

We're still using the JSON files to offer backward compatibility to the data producers. But we map the values of the JSON into the DataHub. We're keeping it simple here and leaving the maintenance and updates of data products' metadata out of the story but, of course, the metadata should be updatable. From here, we could go in either of two directions if we wanted to expand on this direction:

- Keep the JSON files, and expand them to include additional values relevant to additional features in DataHub
- Scrap the JSONs, and allow data product owners to modify metadata via the API right inside DataHub

The second option is more centralized than the first. The first option keeps the metadata close to the data product and "discovers it," whereas the second option means more centralization. In general, we recommend keeping the metadata tightly coupled to the service and using a discovery mechanism akin to the first option.

FEDERATED COMPUTATIONAL GOVERNANCE IN ITERATION 1

Data consumers at Messflix are having trouble understanding data products and are particularly worried about lineage. A centralist way of ensuring that lineage data exists is to simply enforce a policy checking for lineage information in the data product registration.

But for the governance team members at Messflix, that does not seem right at all. They come up with a better solution with the data platform team. The data catalog provides a simple link to the lineage information the teams can provide in any way they want at an endpoint hosted inside their domain.

The data platform team, however, implements a simple script that does a bit of automatic lineage calculation based on SQL and Python code that uses other common interfaces and endpoints at Messflix. This way, teams Yellow and Green are encouraged to simply write good code using common interfaces at Messflix, and then let the data platform team handle the lineage automatically. In addition, this is incorporated into the data mesh, so lineage between data products is automatically detected.

Figure 7.7 describes the one group of functionality we've added so far. You could group by capability, but for simplicity, we choose not to.

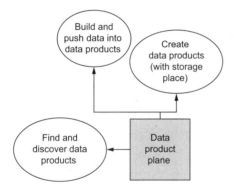

Figure 7.7 The first architecture plane of our platform and its three functionalities

The new workflow for data consumers becomes pretty quick when using the advanced functionality of DataHub. We should now be able to remove the human dependency on the Data team. This also means it is now time to look at the data producers' perspective and make their lives easier. To accomplish that, you'll learn one final concept about platform architectures in the next section.

7.3 *Improvements with platform architecture*

Teams Yellow and Green are quite happy with the current self-serve platform. But the ML engineers are requesting data from team Gray now, responsible for the Advertise capability. They want to help optimize the campaigns.

The machine learners are already big fans of the DataHub data catalog, but team Gray isn't at all a fan of pushing CSVs into some repository. They are big fans of PostgreSQL databases because their data product is huge and will contain many datasets.

The data platform team decides to make that possible. But how exactly? Should everyone from now on use PostgreSQL? Should the CSVs disappear? What is a good approach here? Let's explore the architecture of any kind of platform to understand how we can come up with a quite modular answer to this problem.

7.3.1   *Platform architecture explained*

Carliss Baldwin and C. Jason Woodard, in "The Architecture of Platforms: A Unified View" (http://mng.bz/XaWp), shine a different light on platforms that we'll explore in this section. Platforms are not easy to define, as you can see in this chapter, and ambiguity may exist even in the terms defining a platform.

But the architecture of any kind of platform is surprisingly constant. We can find the same kind of architectural components inside developer platforms, self-serve data platforms, a brick-and-mortar marketplace, or even Stripe.

Take your central town square as an example. In many small towns, it hosts a farmers market, usually at a fixed time. The selling farmers change from time to time, but they know where they have to sign up. The buyers change all the time, but everyone knows the place and time. Additionally, a central town square usually supplies the needed electricity and water taps for farmers to use.

A central town square thus becomes a platform with three components:

- The buyers and the farmers are the *complements,* or participants, of the platform.
- The town square (place) and the fixed time together become the *platform interface,* everything required for buyers and farmers to interact much more easily.
- Everything on the town square and everything around it, possibly the processes around it such as charges for renting a space at the market, make up the *platform kernel.* This component includes everything that provides value, such as water taps and electricity for the farmers or nice decorations for the visitors.

Turns out, these three components—complements, platform interface, and platform kernel—can be found in any platform. The latter two architectural components have the following goals:

- The platform interface is supposed to be kept as fixed as possible to ensure maximal platform activity. Once you change the day of the market, things will go pretty crazy.
- The platform kernel is constantly changed to optimize the platforms' value to the participants. The pricing is optimized, possibly tents are provided, the power sources are upgraded to include other sellers, or maybe Christmas decorations can be provided to make the farmers market a huge Christmas success.

NOTE   In the preceding section, we decided to map the checked-in JSON files into the DataHub and not let people use the DataHub directly. Why? Because the JSON files are part of the platform interface! We cannot change the platform interface without inflicting serious problems. We're aiming to keep it as fixed as possible.

COMPLEMENTS, INTERFACE, AND KERNEL IN OUR ITERATION 1

If we revisit the architecture sketch from the preceding section, we can highlight the complements, the different parts that make up the interface, and the platform kernel with some effort. We've depicted them for you in figure 7.8. Before we get to it, let's consider what we're looking at.

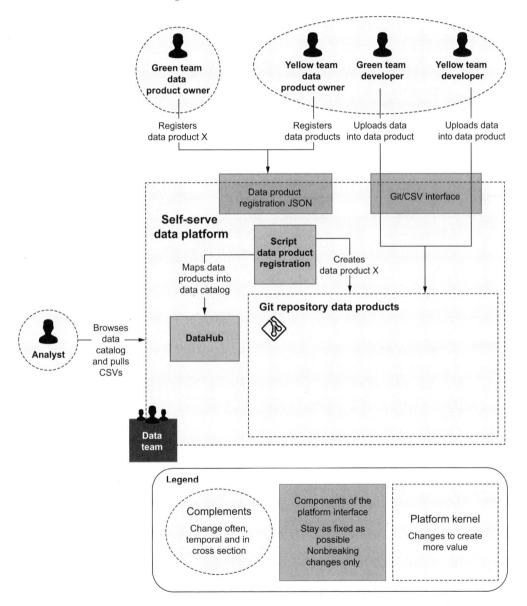

Figure 7.8   Highlighting the very different parts of what is usually considered just one platform

Leaving out parts of the interface is troublesome because if you change a part, you will cause serious value deterioration to the platform. For instance, if we decide to not use the Git repository anymore, teams Green and Yellow will have to redo a lot of their current data products. Analysts won't have them available for quite some time, and we will lose a lot of value over the transition period. If, instead, we keep the old parts of the interface open and slowly introduce additional functionality, we only increase the value of the platform.

Interfaces and why they are so hard to spot

The word *interface* is an overloaded term. In terms of platforms, an interface to a platform X is something really generic; it's "the ways of interacting with platform X."

From the platform perspective, an interface can be much more than a technically implemented REST interface. The central town square becomes a platform, with its interface being the location and the time.

And the same is true of a self-serve data platform. The interface might consist of practices and processes you've put into place to use, such as the central Git repository to upload CSVs.

All of these make up the interfaces, not just the technical parts. All of these are supposed to stay "mostly fixed." That's why they are so hard to spot and so important.

We can now easily point out the *platform kernel*—it's everything hidden behind the interfaces. The actual software running the DataHub and the data product registration script are definitely parts of the platform kernel that we can easily exchange in order to create more value.

And that is exactly what we are going to do in the next section. We will keep the interface fixed, and add a new part to the interface by making the kernel more modular and exposing more parts of it. Let's see that applied.

7.3.2 *Platform architecture applied*

Team Gray essentially wants to be able to configure the data storage. This is an advanced capability of the platform (figure 7.9). Not all teams want to configure their own storage, so we will make that option available only when someone specifically opts in for it. Otherwise, the default option will always be to use the CSV dump.

Infrastructure as code templates: We choose Terraform

To deploy any kind of infrastructure, most technology teams today follow the *infrastructure-as-code pattern*. The infrastructure—like a Docker container, a cluster, some kind of load balancer, or a set of these together with operating systems and all—are configured *as code*.

To do so, teams use an abstraction layer, and tooling that maps that abstraction into reality. One of the most common tooling choices here is Terraform (www.terraform.io), together with its easy-to-read language, HashiCorp Configuration Language (HCL).

To provide an infrastructure template, our Gray team can write a Terraform file in HCL and make a couple of parameters configurable, like names, sizes, optional components, and so on. Any team can then use the template, fill in the parameters, and deploy the infrastructure by using the tool called Terraform.

To add this functionality, we make our kernel into modules of capabilities:

- The data product plane for creating, finding, and discovering
- The data storage plane for the internal creation of the default CSV storage, or the option to create a Terraform template for using a suitable PostgreSQL instance that will autoregister the data products' storage location

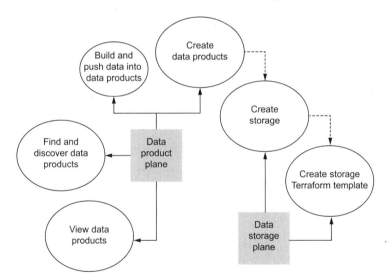

Figure 7.9   The new architecture plane adds two functionalities and interacts with the first plane.

A lot of other options could satisfy the same requirement. Instead of creating a Terraform template, we could include an access policy and let data producers register the data storage location.

But this does the job just fine. Team Gray creates its Advertise data product, using the predefined Terraform template to create its PostgreSQL database, which automatically is checked into the DataHub. Teams Yellow and Green still keep their CSVs.

Figure 7.10 summarizes this approach. This architecture sketch highlights the components of the platform, but omits some details to make it easier to read.

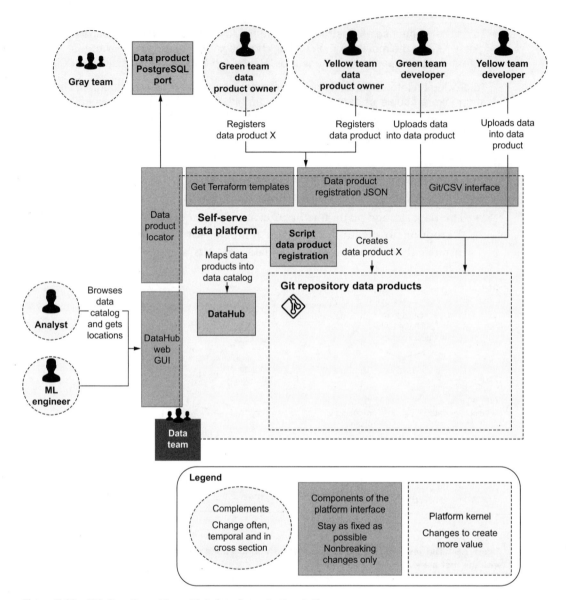

Figure 7.10   This iteration adds multiple interfaces to the platform.

The new changes the data platform team makes are important. First of all, the easy parts: a *data product storage and port interface* do the described Terraform magic. This is a new part and can be used optionally. In this case, it will be used by the Gray team. This team's data product gets a separate PostgreSQL-based port via the PostgreSQL endpoint.

However, this puts the infrastructure of the data ports largely into the hands of the data-producing teams. They are now free to exchange their PostgreSQL instance for a new one, should they have trouble with it. This also means the Data team has to provide some way of keeping track of the distributed data products. This is what they design the *data product locator* interface for.

The data product locator interface, depicted in figure 7.11, is used by the distributed data products to register and update themselves. They specify their location, which usually means the SQL endpoint for the PostgreSQL instance, as well as the location of the datasets, which in this case is schema and table information.

The data product Locator then also checks the data product files, which are still hosted in the central repository for the rest of the data products, and provides the unified information to the DataHub.

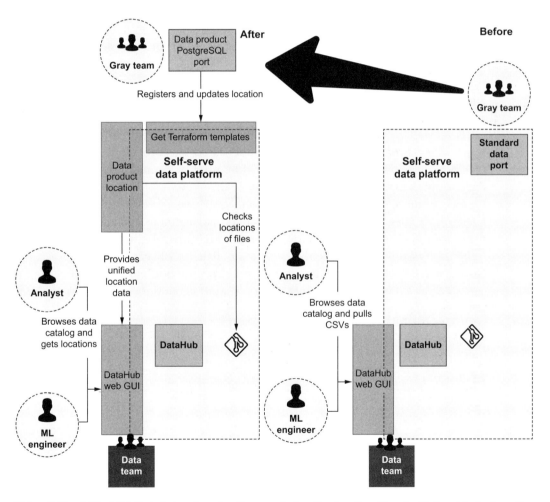

Figure 7.11   Adding distributed storage makes the use of a location functionality valuable by adding automatic location detection for the DataHub as well as for the ML engineers.

Additionally, the data product Locator exposes its API externally. The analysts can keep on working with DataHub, but the ML engineers could use the new interface to programmatically keep track of the location of the data products Team Gray provides.

FEDERATED COMPUTATIONAL GOVERNANCE IN ITERATION 2

Now that the data can be stored outside the central Git repository, the federated aspect of governance becomes increasingly important. The Data team decides to provide some small additional capabilities inside its Terraform template. The team members implement a simple endpoint that provides data about the state of the data product, including the recency of the data, the size, and basic data classification on a column level.

Storage outside the central Git repository also rips open another topic: access policies. In a federated fashion, Messflix could simply decide to let the data producers handle everything on their own. To implement that, Messflix should provide a default "restrict everything" policy for the PostgreSQL instance. In detail, the company would provide a read-only role and group that is essentially able to retrieve only metadata and not even data. This would be used for lineage calculation and listing of datasets, possibly enriching the DataHub.

However, the team chooses to provide a little bit more help to data-producing teams. Right now, there are only two, so they choose to provide two default policies. One is a "restricted access" role. It should be used by teams to mark datasets inside data products as sensitive. The second role is an "open for all" role that is supposed to be used to mark datasets inside data products as open to everyone at Messflix. The company decides to leave the rest of the policy management up to the data-producing teams for now, until the federated governance body provides more guidance.

Finally, we want to take another look at the data producers—this time, all of them. Now that the flow on the data consumer side isn't the bottleneck anymore, the focus should be on enabling the data producers, as we'll see in the next section.

7.4   *Improvements for the data producers*

Messflix realizes that this ML suddenly takes off, together with its data mesh. The company has a recommendation system running, automatically optimized its ad campaigns, and has a bunch of forecasting systems in place.

The needed data products, however, are pretty intense in the sense that all three teams (Green, Yellow, and Gray) start to complain about the amount of transformation work they have to do. They feel like they don't have the right tools to handle intense and complex data transformations. In particular, they have problems handling a bunch of computations in sequence to compute their datasets.

And they might be right. Data teams deploy data orchestrators, transformers, or parallel computing frameworks to handle these kinds of things. The problem the three teams describe sounds like an orchestration problem. So, our Data team decides to provide a data orchestration tool called Apache Airflow to the data producers.

DEFINITION   *Apache Airflow* is an open source platform, a so-called *data orches-trator*, to run, schedule, and monitor computational workloads. It runs on Python and has a UI. Basically, Airflow allows you to schedule a bunch of Python scripts and run them in useful sequences.

The Data team members choose to provide Airflow as a self-service, meaning they would again provide a Terraform template together with an onboarding session. The beauty of the Terraform template is that they are able to include configurations that allow them to directly hook up Airflow to the rest of the data platform.

> **Providing hosted Airflow vs. Airflow infrastructure template**
>
> Our data platform team members choose to provide an Airflow infrastructure template. They do so because all the currently relevant Messflix teams are well educated in DevOps.
>
> The data platform team could have chosen to provide one hosted Airflow cluster maintained by the data platform team (or a third party like Amazon Web Services), with a reasonable separation between the compute environments per team.
>
> Either option can be valid, depending on the circumstances. The question is simply, is the combination of platform team + flow-aligned teams able to increase their throughput with this option? And that includes answering whether maintaining a central service is feasible and whether flow-aligned teams (in this case, development teams) are able to manage things on their own.

We will now take a look at the final architecture of our self-serve data platform. Again, what the data platform team does is modularize and extend another part of the capabilities of the platform. Our new platform kernel contains three capabilities, pictured in figure 7.12:

- A data product plane for creating, finding, and discovering.
- A data storage plane for the internal creation of the default CSV storage, or the option to create a Terraform template for using a suitable PostgreSQL instance that will autoregister the data products' storage location.
- A data transformation plane can be used optionally. In this case, it creates and links a Terraform template for Airflow.

This new architecture plane means a lot of new possibilities for the data-producing teams. Figure 7.13 zooms into a few relevant parts for the Gray team before turning to the complete picture.

The Gray team members utilize the Terraform templates to create the PostgreSQL instance for the data product storage and the SQL port. They also utilize the Airflow template to create ingestions and transformation tooling. Finally, they utilize the actual tool Airflow to ingest and transform the data from various operational systems and write the results into the port.

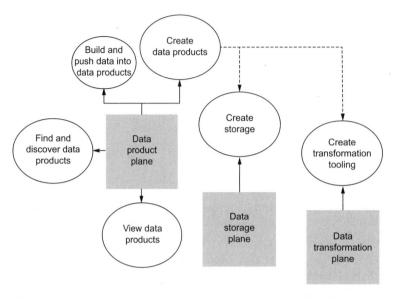

Figure 7.12   The third architecture plane adds one more functionality.

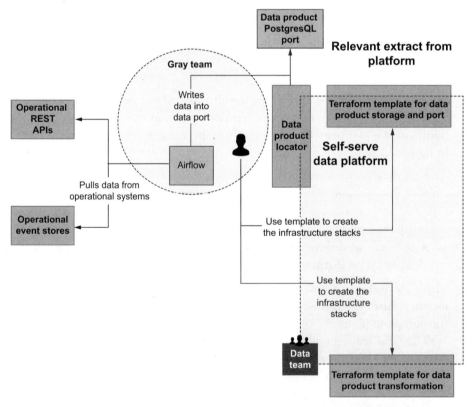

Figure 7.13   By adding the transformation tooling template, the data-producing team can easily set up complex transformation processes and pull in data from a variety of sources.

The final architecture, shown in figure 7.14, now allows for each data-producing team to have decently equipped data products.

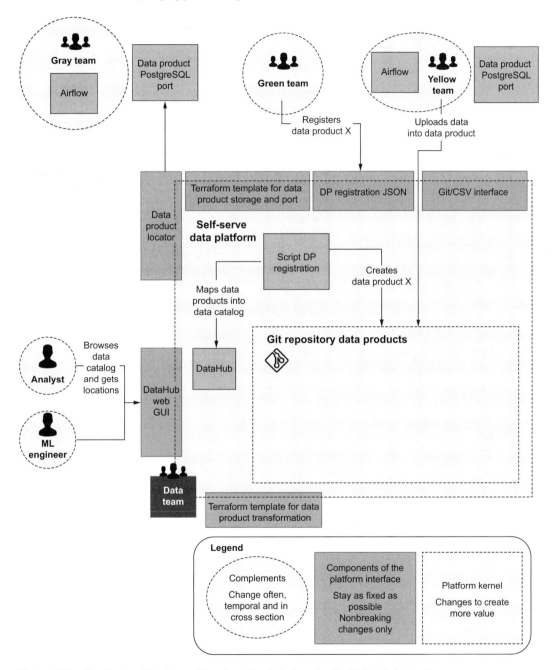

Figure 7.14   The final architecture adds yet another interface for the Airflow infrastructure.

They now include the following:

- An optional CSV output port
- An optional SQL output port in the form of the SQL endpoint of a PostgreSQL instance
- An Airflow instance to easily manipulate data to prepare it for consumption
- The centralized metadata endpoints inside the DataHub

The data consumer stack consists of the DataHub and related tooling to mainly focus on finding and understanding the right data.

The workflow for data producers changes a lot with this newly provided interface. Both the Yellow and Gray teams decide to use the provided templates to start an Airflow instance inside their team context. They are using Airflow to quickly churn out new data products using their operational systems' REST APIs and event stores as input ports. Here are the details:

- Team Gray is now using just the SQL ports.
- Team Yellow opts to use the SQL endpoints in addition to the CSV port as output ports because the team is now free to create so many more valuable data products.
- Team Green keeps on using the CSV dumps, as it doesn't have the need for anything else right now.

The data consumers, both the ML engineers as well as analysts, use the central DataHub to locate datasets and then use their personal weapons to consume and combine them.

FEDERATED COMPUTATIONAL GOVERNANCE IN ITERATION 3

The Data team now realizes that the data products are becoming increasingly more decentralized. For this iteration, they decide to do two things in terms of computational governance.

Previously, the team members helped to calculate lineage based on the SQL script. With the provisioning of Airflow as a service, it makes sense for them to extend that calculation to the new way of modifying data. So they extend their calculation to include the checked-in Airflow scripts as well. Second, they start to ping the provided endpoints of the data products on a regular basis and pull that information into the DataHub.

> ### Architectural quantum
> In another iteration, the Data team could also enable the movement of the JSON files with data product metadata into an endpoint residing inside the data products, which are now also technically completely inside the teams' contexts.
>
> This would complete the architectural decoupling of the data products into one single unit called the *architectural quantum*. (We could argue this would also have been possible beforehand, depending on how we define *ownership*.)
>
> But this decoupling would offer more freedom to the decentralized teams. In that setup, they could provide the endpoint any way they want, following a standardized schema, and simply register the URL of the endpoint at some central service.

And we're done! Except, we're never done. But now we hope you are equipped with the general mindset to build a self-serve data platform yourself. In the next chapter, you will be able to gain a lot of inspiration from real-world examples that are outlined with a lot of detail.

We went through a long journey in this chapter by first identifying the key concepts of the thin platform we began with. We then went on to do three iterations on it until we arrived at a platform for Messflix.

We've also covered a lot of ground with our self-serve data platform. Table 7.2 shows a short summary of the stages. The three iterations, starting with our MVP look like this.

Table 7.2 Iterations, components, and added value of the platform

Number of iterations	Components	Value added
0—MVP (chapter 3)	**Data product plane** Git repository for CSVs	**Data consumers** Single point of access
1—Iteration 1	**Data product plane** Git repository for CSVs DataHub data catalog	**Data consumers** Speed up finding and understanding data
2—Iteration 2	**Data product plane** Git repository for CSVs DataHub data catalog Data storage plane Terraform template for PostgreSQL DB	**Data producers** Speed up providing data products
3—Iteration 3	**Data product plane** Git repository for CSVs DataHub data catalog **Data storage plane** Terraform template for PostgreSQL DB **Data transformation plane** Terraform template for Airflow	**Data producers** Speed up providing complex data products

Summary

- Platforms are essentially mediating interactions between parties.
- The architecture of a platform consists of complements, the platform kernel, and the interface.
- X as a service is a great concept for understanding the interaction modes of platform teams that maintain self-serve data platforms.
- Platform thinking is an approach to thinking about products in terms of development flow and speeding up development by providing shared tooling.
- You can build a self-serve data platform iteratively, starting with a small seed, or MVP. But concepts like X as a service also can help you quickly make the right decisions for your self-serve platform.
- Combining tooling can create value with your data mesh, quickly leveraging the power of the self-serve platform.

Part 3

Infrastructure and technical architecture

This third part of the book focuses on all things technical. You will learn different blueprints for data mesh platforms, depending on, for example, your cloud provider or the size of your company.

You will also learn how to approach the migration from your existing system to various different kinds of architectures, step by step and component by component.

We highlight different architectures and discuss multiple different options for moving from your existing structures, such as data lakes and data warehouses, to a data mesh.

Comparing self-serve data platforms

8

This chapter covers

- Platforms leveraging Google Cloud Platform
- Platforms leveraging Amazon Web Services
- Platforms leveraging Databricks
- Platforms leveraging Apache Kafka
- Pros and cons of each platform

In the first part of this book, you learned all the basics of the data mesh. In chapter 7, you did a deep dive into building self-serve platforms using the example of Messflix. You learned how to iterate on one specific example and build up a fully functioning platform.

This chapter is different. While the data mesh paradigm is not tied to any one implementation, we believe it's necessary to see it in action more than once to really find a suitable architecture for your platform.

This is the focus of this chapter: supplying you with multiple architectures and technology stacks to make it easy for you to choose a good architecture. We will walk you through four possible architectures that all are inspired by real-world examples implemented at multiple companies throughout the world.

> **NOTE**   Each section highlights a specific choice of cloud provider, data catalog, and programming language to make these rather complex architectures easy to understand. However, all architectures can be mixed and matched or translated to different technology combinations. The architecture in section 8.1 on Google Cloud Platform, for instance, could be translated almost one-to-one to Amazon Web Services. But also keep in mind that building the technical side of data meshes is unusually hard compared to other technology projects. From our perspective, the reason is that we simply don't yet have many data mesh-specific tools, so we are using and reusing a lot of basic tools and need to be mindful of their exact usage. You will experience that directly in the first section, where a minor detail like service accounts becomes essential for the data mesh.

Section 8.1 contains an introduction using technologies from Google Cloud Platform (GCP). This part is based on a publicly available two-part workshop by Thoughtworks as well as a data mesh built by Delivery Hero. This platform puts the ownership of the underlying infrastructure into the data-producing teams and utilizes the underlying cloud providers' tooling and integration.

Section 8.2 focuses on Amazon Web Services (AWS) and its object storage, Amazon Simple Storage Service (S3). This part is inspired by a few of the very first data meshes that appeared, like the ones from BMW Group and Zalando. This platform puts the ownership of the infrastructure into the data-producing teams but loosens itself a bit from the underlying cloud provider to allow more freedom.

Section 8.3 explains how Databricks can be used to build up a data mesh. This section is inspired by companies like DPG Media Group, which appeared early on the data mesh stage, but also many more. This section turns the focus away from specific cloud providers, as this technology can be combined with all of the large cloud providers today. This architecture does not put the ownership of the infrastructure into the teams' hands.

Section 8.4 focuses on Apache Kafka, a technology that offers great potential for building data meshes. This example is inspired by a few smaller companies such as Gloo.us that have implemented a data mesh. This last architecture will also not put the ownership of the infrastructure into the teams' hands but will put the data emission and storage of the central system into their hands.

Even though the self-serve data platform is "just" a piece of technology, it has components that enable other elements of the data mesh to work, especially when it comes to (federated computational) governance, data as a product, and (data) domain ownership. So in each section, we will first sketch the architecture, discuss how it works with one or two examples, and then show how these various elements play out in this architecture.

One final note about the word *centralization*, which we will use a lot in this chapter.

DEFINITION *Centralization* in this chapter means physical and technological centralization—and never means logical centralization. Logically, every setup separates data products into their proper domains. But it is important to talk about physical and technological centralization because they sometimes make it harder to enforce or enable logical decentralization, which is what we want to achieve in the end.

Let's dive into the first architecture.

8.1 Data mesh on Google Cloud Platform

The self-serve data platform presented in this section is inspired by real-world examples showcased by Delivery Hero and Thoughtworks. Thoughtworks held workshops at Woman Who Code in 2020 and 2021 and presented an introduction to the data mesh using GCP, whereas Delivery Hero has presented a full-fledged enterprise-level data mesh.

What we're presenting here is mostly a middle ground. GCP is a great data platform to start off utilizing a lot of well-integrated services from Google Cloud. This will enable teams to quickly get off the ground. We address how to enlarge the data platform in this section as well as adding elements that are used at larger enterprise-level implementations.

In particular, the platform here puts a focus on having a good balance between being easy to set up and providing a certain level of autonomy to data-producing teams (unlike the Databricks-based platform you will see later).

8.1.1 Self-serve data platform architecture

Our data mesh has a few participants:

- *Black team*—A development team also tasked with creating and maintaining data products.
- *White team*—A data science team that creates and consumes data products.
- *Gray team*—Owns the self-serve data platform and provides a configurable Terraform template.
- *Business analysts and a recommendation system*—All of these mostly consume data.

Figure 8.1 presents a fairly detailed overview of the architecture and the teams' interactions. You will find the context of the Gray team's platform utilizing Terraform, and a lone business analyst using one of the data products through Google Cloud BigQuery. You will also see a recommendation engine that again is using one of the data products through BigQuery.

The three data products, two built by the White team and the Black team, are built using Google Cloud internal services. Take a look at how the technical setup with GCP products can work.

Let's identify the components a data mesh usually has. We'll do this in two steps: first the components of the platform and then the components of the data products in detail. Then we will present the user flow for multiple personas and finally consider a few variations to this platform.

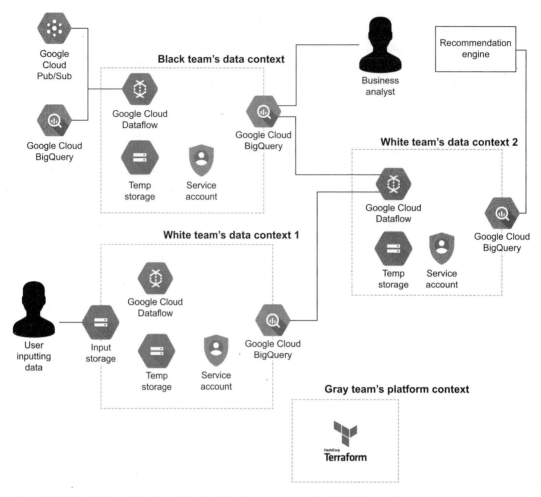

Figure 8.1   Detailed architecture of the technical components of a GCP data mesh

Explanation of GCP technologies

The following are short descriptions of the GCP technologies used in this section:

- *BigQuery*—Highly scalable data warehouse, serverless
- *Dataflow*—A serverless batch- and stream-processing system. Works with Python and SQL or through a software development kit (SDK)
- *Pub/Sub*—A Kafka-like event messaging system with great integration into Cloud Storage and BigQuery
- *Service account*—A wrapper to manage access, rights, and policies for any kind of Google Cloud technology
- *Cloud Storage*—Object storage on Google Cloud

8.1.2   *Identifying the components of the platform*

As you learned in chapter 7, a platform consists of a platform kernel, a platform interface, and complements. The first two are the technical components.

In our architecture, the platform team Gray provides is a configurable Terraform template. The team chooses to put up the latest template inside a Git repository. In this case, the Git repository together with its README file becomes the platform interface. The template becomes the platform kernel.

It is not necessary to have a full team working on such a minimal platform. The platform kernel can be upgraded by providing a new version of the Terraform template and letting teams upgrade their stacks. This platform has a very low degree of abstraction right now.

However, the templates already provide a lot of benefits to the data producers as well as consumers, thanks to the architecture of the data products.

8.1.3   *Identifying the components of the data product*

The data products all share common tooling based on Google Cloud Dataflow and its associated temporary storage. This enables a team to easily create data products. Dataflow allows teams to create pipelines that output data products in Java, Python, or SQL.

For the data product owned by the Black team, the team chooses to directly connect to the sources, using the Dataflow pipeline. Its upstream data sources are Pub/Sub and the BigQuery dataset.

The Dataflow pipeline produces one BigQuery dataset. This platform uses datasets as containers for data products. One data product has exactly one BigQuery dataset. BigQuery datasets can hold multiple tables and views, but the access permissions can easily be handled at the dataset level. Having multiple tables inside one data product is totally normal. This dataset becomes the first data output port, as you can see in figure 8.2.

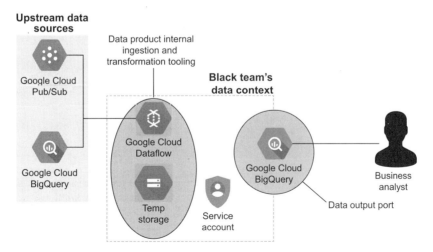

Figure 8.2   The Black team uses GCP to build a data product.

Since this platform uses a shared service, BigQuery, it is important to include one specific Google service account inside each data product. This allows managing the permissions at the data product level.

The first data product of the White team uses a Google Cloud Storage (GCS) bucket as an input, as you can see in figure 8.3. This bucket allows users to upload files in a predefined schema. On upload, the Dataflow pipeline starts to do its work and transforms the data into a new data product inside BigQuery.

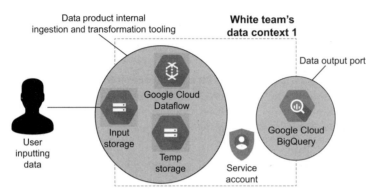

Figure 8.3   The White team adds a push data mechanism to the data product.

You can see here, as we explained in chapter 4, that data ports are an ambiguous concept. We have a push input port in the form of a GCS bucket, a pull input port in the form of Dataflow, and upstream datasets. Finally, in the second data product of the White team, displayed in figure 8.4, we're combining the two data products and taking as an input port again Dataflow together with the two upstream data products created first.

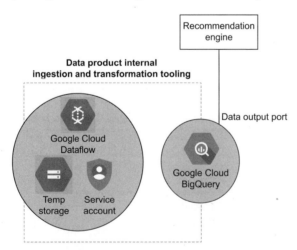

Figure 8.4   A recommendation engine interacts with the second data product of the White team.

Access to all three data products is managed with the service accounts. Each is individually configured to allow access (e.g., for the business analysts) to certain important data products or to let the recommendation system do its work.

8.1.4   Workflows

Data producers looking to create a new data product will head over to the platform interface, the GitHub repository. They read the README, pull in the newest Terraform template, and apply it to create a new stack for their new data product. Doing this, they, for instance, configure whether they want to use input storage or not.

Then they configure their Dataflow pipelines, connect to possible upstream data sources, and configure their service account to allow access to the necessary set of consumers.

Data consumers, on the other hand, use the BigQuery SQL interface to browse data products. If they need access to a new data product, they request that from the owning team.

As explained before, this is still a minimal platform.

8.1.5   Variations

One simple variation is to include a set of data products and their owners into the platform repository. This way, data consumers would directly know whom to request access from.

Another set of variations is depicted in figure 8.5. This example shows the platform context with possible add-ons that could be used in no particular sequence.

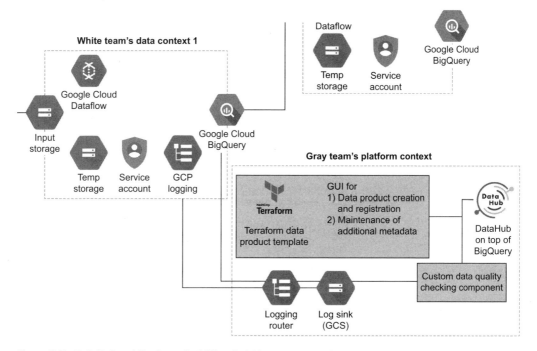

Figure 8.5   Detailed architecture of additional platform components

For one, a tool called DataHub can be used and directly connected to BigQuery to serve as a central data catalog for the distributed set of data products. This component can work in isolation without any additional components added. It would help consumers quickly discover the data products.

Second, the platform could be enriched through "popular datasets" or "most frequent data user" statistics by accessing the BigQuery logs. This can be done by using GCP logging and configuring a logging router together with a log sink in the form of a GCS bucket. From the GCS bucket, a custom component can compute these statistics and push them into the DataHub.

> ### Explanation of GCP technologies
> The following is a short description of the GCP technologies used in this section:
>
> *Google Cloud log router and sink*—The log router is a service utilizing a logging API and inclusion and exclusion filters to send log entries to a certain location. A *sink* is the location to put the log entries, sent via the API either from custom applications or one of the Google Cloud native services.

Third, another custom component with access to all data products could run custom data quality checks on the components, counting not-a-number (NaN) values or running custom checks registered by the data products' owning team. For instance, a team responsible for a Customer data product could make sure the customer numbers inside that product are always in the right format. This test and the result would then be exposed in DataHub as well.

Fourth and last, the bare Terraform template could be wrapped into a slim GUI. This GUI could then be used to enrich the metadata pulled from BigQuery through important fields that need to be set manually.

8.1.6   *Relation to data mesh ideas*

Even though this chapter is just about the platform and the technical implementations, technology does have an influence on what is possible within the other principles of the data mesh.

Platform thinking as a principle is about making the lives of all platform participants easier, while not restricting their freedom. This architecture enables other teams when it takes a load off their shoulders. That would, for instance, be the case if all of the development teams inside a company are on GCP and are heavy users of shared services like Pub/Sub and BigQuery. In that case, the template will help teams to quickly access these sources with Dataflow and turn them into datasets for data products.

In the variation outlined previously, data-producing teams would likely check in new data-quality tests to a central repository to then let the central quality component run them. This might turn into a bottleneck because it might lead to pull requests

(PRs) that need approval and failures. If that becomes the case, quality checking should be made part of the data products themselves. Only the results of the checks would then be exposed to a GCS location and picked up by the central component to get pushed into DataHub.

Federated computational governance is discussed only briefly in this architecture, but with the central DataHub, and specifically a GUI for registering data products, as well as the central component running checks on the datasets itself, there is a lot of space to inject automatically executable policies into this platform.

Data as a product in this architecture hinges a lot on each team having easy ways of manipulating its data. We believe Dataflow serves that purpose in this example.

Data domain ownership in this architecture ironically hinges on the service accounts and the access control, because the architecture is using a large shared service. It is critically important to have technological boundaries to access; otherwise, the ownership would not truly fall into the hands of the data-producing teams.

8.1.7 GCP architecture summary

This platform architecture uses shared cloud services, mostly native to the GCP environment. It uses a few components that are not GCP specific, Git and Terraform, and in the variations, custom code and DataHub.

This architecture provides data producers with a set of tooling for transforming data, but only one standardized data port. The data ports, however, could be easily extended to use Pub/Sub and GCS as well, giving you a large range of target formats and satisfying most consumer needs.

The setup can be translated, with minor differences, to the other large cloud providers AWS and Microsoft Azure as well. Since they would look similar, we chose not to display them here as a one-to-one mapping. Table 8.1 summarizes the GCP architecture profile.

Table 8.1   GCP architecture profile

Short description	This platform utilizes multiple cloud provider–specific services that integrate well together.
Pros	A large degree of autonomy for data-producing teams. Components run as a service. Easy integration of GCP services. Low maintenance effort.
Cons	Lock-in effect into cloud-provider-specific services. Extra effort necessary to integrate multiple data sources.
Suitable situations	Small- to medium-sized companies. This architecture is the middle ground between team autonomy (displayed in the AWS section) and cost/value ratio for data workloads (displayed in the Databricks section).

Next, we will look into AWS as a platform and how a possible infrastructure architecture looks on that platform.

8.2   *Data mesh on AWS*

This section's architecture is inspired by real-world implementations by Zalando, BMW Group, and JPMorgan Chase. The data mesh will share a few key characteristics of the data mesh on GCP—namely, using a bunch of AWS-native services and being more decentralized. But we will also focus on a few key differences. In particular, we will take a deeper look into the data-consuming side of things.

8.2.1   *Self-serve data platform architecture*

We're going to keep the teams as before, with a small modification. The Black team is a development team, the White team is mostly focused on data science, and the Gray team owns the self-serve data platform. We also have a recommendation system that would like to use some data.

But this time, our business analysts are more advanced; they don't want to just analyze data, but also create a few ETL jobs and pump some new data back into the data mesh. Their team consists of one or two data scientists and one or two analysts. They too become both data consumers and producers, even though they are less technical than the producers we've met in the preceding section, at least with respect to infrastructure setup.

Figure 8.6 depicts the architecture. Take a look at how you can set up this kind of data mesh on AWS. We won't consider add-ons for this architecture but instead will discuss variations that we also discussed in the GCP version. Try to identify the components of the technical platform as well as the data products yourself before reading on.

> ### Explanation of AWS technologies
> The following is a short description of the AWS technologies used in this section:
>
> - *Simple Storage Service (S3)*—The AWS-based object storage akin to Google Cloud Storage.
> - *Glue*—Cloud-hosted and -managed ETL solution based on Python/Spark, somewhat similar to Google Dataflow.
> - *Glue Data Catalog*—An integrated schema-catalog for S3 integrated with Glue and *crawlers* that create schemas from structured data inside S3 buckets.
> - *Lake Formation*—A right management solution enabling data lakes across AWS account boundaries.
> - *Kinesis Data Streams*—A Kafka-like streaming solution. Amazon Kinesis Data Firehose can use the streams to push them to other AWS resources like Amazon S3 buckets or databases.
> - *Athena*—A query engine with native AWS integrations. It provides an SQL interface as well as a UI.

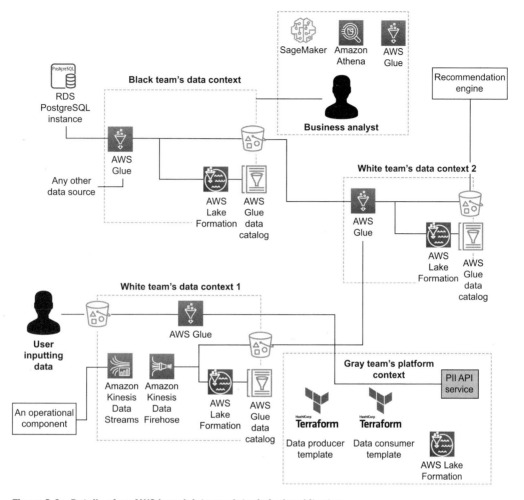

Figure 8.6   Details of an AWS-based data mesh technical architecture

If you compare this architecture to the GCP-based architecture described in the preceding section, you should notice four important points:

- This architecture is based on S3 object storage, whereas in the previous section, we were building on a tabular storage format.
- This architecture allows ingesting data from any kind of data source into the data products by using AWS Glue.
- This architecture allows pushing data into a data product by using Amazon Kinesis Data Streams (the SDK).
- This architecture also provides a data consumer template.

Let's again identify the components of a data mesh: first the components of the platform and then the data product part.

8.2.2   *Identifying the components of the platform*

As you learned in chapter 7, a platform consists of a platform kernel, a platform interface, and complements. The first two are the technical components.

In our architecture, the platform team Gray provides four things. One is a data producer Terraform template containing the possible configuration to deploy a new data product into any AWS account. The second is a data consumer Terraform template containing the tools necessary to analyze and transform data from a data consumer perspective. Third, the Gray team provides the central AWS Lake Formation together with an identity and access management (IAM) role repository to let teams grant access to both metadata and data inside their own data products. Finally, the team provides a central PII service, which is a simple API that hashes personalized data that is flagged as such. This is a helper function for data producers, making staying GDPR compliant easy.

Again, the Git repository hosting the templates and its README, as well as the REST API of the PII service, become the platform interface. The templates as well as the inner workings of the PII services and the deployment process for the IAM roles become the platform kernel.

Maintaining this platform might already require one or more full-time engineers.

8.2.3   *Identifying the components of the data products*

The data consumer Business Analysis team has used the Terraform template to set up a full-fledged stack of tools. The team has Amazon Athena to query the data directly through the AWS interface using SQL. Athena is hooked up to the central Glue catalog and supplied with a role from the central repository. In addition, the Business Analysis team has both SageMaker and Glue for direct usage, deeper exploration of data using notebooks, and possibly transforming data into new data products.

The data products all share common tooling based on Glue and Lake Formation. Glue functions in two roles here, first for interacting with Lake Formation, and second, as data ingestion and transformation tooling. Glue supports both PySpark (Python) and Scala code. Let's look at the details.

In the data product owned by team Black depicted in figure 8.7, Glue is used first to get data from upstream data sources like an Amazon Relational Database Service (RDS) instance or any other data sources that can be accessed via Python or Scala. At this point, a team might choose to inject temporary S3 storage, or might choose to go directly into an ETL workflow. Glue is then used to transform this data into files hosted inside an S3 bucket. This S3 bucket becomes the data output port of the data product. Finally, a Glue crawler is used to update the metadata inside the federated Glue catalog, which is hooked up to Lake Formation. The federated Glue catalog thus becomes the discovery port of this data product.

Thanks to Lake Formation, the federated data catalogs sync back to the central one inside the Gray team's data platform context.

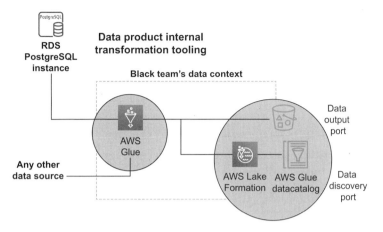

Figure 8.7   The Black team uses Glue and Lake Formation to build a data product.

For the data product owned by the White team, we have all the same components that we can see in the Black team's data product. This time, our team has a push mechanism listening to an S3 bucket, just as in the GCP section. However, the data product has a second important addition, as shown in figure 8.8. This team opts to use an optional component inside the Terraform template used for streaming data. A Kinesis data stream is used to get real-time event-based data from operational components used in the White team's bigger domain. These operational components use the Kinesis SDK to push data into this stream.

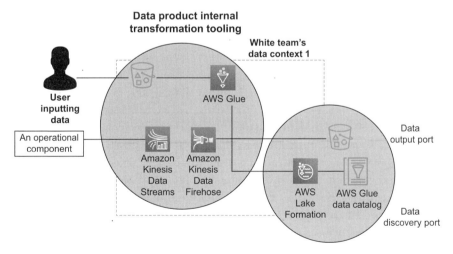

Figure 8.8   The White team adds Kinesis Data Streams to the mix to ingest streaming data into the second data product as well.

Then Amazon Kinesis Data Firehose picks up the streaming data and dumps it into a temporary S3 bucket, where Glue can pick it up and transform it and push the necessary metadata into the Glue data catalog, akin to the process used by the Black team.

The second data product of the White team is straightforward, using the same components we've already discussed. The more interesting part is now on the data consumer side.

8.2.4   Workflows

The data producer workflow in this technical architecture is similar to the one in the GCP section. Data producers pull the latest template from the central repository, configure it to meet their demands, opt in or out of possible Kinesis data stream creation, and apply the template to their AWS accounts.

The new addition is the PII service they can opt to use. If they want to use this service, they can integrate calls into the Glue code to the central service, which makes sure to hash personalized data equally.

The regular data consumer by default can use an open-for-all IAM role to access the metadata catalog. Then they use their own tools or the central Athena interface to query the related data. If they don't have access to a certain data product, they can request it from the owning team. That team would then modify the IAM to provide access.

However, the data consumer can also opt to use the Terraform template to get a larger toolset. If they choose to, they need to configure it and then apply it to their account. Once done, they will have access to a ready and set SageMaker to explore data using Python inside a notebook. Once they are done with their analysis, they can also opt to create their own data products out of their analysis and publish them to the Lake Formation, following the same process the other teams are using.

8.2.5   Relation to data mesh ideas

Let's discuss the data mesh principles indirectly used in this architecture.

Platform thinking, as a principle, is about making the lives of all platform participants easier, while not restricting their freedom. This architecture is aimed not just at data producers but also at data consumers, making it easy for a non-AWS savvy team to get going. It also goes slightly further than the Google Cloud version by allowing data producers to easily ingest arbitrary data sources.

Federated computational governance is again taken a step further with the provisioning of a central PII service. The computational side!

Data as a product is supported to roughly the same degree as in the Google Cloud data mesh architecture.

Data domain ownership is taken to a different level using Lake Formation and separate AWS accounts. Whereas in the Google Cloud version ownership is truly achieved only by adding additional boundaries with the service accounts, on AWS with separate accounts we actually need to have Lake Formation to even be able to allow cross-account access in a manageable way.

8.2.6   *Variations*

All of the variations introduced in the Google Cloud section can be applied to this architecture as well, and probably should. The DataHub can integrate the metadata from Glue, and adding a proper GUI would be especially important for the data consumers, who usually are less infrastructure savvy.

If you're a fan of more coupling to the cloud provider, you could opt to use the AWS Cloud Development Kit (CDK) and/or CloudFormation to provide the templates. In that case, you could then follow up with AWS CodePipeline, which can automatically apply these templates into accounts of data consumers and producers. This way, you can end up with a short GUI configuration and an almost completely automated process behind that.

Of course, you can build the same thing using Terraform. It just would be a bit more involved.

Another important variation concerns the stream's data ingestion the platform currently provides. In the previously sketched version, the only way of getting data into the AWS-based streams is to push it. If you happen to have legacy applications flying around that already emit streaming data, but not based on AWS, rewriting these applications will likely not be the easiest option. Instead, the platform could provide other ways of integrating data sources. Depending on the data sources, a variety of solutions can be chosen; for instance, the platform could provide an AWS Fargate template, which would spin up a few hosted Docker containers, which then would pull legacy streaming data in and write it into the correct Kinesis data stream continuously.

Another variation could include a lot more SQL-focused work. If that is the focus of your company, you could add a separate query engine like Trino, replacing Athena. Data consumers could then check in materialized views and basically do their computations inside Trino.

If that becomes too cumbersome, you can provide data consumers with a template for a database coupled with a `dbt` instance to push their own analysis through the `dbt-trino` adapter into a database.

Finally, you could think about providing a more centralized platform for data analysis and exploration. We will look at that option in section 8.3, using Databricks.

8.2.7   *AWS architecture summary*

This platform architecture uses shared cloud services, mostly native to the AWS environment. It uses a few components that are not AWS specific, Git and Terraform, and in the variations, custom code and DataHub.

This architecture provides data producers with a set of tooling for transforming data and two standardized input ports, but only one output port. It provides data consumers with a lot of tools to do their work with the less required knowledge of infrastructure in general.

This setup can be translated to other cloud providers like Google or Azure. Table 8.2 summarizes the AWS architecture profile.

Table 8.2 AWS architecture profile

Short description	This platform utilizes cloud provider–specific services, but offers data integration from any source and has additional platform offerings (e.g., the PII service).
Pros	A large degree of autonomy for data-producing teams. Runs as a service. Extremely low maintenance effort. Wide support for both data analytics workloads. Wide support for development teams.
Cons	Lock-in effect into cloud provider–specific services (but much less than in the previous setup). Requires a team to run the platform.
Suitable situations	Medium- to large-sized companies prioritizing maximum flexibility for data-producing teams.

As promised, we're now going to explore a more centralized approach with a larger central platform in the middle.

8.3 *Data mesh on Databricks*

This section's architecture is inspired by real-world implementations by DPG Media, Zalando, and many more. Unlike the AWS and GCP versions of the data meshes, a data mesh on Databricks looks a lot like a centralized data setup—at least with respect to technology.

That brings obvious benefits: namely, ease of setup and typical centralization benefits. This approach also has two big but not-so-obvious drawbacks:

- By centralizing large parts of the infrastructure, we're again subjecting ourselves to central bottlenecks. The effect of this is much smaller when using a hosted shared service, but it is still there. Additionally, we are physically centralizing the data in one place.
- By centralizing parts of the process, we're making the data domain ownership a lot harder to understand. In such a technical architecture, it is of prime importance to put the focus on the processes, the people, and the organization.

In the AWS data mesh, data producers are pretty much forced into owning their data, because they also own the infrastructure. That will not be the case here.

On the flip side, this data mesh likely doesn't need more than one data engineer to maintain the technical infrastructure inside a small- to medium-sized company. Inside domains, you should be able to cover the needs with one data scientist/engineer per domain.

8.3.1 *Self-serve data platform architecture*

We're going to make a small modification to our teams. Teams Black and White are both development teams with one data scientist. Team Gray is just a one-person team maintaining the platform on its own. Our business analysts are SQL savvy and can do some work with Python inside notebooks.

Figure 8.9 depicts our architecture this time. Notice how the contexts are a bit more blurry. You could, of course, separate out the contexts of teams Black and White, but we chose not to in this case.

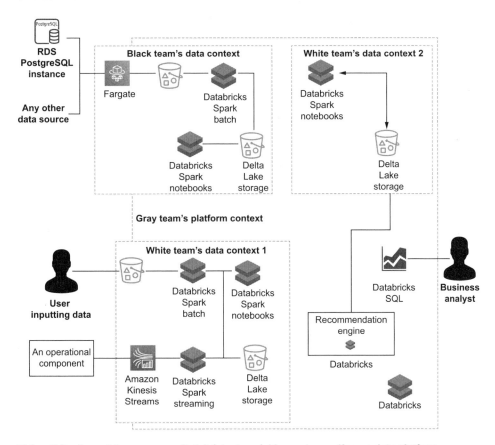

Figure 8.9   A small team can use Databricks to quickly create a self-serve data platform.

Explanation of Databricks technologies
The following is a short description of the Databricks technologies used in this section:

- *Databricks in general*—Databricks is a comprehensive analytics platform that can run on every major cloud. We're using only a part of the platform offering here.
- *Databricks Delta Lake*—This smart object storage format used by Databricks provides a bunch of database-like guarantees for your analytical workloads.
- *Apache Spark*—This is a multilanguage framework for executing analytical workloads.

(continued)

- *Databricks notebooks*—These are notebooks you can use to write Python- or Scala-based Spark code. This can be scheduled as a batch or streaming job.
- *Databricks SQL*—This is basically a wrapper around the BI tool Redash, well integrated into the Databricks landscape.

Comparing this architecture to the AWS and GCP-based architectures, you should be able to notice the following:

- This architecture is very intertwined in terms of the technology different teams use. The teams share Delta Lake, so separate (folder-based) boundaries have to be put in to mark the domains.
- But in turn, it is easy to set up and maintain.
- Most technology choices work inside the Databricks context.
- We need a few additional technologies (here, AWS based) to get the same scope as we had in the other data meshes. These concern getting data into the centralized data structures.
- A lot of out-of-the-box technologies assist analytical working, like notebooks and Databricks SQL for graphical analysis. Even the recommendation engine can be built inside Databricks.
- This architecture, unlike the previous two, doesn't utilize infrastructure provisioning templates.
- This architecture doesn't utilize a data catalog. A Databricks internal data catalog can be used, but *data catalog* in the data mesh context usually refers to technologies aiming to cover physically distributed data pieces. Since this is not the case here, the platform can work without it for now. See section 8.3.5 for more details.

Let's again identify the components of a data mesh: first the components of the platform and then the data product part.

8.3.2   *Identifying the components of the platform*

In our architecture, the platform interface and the kernel are largely composed of Databricks and related services. The team of one could start to provide templates or some kind of service for provisioning of the Kinesis and Fargate components, but that would probably clash with the idea of having a very lean platform team.

What the platform team will have to do is to provide guidelines, a one-pager of how to use Databricks inside the data mesh. These guidelines will indicate how to work with access rights, where to store all data products, and the likes.

8.3.3   Identifying the components of the data product

All data products are built on top of Databricks. Let's describe them in detail.

The data product owned by the Black team is a bit more involved. The upstream data is sourced from an operational RDS instance and some other systems. The team uses a custom Fargate task to load the data periodically into an S3 bucket. From there, a Databricks Spark batch job picks up the data and shoves it into Delta Lake. Then a Databricks notebook is used to transform the data into a data product and put it again into Delta Lake, from where it is exposed to others to use. The Delta Lake dataset in this case forms the data output port.

The data product owned by the White team uses two upstream datasets, as you can see in figure 8.10. A user periodically inputs data into an S3 bucket, which is picked up by a batch job and delivered into Delta Lake for temporary storage. This forms a push interface for the data product. On the other side, the team has provided a custom Kinesis Data Stream. Operational components push data in real time into the stream, which then is picked up by a Databricks streaming job. Again, a notebook is used for transformation and to produce the data output.

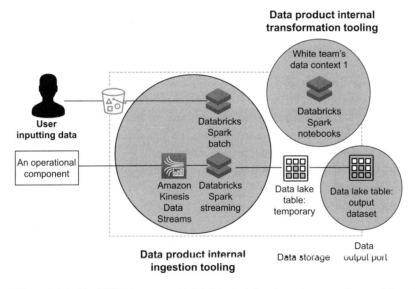

Figure 8.10   The White team uses Databricks to take streaming as well as push-based data to build a new data product.

The second data product of the White team shows how simple it is to build additional derived data products using Databricks. The team simply has to pick up another notebook, source the two data products already provided, and transform them into a third new data product inside Databricks.

Business analysts can easily use Databricks SQL to access and browse the data products. They can also create reports and dashboards inside that framework.

On Databricks, the workflows are quite Databricks-specific, and the principles work out a bit differently. So we'll cover them together in one section, highlighting why this change can be a pro for this architecture.

8.3.4   *Workflow considerations*

As we have said, the workflows on Databricks are very Databricks-specific. Teams can use the infrastructure to manage access rights for data products, and analysts can use the unity data catalog to explore data.

The data mesh principles work out a bit differently if we employ an architecture like this. The Databricks-centric architecture limits the freedom of teams quite a bit, and there is no easy way to opt out of the platform. Hence, this setup works well only if you either work around these limitations or make sure via governance measures that the teams are aligned in the tool choice. With this, this architecture does bring the risk of slipping back into a non-data-mesh-like mode of operation.

This makes this architecture much more suitable for younger companies. This architecture is also aimed more at data engineers and data scientists. This means it targets companies with a higher percentage of data people inside, whereas the GCP and AWS options are also accessible for software engineers.

8.3.5   *Variations*

Databricks in itself could be replaced by other bigger data platforms like the Snowflake ecosystem, which already offers almost all of the components needed to implement the preceding architecture.

To scale up this kind of data mesh architecture, you'll need to enable the opt-out option for every participant. This can be achieved by adding an external data catalog and reducing Databricks mostly to the transformation tooling, which still is a powerful toolset. Your setup could look like this:

1 Teams store data in their own data stores.
2 Ingestion tooling takes that data and puts it into Databricks-accessible data stores.
3 Databricks is used to do transformations on these datasets and to produce data products.
4 A query engine like Trino is used to connect various data products together.
5 A central data catalog makes sure data products can be stored anywhere and still be accessible and findable.

8.3.6   *Databricks architecture summary*

The architecture described in this section is focused on using the data-transformation powers of Databricks to the maximum. It is thus intertwined with the Databricks platform. We also saw that we need a bit of help in getting data into the central Delta Lake to unleash the Databricks' powers.

The one big strength of this setup is the minimal maintenance effort with great support for all the analytical workloads companies usually want to take on. On the flip side, we see limited support for development teams and the lock-in effect into the Databricks platform. Take a look at the summary profile in table 8.3.

Table 8.3   Databricks architecture profile

Short description	Platform is technologically very centralized but needs a bit of support on the ingestion part. Technologically, getting data into the data product isn't owned by the data producers.
Pros	Runs as a service. Extremely low maintenance effort. Great support for data engineering, data science, and analysts' workflows.
Cons	Lock-in effect into Databricks. No native support for development teams.
Suitable situations	Small- to medium-sized companies focused on building analytical data products fast, whether they're ML systems or reports and dashboards.

Finally, we will take a look at a setup utilizing the whole Kafka ecosystem. Whereas the focus on this setup is more on data engineers and scientists, the next setup is more geared to including software engineers as well. In particular, it is an interesting setup for companies with data-intensive applications.

8.4   Data mesh on Kafka

Whereas the data mesh on Databricks described in the preceding section was effectively using a central technology piece for transforming data, but not for the initial collection, the architecture in this section starts at the initial collection of data.

With this, we're providing an even larger degree of centralization, which enables very fast building of data-intensive applications. Remember, we're talking about physical and technological centralization, not a logical one.

This setup will provide standardized input and output ports, without forcing Kafka onto a team. It will enable SQL-based transformation tooling and will bring the possibility to work nicely with legacy data sources that aren't yet migrated into the data mesh itself.

8.4.1   Self-serve data platform architecture

Our teams are equipped similarly to the setups in the first two sections. We have two software engineering teams, Black and White, and a platform team responsible for operating a few additional components that round up the Kafka-based data mesh.

Figure 8.11 depicts the setup. Take some time to see how data flows between the data products. Note that the figure is a bit reduced. Just as in the Databricks setup, the Kafka cluster here is a physically central piece of infrastructure, with logical separation

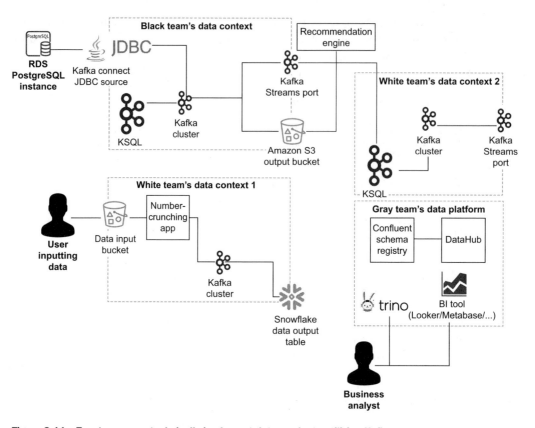

Figure 8.11   Two teams can technically implement data products utilizing Kafka.

on the levels, called *streams* and *topics*, the organizational units inside Kafka. The architecture uses two key Kafka technologies:

- Using either event streams with a Kafka topic carrier as data output ports, or directly mapping the topic into a provided output format like a Snowflake table or a CSV file inside cloud storage using Kafka Connect sinks.
- Defaulting to ksqlDB as SQL-syntax-based transformation tooling inside the data product. Additionally, ksqlDB is used as a tool for ingesting data from event stream data output ports that are carried by a Kafka topic.

Explanation of Kafka components

The following is a short description of the Kafka components used in this section:

- *Apache Kafka*—An open source streaming platform for high-performance streaming and analytics. Data inside Kafka is organized into *topics*. The default way of getting data into Kafka is to use the Producer API, e.g., inside Java. Similarly, the Consumer API can be used to get data out of Kafka.

- *Kafka Connect*—For diverse data sources, Connect offers a variety of connectors to import data into topics as with any Java Database Connectivity (JDBC) source, as well as export data (called *sinks*) into other data systems (for instance, typical object storage systems).
- *ksqlDB*—This distributed open source streaming database, built on top of Kafka, allows transforming data inside Kafka by using a SQL syntax.

You should be able to quickly figure out a few important highlights in this architecture:

- A lot is going on inside the Kafka ecosystem.
- The data inputs are standardized using Kafka sources, which is something that wasn't the case in most other setups.
- The data output ports are standardized using Kafka sinks and the event streams carried by Kafka topics.
- KSQL is used for transformations inside the ecosystem.
- Additional capabilities—like a central data catalog that utilizes the Confluent schema registry, Trino, and some BI tools—are necessary to enable business analysts to work. This is more straightforward in other setups.

Let's now take a look at the platform itself and then the data products in detail.

8.4.2   *Identifying the components*

Akin to the Databricks data mesh architecture, this platform interface consists mostly of documentation, and the rest of the interface is the Kafka-specific interface. The team might set up a README file for easy navigation of the company-specific Kafka setup.

The Black team's data product sources data from an upstream SQL-based database, as you can see in figure 8.12. It uses the Kafka Connect built-in JDBC source connector to stream the data into a Kafka topic. ksqlDB is used to transform the data and write datasets into a new Kafka stream as well as into an S3 bucket. For the latter, again a Kafka Connect S3 connector is used. The Kafka stream is accessible via, for example,

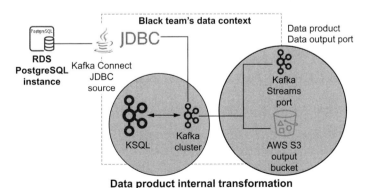

Data product internal transformation
tooling and data storage

Figure 8.12   The Black team implements its data product on top of Kafka.

the Kafka Streams API, or from ksqlDB. Thus the Kafka Streams port becomes the data output port together with the S3 bucket.

The White team's data product sources data from an S3 bucket; the sourcing is done via a custom number-crunching application. The app uses the Kafka Producer API to write the datasets into a Kafka stream. A Kafka Connect sink is configured to dump this data into a Snowflake table as well. These two components, the Snowflake table and the Kafka streams port, become the data output ports.

The second data product from the White team is really simple in its architecture. It uses ksqlDB to connect to the existing event stream from the team's first data product, transforms the data using SQL, and then writes it again to an event stream that functions as the data output port. The data product is depicted in figure 8.13.

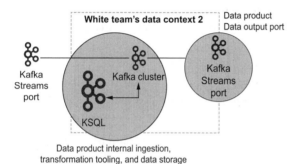

Figure 8.13   The White team uses ksqlDB to source another team's data to produce a second data product.

The recommendation engine in this case could just source the Kafka streams, but in our case, it is easier for it to take batch data that is put into the S3 bucket via a standard Kafka sink.

The business analysts are a bit special in this case. They have no direct way of consuming data products, not inside the Kafka ecosystem. For that, we utilize Trino as a query engine to query across all data products and allow joining between them in native SQL. On top of Trino we can then place a standard BI tool like Tableau, Looker, or Metabase to also make the data available in the form of dashboards and the like.

As in the preceding section, this architecture is a more specific tool than the first two explained in this chapter. So instead of discussing the workflows and data mesh principles, we'll focus on why this architecture is more of a special-purpose tool.

8.4.3   Considerations

This architecture is powerful if your company is focused on building data-intensive applications, especially in real time, as the native integrations provided by Kafka make building and combining these easy.

This architecture is designed to be used a lot by development teams. To accommodate data engineers and data scientists, we need to add a few extras, like Trino. We also do not have any native integration into a notebook-like environment as the Databricks-based architecture had. We can make all of this work; it just requires extra attention.

Another consideration is the schema registry and the data catalog. Kafka will need its own schema registry to be fully useful. The schema registry then needs to be integrated into an external data catalog. This is also the case for all other architectures, but in all other architectures, the data catalog could also serve as a schema registry; in this case, we do need the Kafka-specific registry.

Most variations used in other architectures are possible here as well. In particular, installing more data engineering–heavy components is the one that will make the most sense here.

8.4.4   Kafka architecture summary

The Kafka architecture is different from the other three we have covered. While the focus of the other three is to enable analytical work, this architecture focuses more on building data-heavy applications, which do not necessarily need to be analytical in nature.

This architecture is aimed at companies that want to extract value from data in almost every part of their product and thus build mostly data-intensive applications. Therefore, the primary focus becomes development teams and making their lives a lot easier. This also means that the life of the data engineer is a bit harder or at least will require extra attention.

These are tradeoffs that are hard but necessary. Table 8.4 presents the summary of the Kafka data mesh.

Table 8.4   Kafka architecture profile

Short description	Platform is technologically very centralized. Technologically, getting data into the data product *is* the responsibility of the data producers.
Pros	Possibility to run most components as a service or self-service. Low maintenance effort of self-serve platform. Native support for development teams. A lot of sources and targets are supported within the ecosystem.
Cons	Extra work necessary to integrate data science and analysis workflows. Strong technological centralization means less autonomy for the development teams. Steep learning curve of using stream processing and Kafka.
Suitable situations	Small- to medium-sized companies focused on building data-heavy applications in most parts of the business.

In this chapter, you explored four architectures and four technology stacks. In the next chapter, we will head into further technical details of data meshes and look at how to migrate from legacy patterns to data mesh patterns.

Summary

- You got to know four architectures of self-serve platforms: a cloud-native architecture, a cloud-native architecture with larger autonomy for the data producers, a much easier-to-deploy architecture using a certain degree of centralization, and finally an architecture focused on building data-intensive real-time applications.
- We've covered a variety of toolkits—most importantly GCP, AWS, Databricks, and Apache Kafka—but also Terraform and DataHub.
- All of the architectures, as well as the toolkits, can be mixed and matched to solve your specific problems.
- Building a self-serve data platform is serious work simply because no appropriate out-of-the-box tooling is available.
- Because your underlying data landscape will likely be unique, you will end up customizing a solution for your company anyhow.
- The architectures and toolkits in this chapter will help you take a good stab at the first few iterations of building your own self-serve data platform, whether you start with a platform that needs almost no maintenance to maintain (like the Databricks-based example) or you want to build multiple real-time data-based applications (and thus opt for a Kafka-based setup).
- Whatever architecture you choose, you will end up facing a tradeoff of the data-producing teams' autonomy and flexibility against the cost and maintainability of the platform itself.

Solution
architecture design

In this chapter, we will come much closer to the code and technical details. We will step into the Messflix software architect's shoes to design technical architecture for our data products.

In the previous chapters, you learned the principles, such as what data product boundaries should look like, how to apply product thinking, how governance should be set up, and what an underlying platform is. We can imagine you are now looking at diagrams of your current systems and asking yourself: how should we extend this particular system to the data product? What should the design look like? In this chapter, we will help you answer these questions. After this chapter, you will be able to do the following:

- Organize a design session for your team
- Choose the proper notation to capture architecture
- Capture architectural drivers of planned data products
- Make design decisions based on architectural drivers
- Choose between design patterns using tradeoff analysis or a pro-con-fix exercise
- Design the technical architecture of a data product

Let's start by explaining what software architecture is and how to capture its current state in your organization.

9.1   *Capturing and understanding the current state*

Whenever someone is planning a major renovation of their home interior, they usually hire an interior designer. But before the designer can start work, they have to capture a current floor plan. To make meaningful decisions about what can be changed, they need to understand the current state. As an example, you might not be able to remove every wall, because you cannot easily change load-bearing walls. Only partition walls can be easily moved.

This planning process is similar to the work done by software architects. If you do not understand the systems that are already in place and how they are connected, you cannot plan any changes. This is why we will start this chapter by capturing the current state of the Messflix architecture. Furthermore, it will not be enough to understand the end state. We also need to understand the reasoning behind decisions that were made so we can make conscious choices about changes. We will also have to understand architectural drivers for our data products.

This section will show you the kind of architectural information you need to gather before jumping into the design of data products. If your systems are already well documented, good for you! This section will help you navigate through this documentation and look for pieces of information that matter. If you are not so lucky, and the complete documentation is in the heads of developers and architects, this section will help you capture that documentation. But before we do that, you need to understand what architecture is.

9.1.1   *What is software architecture?*

Let's start by clarifying what we mean by *software architecture*. For us, architecture is the structure of the software and the process of designing it.

By *architecture* as a *structure*, we mean the building blocks of the system; the relations and interfaces between them; the patterns applied; the technology stack for the building blocks, platform, or infrastructure used by these components; and finally cross-cutting concerns like security and logging. By *architecture*, we mean elements of the structure that take time to change.

By *architecture* as a *process*, we mean an act of translating architectural drivers into the architecture design and architectural decisions that shape the structure.

What do we *not* consider architecture? Details of the code, or how the particular line of code was written. Everything that can be easily changed within minutes is usually not an architectural concern.

In this chapter, we focus on both sides: architecture as a structure of related building blocks, and architecture as a process of designing and making conscious decisions.

9.1.2 How to document architecture: The C4 model

One great author who strongly influences our understanding of software architecture is Simon Brown. In *C4 Model for Visualising Software Architecture* (Leanpub, 2022), he shares a brief yet powerful notation that can be used to capture architecture diagrams: the C4 model.

We describe this notation here for two reasons. First, to explain to you ways of designing data products in our Messflix example. Second, it is common that in big organizations, architecture of every project is documented differently, which makes an exchange of knowledge and cross-reviews problematic. By using the C4 notation, you can introduce a common language to talk about architecture in your organization.

The C4 model is built with four levels of abstraction:

1. *Context*—It shows a software system as a black box with people and other systems interacting with it.
2. *Container*—It is similar to a context diagram, but reveals the containers that form the software system. By *containers*, Brown usually means applications or data stores. In the container diagram, we also extend that definition with descriptions of used technologies (like Java with Spring Boot or Oracle Database) and communication mechanisms (REST call or Kafka message).
3. *Component*—It zooms into one of the containers and shows its building blocks, the components. You can treat components like modules in your codebase.
4. *Code*—It zooms into one of the components. It is a UML class diagram that describes the internals of a component. In this diagram, you describe the code's structure, classes that reside in the code, and their relationships.

In addition, Brown describes a few additional diagrams like deployment, infrastructure, and system landscape.

We usually use levels 1, 2, and 3, and additionally system landscape, deployment, and infrastructure. We usually skip level 4, because we prefer that code speaks for itself. By this, we mean writing code in a self-explanatory way, with names of classes and methods that are meaningful from the business domain perspective, and with tests that should be living code documentation. But sometimes when the model is a bit more complex, it is beneficial to visualize relations between classes as well.

Notation in levels 1–3 is simple: human icons, rectangles, and arrows. Each diagram has only a few elements: system, container, component, person, and their relations (arrows). Remember that relations with the explicit intent behind them are as important as boxes. You can check the examples in figures 9.1–9.3. On levels 1 and 2, we mark with a magnifier the building block zoomed in on the next level.

We begin at the context level (C1) in figure 9.1.

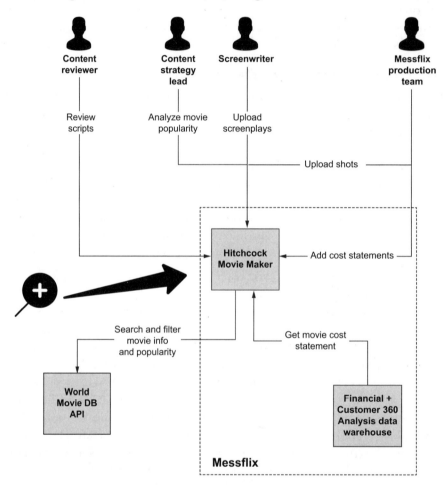

Figure 9.1   A C1 (context level) example in the Messflix domain

Now let's zoom into the container level (C2) in figure 9.2.

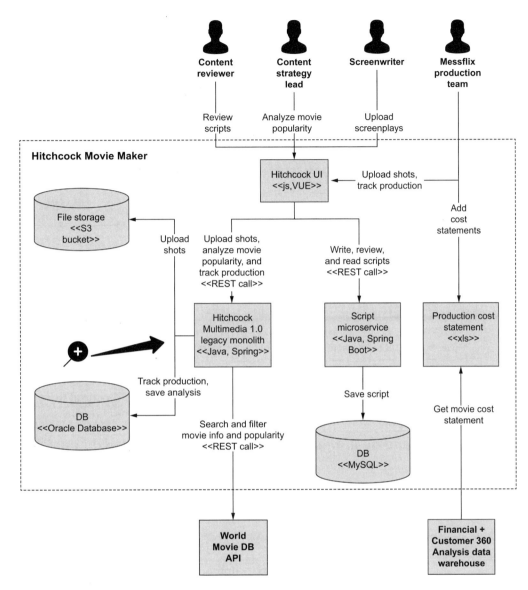

Figure 9.2 A C2 (container level) example in the Messflix domain

Finally, we zoom into the component level (C3) in figure 9.3.

With such diagrams, we can understand the static structure of the Messflix architecture, but architecting is a process of decision-making, and to fully understand the design, we need to understand the architectural drivers (functional requirements, quality attributes, constraints, and principles) that lead us to those decisions.

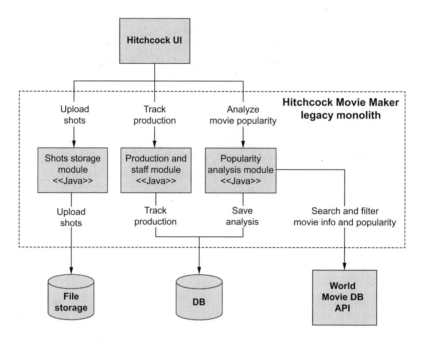

Figure 9.3   A C3 (component level) example in the Messflix domain

We already know the structure of current solutions. But before we jump into the design of a data product, we need first to understand the architectural drivers that will guide our design.

9.2   *Understanding architectural drivers of a data product design*

Imagine you are an army commander. It is the day before a battle. Before you plan tactics for your upcoming battle, you need to gather important information that will drive these decisions. You require a map of the surrounding terrain, a weather forecast for the next day, information about the enemy army from intel, and a report from your officers about the morale of your soldiers. You will have to analyze all this information to make good decisions.

As a software architect, much like a military commander, you rely on the contextual information of the specific "battlefield" before you can make your plans. Architecture design is your battle, and architectural drivers are the information you need to choose the best architecture.

In this section, we will teach you about architectural drivers. These drivers will be an input needed for your design.

9.2.1   *Architectural drivers*

We can divide architectural drivers into four categories: functional requirements, quality attributes (also called nonfunctional requirements), constraints, and principles.

FUNCTIONAL REQUIREMENTS

For the system of records, functional requirements are usually gathered in a backlog in the form of features or user stories. In the context of a data product, *functional requirements* are the information needs of (potential) data consumers together with the value they derive from it, and they are the preferred ways of consumption. Functional requirements can be segmented by different types of consumers, and each comes with possibly different needs of information, different ways they prefer to consume data, and different ways they can consume data.

QUALITY ATTRIBUTES

Quality attributes, sometimes called *nonfunctional requirements,* are more technical. You can think of them as qualities or technical requirements of the system. The list of examples in table 9.1 is a good starting point, but it's by no means a complete list.

Table 9.1   Quality attributes

Type	Requirement description
Auditability	Datasets should be persisted for at least five years because of possible legal audits.
Availability	Data will be used for near real-time decision making. Endpoints should be available for consumption 99.99% percent of the time.
Compliance	We are storing user-sensitive data that should comply with GDPR. This means that we should be able to remove all user data on demand.
Extensibility	At the beginning, data will be consumed through the REST API port, but we know that two other types of consumers will require access using different ports: S3 bucket files and streams of events. We should design a data product to extend it in the near future easily. Adding a new port should not take more than two weeks.
Inter-operability	Every controlled vocabulary used in the datasets should be defined in a terminology service.
	Data models and datasets should be defined using open source ontology (e.g., https://openontology.org/).
Support-ability	We want to track down the reason data is missing in the exposed datasets, we want to be notified when data is not passing validation, and we want to analyze logged reasons for that.
Performance	Downloading yearly financial reports should have a response time below 10 seconds.
Privacy	Only people with a manager role can access employee personal data.
Resilience	Data not complying with the contract coming from the system on the input of a data product should be logged, and support should be notified. The data product should omit that part of the data, but it should continue providing data to consumers without interruptions.
	If, during the processing of the event, the value of the Item Price field exceeds the maximum value, it should be replaced with a default value and processing should proceed.

Table 9.1   Quality attributes *(continued)*

Type	Requirement description
Scalability	Usage of the data product will have its peaks during weekends. Data products should scale down during the week and scale up on the weekend to handle up to 1,000 calls per minute.
Security	The data product can be consumed only by users with a data scientist role.
	The REST API will be secured using the OAuth 2.0 protocol.
	All PII has to be masked before exposure.
Testability	Data product tests should be fully automated. No manual tests should be required before production release.
	Every input validation scenario should be reflected in automated tests, and the data product should be treated as a black box.
	Data product tests should be a part of integration tests, starting from calling the System of Record API and asserting the end result in the data product output port.
	Data product tests should be autonomous and should not require an environment with other systems running on it.

Most quality attributes are limited to just a system/product level. Still, quality attributes are so important from the company strategy perspective that they are established at the level of the governance team or top management.

CONSTRAINTS

Constraints are usually independent of us and are imposed by a governance body or top management. You can divide constraints into the following categories:

- Time and budget constraints
- Technology constraints
- People and organizational constraints

Time and budget constraints are self-explanatory, and we believe everybody is familiar with them. An example of such a constraint is a deadline for delivering solutions. A widespread example of technology constraints is how an organization hosts its applications. It might be an on-premises solution versus one of the cloud vendors like Google, AWS, or Azure. Last, people and organizational constraints can be the technology stack of your solution because of the limited skills of development teams (e.g., you can use only Java as a general-purpose programming language on the backend).

PRINCIPLES

If your organization has strong technical leadership or some kind of architecture or data governing body, an explicit list of *principles* should drive your design decision. You can see examples of such principles in table 9.2.

Table 9.2 Guiding principles

Name	Description	Rationale	Implications
Cloud-native	Use cloud-native technologies of our provider of choice.	It enables the rapid development of solutions without worrying about capabilities, like hosting, that are not the core of our business.	Prefer open tooling for deployment suitable for our cloud provider. Prefer platform-as-a-service and function-as-a-service solutions.
Mature technologies only	Don't use immature technologies or frameworks unless necessary.	Our products and systems are critical, and once developed are planned to serve and be maintained for multiple years. We value stability more than rapid development.	Choose frameworks and libraries that have more than 1,000 stars on GitHub. Use a framework or library only after first applying a minor/patch release with fixes.
Automate everything	All manual work should be automated whenever possible.	Manual work, like deployments, is always more error prone and less repeatable than automated work.	Deployments from development to production environments should be fully automated using pipeline as a code. All tests should be automated.

9.2.2 *Capturing architectural drivers for a data-product design*

In section 9.2.1, we described what we mean by architectural drivers with simple examples. This section focuses on capturing architectural drivers for our data products, using the example of a Cost Statement data product, which is a merge of cost statements from preproduction, production, and postproduction. Cost statements are about spending during the whole process of production.

ANALYZE FUNCTIONAL REQUIREMENTS

Let's imagine you are the software architect responsible for designing a newly established data product. The data product owner already knows the data scope of the product and has already interviewed all possible users, and so knows their needs. It is your responsibility as an architect to meet the data product owner to help extract more technical requirements. To do that, you need to analyze functional requirements gathered by the data product owner.

Such requirements can be gathered in many forms, but let's assume that our data product owner gathered these in the form of plain text combined with a simple picture and data product canvas. In figure 9.4, you can see the Cost Statement data product with its source and envisioned consumers.

In figure 9.5, you can see the requirements and data product canvas (described in chapter 5) that you received from the data product owner.

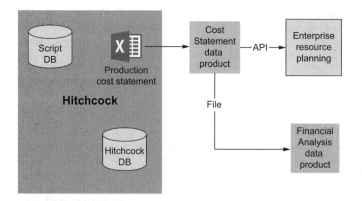

Figure 9.4   The Cost Statement data product, its source, and consumers

Name	Description	
Cost Statement	Contains the cost breakdown of a given production run by Messflix	
Data Product Owner	Business Capability/ Domain/ Bounded Context	System
Jane Doe	Produce Content	Hitchcock Movie Maker
Classification (source aligned/consumer aligned/shared core) Source aligned	Classification (virtual or materialized) Materialized	Life-Cycle Classification (experimental / stable) Stable
Input Interface Excel file	Output Ports REST API and CSV file	Security Private
Inbound Flow Production cost statements	Outbound Flow Aggregated cost statements	Volume 100 MB
Datasets Production cost statements		

Figure 9.5   The Cost Statement data product canvas

SET COST STATEMENT DATA PRODUCT REQUIREMENTS

The Cost Statement data product is derived from cost statement spreadsheets that are stored by the Production team as a part of the Hitchcock Movie Maker on the online drive.

> **NOTE**   If you are not sure how we designed boundaries of data products that we introduce in this chapter, refer to chapter 4.

Data will be exposed to two consumers: ERP for accounting purposes through the REST API, and the Financial Analysis data product for yearly and monthly financial reports prepared for the CEO.

ERP will consume new cost statements daily, and it will require REST API for integration because of its limitations. The cost statement will contain private information like the payrolls of the cast.

The Financial Analysis data product is consuming monthly aggregations. A CSV file port is the preferred port.

As a good data product owner or software architect, you should know that such a description is not enough to understand what kind of quality attributes should be your priority during the design. You should reread the description, talk to the stakeholders or consumers if needed, and try to list them explicitly.

We already can tell what kind of quality attributes we don't have to emphasize. They are scalability, performance, and availability. They are not a priority for us because data will be accessed by just two consumers and not more often than daily. This is good information for you because these quality attributes are usually tough to achieve and costly.

From the description, we can see that privacy is important because of the private data.

We will have to review the details and apply critical thinking to extract more. Cost statements will be used in financial reports, which the CEO will use to make decisions worth millions of dollars; the data product owner, together with you, decide that auditability will also be important. We want to analyze what data drove particular decisions retrospectively.

So we want to propose two quality attributes: *privacy* and *auditability*. As an architect, you also look for quality attributes in system-of-record documentation as an inspiration. In the case of Hitchcock Movie Maker, you would probably find its privacy quality attribute as well.

> **NOTE**   We recommend practicing skills to extract quality attributes the same way developers practice their coding skills. You can use an exercise designed by Ted Neward called *Architectural Katas* (https://nealford.com/katas/). Many examples of these exercises are available on the internet for free.

CHOOSE THE MOST IMPORTANT QUALITY ATTRIBUTES AND DECIDE ON THE METRIC

When you, with the data product owner, establish a list of possible quality attributes, try to limit them to only those that are crucial. Keep the list short and simple. A too-big list of quality attributes leads you to a data product that is optimized for everything and nothing at the same time.

When we have a list of important quality attributes, prepare a straw man's proposal of metrics or measures of success for these nonfunctional requirements.

DEFINITION   Making a *straw man's proposal* is a technique to propose a solution that is obviously wrong. Because it is wrong, it will usually trigger the recipient to provide a better proposal.

As you can see in table 9.3, the values in the "Straw man's proposal" column will trigger discussions with the data product Owner and Business Stakeholders. The result of these discussions should be collected in the form of two measures of success: worst possible but still acceptable, and optimal. This way, you will know your boundaries as a designer.

Table 9.3   Quality attributes, measures of success, and straw man's proposals

Quality attribute	Measure of success	Straw man's proposal	Worst acceptable	Optimal
Auditability	Persistency	One week	One year	Five years
Privacy	Access to personal data	Everyone in Messflix has access.	The production team has access.	Only HR people in the production team have access.

For auditability, the straw man's proposal that you show to stakeholders is to keep the cost statements for one week. Because you plan to use cost statements for financial reports, this option is obviously wrong; usually this report is created with data from at least the past year. This is why the worst acceptable persistence of data is set by stakeholders to one year. When you ask them about the period of time sometimes required to recalculate some reports, they say five years, and this is how you come up with five years as an optimal value.

This process is similar for privacy. Saying that everyone at Messflix has access to personal data is obviously a wrong statement. If you keep that access to only the production team, it's a bit better and more acceptable, but the preferred way is to give access only to HR staff, because they know how to deal with it.

To summarize, here are the steps that you, as an architect or data product owner should follow:

1 Analyze functional requirements.
2 Extract nonfunctional requirements from the requirements and discussions with stakeholders.
3 Limit the list to only crucial nonfunctional requirements.
4 Prepare a straw man's proposal with measures of success and review it with possible consumers and stakeholders.

LOOK FOR CONSTRAINTS, PRINCIPLES, AND QUALITY ATTRIBUTES ON THE ORGANIZATIONAL LEVEL
Constraints, principles, and quality attributes can be defined on the level of the product, as we showed in previous sections, but they also can be defined on the level of the whole organization. This is usually the case when your organization has a governance

body and strong individual or collective technical leadership. When you are designing your data product, you consider not only the product-level architectural drivers but the organization-level ones as well.

At Messflix, we have a case of strong technical leadership; let's see architectural drivers those leaders defined at the level of the organization.

First, here are the constraints:

- *Java and Python as our general-purpose programming languages*—The company has many Java and Python developers with dedicated communities of practice. Using these two languages facilitates transferring knowledge, sharing experience, and moving employees between projects/products.
- *Single cloud provider*—Moving to a new provider requires a lot of learning and investments, and the company would like to avoid that if possible.

Next, here are the principles:

- *Platform over custom solutions*—Whenever possible, prefer to use your data platform instead of writing custom solutions.
- *Openness to open source*—When choosing a new tool, library, or framework, always consider open source alternatives.
- Everyone is an architect and can make architecture decisions (within constraints), but every architecture decision has to be discussed with those affected by the decision and with experts in the subject. We want to empower teams to make their own decisions.

Finally, here are the company-wide quality attributes:

- *Usability means user satisfaction is the king*—Messflix relies strongly on user satisfaction, so whenever you make technical decisions, analyze whether that decision will improve or worsen the user experience.
- *Findability of data*—All data within an organization has to be findable in a data catalog.

We gathered everything needed to start the design, so let's jump into it!

9.3   Designing the future architecture of a data product and related systems

In the previous section, we showed you the process of capturing current architecture and collecting architectural drivers, through the example of the Cost Statement data product. In this section, we will follow up on that example to show you the process of designing the data product architecture. We will not limit ourselves to only one example. The following sections present multiple examples from Messflix, and we will try to touch on as many commonly used architectural patterns as possible. We will discuss the following cases:

- File-based data product (spreadsheet)
- Existing monolithic and microservice architecture as a source of data for a data product
- Stream- and batch-processing examples

In each example, we will analyze architectural drivers, possible solutions, and tradeoffs related to these solutions. While reading, don't focus too much on the specific technologies used (e.g., MongoDB); they are provided just as examples. Now let's delve into what the design activity looks like.

9.3.1 Design session

We strongly believe that design should be a collaborative and collective effort done by the whole or by most of the development team. This helps avoid the pitfall of the ivory tower architect.

> **DEFINITION** An *ivory tower architect* is a software architect who is isolated from others, mainly the development team, because of organizational structure, company culture, or personal approach.

When everyone is involved in the design of a data product, the team will feel connected to it; it will be their child. This is why you should invite the whole team to the design session. During the session, it is important to make the exercise inclusive and allow each team member to have a voice.

The following is a simple example agenda for a design session meeting:

1 Architectural drivers presentation and Q&A session.
2 Brainstorming possible design options in pairs, where every pair creates their proposal.
3 Cross-review between teams to determine the pros, cons, and fixes of solutions.
4 Collective decision to decide which design is best.

> **DEFINITION** A *pro-con-fix exercise* provides a way to compare options without overfocusing on the negatives. In this extension of a pro-con exercise, you not only list the pros and cons, but also try to identify a mitigation for each con. See "Pro-Con-Fix List, a Simple Tool for Visualising a Trade-off" by Gien Verschatse for more details (http://mng.bz/GEav).

Now you know the process, but we are still missing some tangible examples. Let's go back to the Cost Statement data product example.

9.3.2 File-based data product: Spreadsheet

Let's summarize what you've learned about the Cost Statement data product:

- Currently, it is stored as a spreadsheet in the virtual drive and manually uploaded to the data warehouse.

- In the future, we want to integrate with the Financial Analysis data product (REST API) and ERP (file-based CSV port).
- Both ports will be consumed not more often than daily. We don't care much about the scalability, availability, or performance of the solution.
- We need to base our design on two nonfunctional requirements: auditability (we need to persist all statements for at least the year) and security/privacy (only the production team can access personal data).
- We are constrained to Python and Java solutions.
- We should use the platform whenever possible.

Your team is guided by these points and comes up with two possible solutions. Each solution goes through cross-review, and as a result, the team comes up with pros, cons, and possible mitigations/fixes for the cons. Let's look at the first solution.

COST STATEMENT DATA PRODUCT: SOLUTION 1

In this solution, we are taking advantage of a platform. We are using an Airflow workflow written in Python to periodically read spreadsheet files prepared by the Production team (figure 9.6).

The workflow stores the raw files in the internal repository. It guarantees the auditability of the data; we can re-create financial aggregations whenever needed. The workflow is also responsible for saving detailed statements in MongoDB in a form optimized for reads, done through the API by ERP. The workflow also performs simple aggregations and saves them in the shared repository as weekly and monthly summaries, consumed later by the Financial Analysis data product. Privacy is ensured at the level of the Airflow workflow; we are removing all sensitive data from the datasets.

> **DEFINITION** *MongoDB* is a document database, classified as a NoSQL database program.

> **NOTE** As you remember from chapter 5, each data product is responsible for exposing not only data but also metadata. Because this metadata was already described in chapter 5, we omit it here. But remember that it is still crucial to have metadata implemented in real data products.

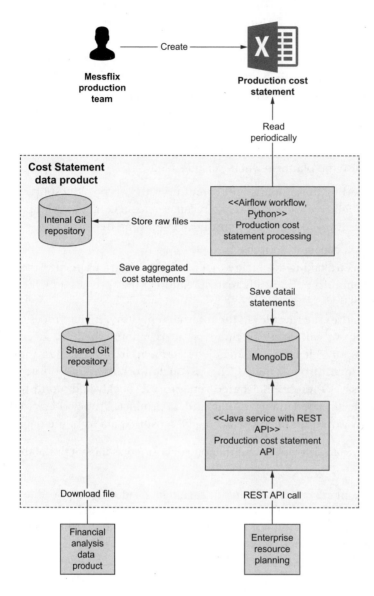

Figure 9.6   Design option 1 for the Cost Statement data product

We can see in figure 9.7 what other dev team members are thinking about the design. The main quality attributes have been auditability and privacy, which are secured by this design.

We can see that we also conformed to our set of principles:

- *Platform over custom solutions*—We use Airflow and storage templates provided by the platform team.
- *Openness to open source*—We use MongoDB.

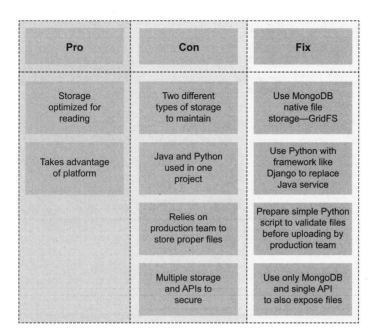

Pro	Con	Fix
Storage optimized for reading	Two different types of storage to maintain	Use MongoDB native file storage—GridFS
Takes advantage of platform	Java and Python used in one project	Use Python with framework like Django to replace Java service
	Relies on production team to store proper files	Prepare simple Python script to validate files before uploading by production team
	Multiple storage and APIs to secure	Use only MongoDB and single API to also expose files

Figure 9.7 Pros, cons, and fixes for the first design option of the Cost Statement data product

We also followed imposed constraints:

- *Java and Python as our general-purpose programming languages*—Only Java and Python are used.
- *Single cloud provider*—The whole infrastructure is set up on our favorite cloud provider.

We also validated our design against company-wide quality attributes:

- *Usability*—User satisfaction is the king. This is not relevant here, because this system is not exposed to the end user.
- *Findability of data*—We achieve this with metadata ports exposed from our data product and connected to a DataHub.

Let's look at solution 2.

COST STATEMENT DATA PRODUCT: SOLUTION 2

In this solution, the things that stand out are the different storage engine—PostgreSQL (an open source, relational database management system)—and the single Java service responsible for processing and data exposure (figure 9.8).

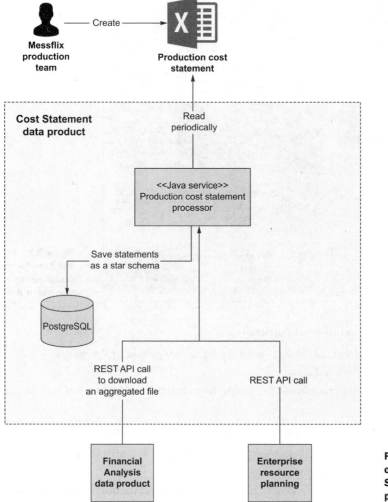

Figure 9.8   Design option 2 for the Cost Statement data product

We will not deeply analyze every part of the following design and pro-con-fix exercise; we just want to explain our way of thinking about the design process (figure 9.9).

As we look at the pros and cons, we can see one crucial con: "Does not take advantage of the platform." This is an important con because it breaks the organization rule: "Platform over custom solutions." In this option, we do not take advantage of the platform because instead of Airflow proposed as a platform, we are implementing a custom Java solution.

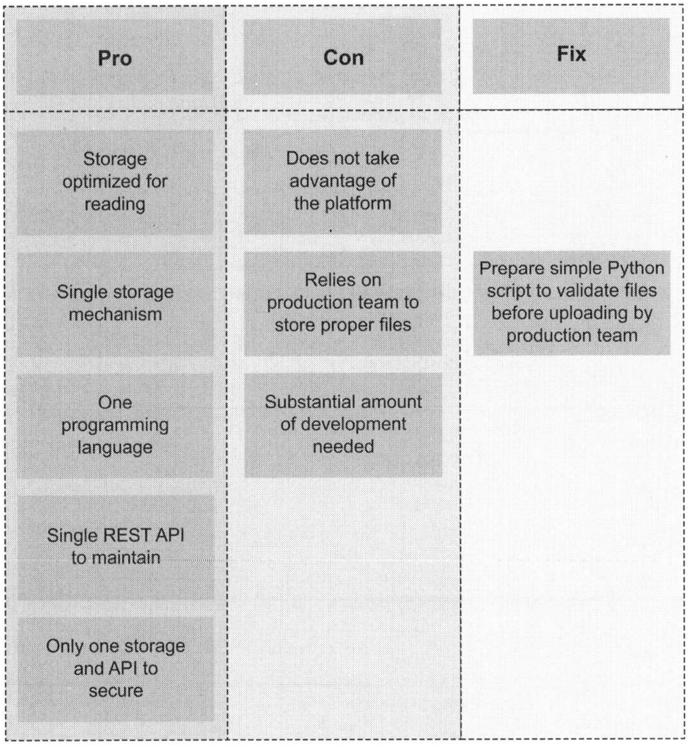

Pro	Con	Fix
Storage optimized for reading	Does not take advantage of the platform	
Single storage mechanism	Relies on production team to store proper files	Prepare simple Python script to validate files before uploading by production team
One programming language	Substantial amount of development needed	
Single REST API to maintain		
Only one storage and API to secure		

Figure 9.9 Pros, cons, and fixes for design option 2 of the Cost Statement data product

After a long and inclusive discussion, the team decides to prepare yet another design, mainly based on design option 1 (we'll skip over the thought process since it's beyond the scope of this chapter). You can see the output in figure 9.10.

We decide to use a single database and a single programming language and take advantage of the Airflow cluster platform.

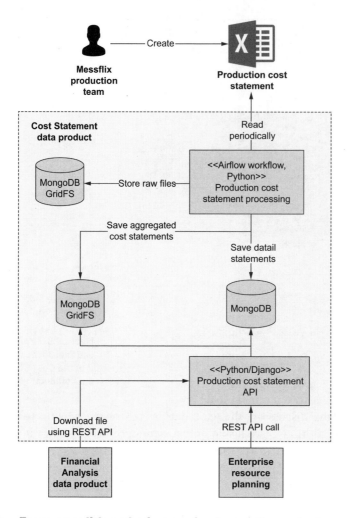

Figure 9.10   Final design of the Cost Statement data product

9.3.3   *From monolith and microservice to a data product*

After the first example, you already know the drill. So with the second example, we will not repeat ourselves, and we will go straight into the summary of the current state and architectural drivers to focus more on the design options.

We will again focus on Hitchcock Movie Maker, but this time on the legacy monolith and script microservice. You can remind yourself of its current architecture in figure 9.11.

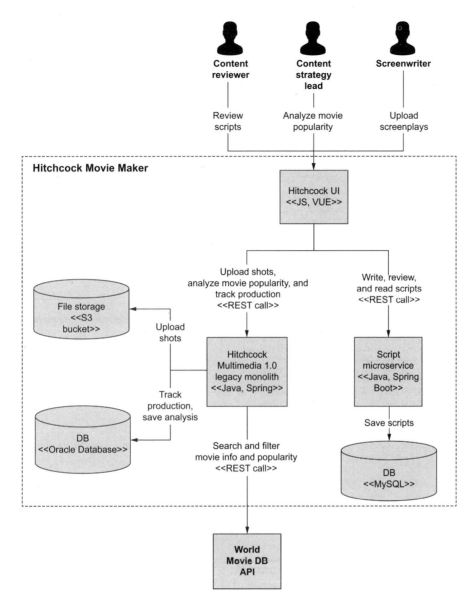

Figure 9.11 **Hitchcock Movie Maker container diagram, focusing on the legacy part and script microservice**

In figure 9.12, we visualize two data products for which we want to design the architecture: the Scripts data product, responsible for aggregating all scripts with their life cycle; and the Cast data product, which focuses on the details of the cast, their preferences, agreements, and movies.

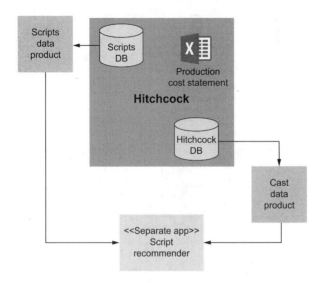

Figure 9.12   The Scripts and Cast data products with their source system, Hitchcock Movie Maker

Let's start with the Cast data product.

CAST DATA PRODUCT

Here's a summary of architectural drivers for the Cast data product:

- The script recommender will consume the data product through a REST API.
- Data analysts want to consume it using SQL statements to help in salary negotiations.
- We discover the following quality attributes:
  - *Privacy*—Only the production team and analyst can have access to cast personal data.
  - *Security*—The payrolls of a cast include sensitive data. A data breach would lead us to million-dollar lawsuits from movie stars.
  - *Compliance*—We are keeping sensitive personal information. This is why GDPR and other privacy regulations apply here.
- The script recommender and other potential consumers are not real-time applications. They will be consuming data no more than once a day. Scalability, availability, and performance are not problems.
- Data analysts will perform their analysis a few times a year.

In this Cast data product example, we deal with a prevalent problem: how to expose data from monolithic, usually legacy, applications. Before we jump into the solution, we want to explain an interesting pattern called *turning the database inside out*.

TURNING THE DATABASE INSIDE OUT

Turning the database inside out is a pattern introduced by Martin Kleppmann (http://mng.bz/z4WB). In this pattern, Kleppmann combines four ideas:

- A database replication mechanism, whereby databases are replicated using asynchronous events transferred between the leader and a follower
- Secondary indexes
- Caching
- Materialized views

All of these are derived data, exactly like a data product. His premise is to create a magically self-updating cache. The way to do that is to expose a stream of events or change data capture stream or transaction log from the system-of-record database and consume it on the other side asynchronously in real time, and create a read model or view (figure 9.13).

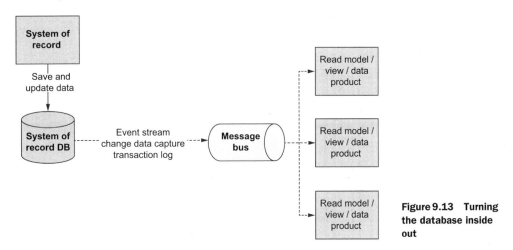

Figure 9.13 Turning the database inside out

So he takes the replication mechanism and applies it outside a database to create something similar to a secondary index or cache or materialized view.

Why are we mentioning this? It is because our team chooses to use this pattern in design option 1, illustrated in figure 9.14. As you can see, we are exposing a stream of events directly from the monolith database cast table. We publish it on the Kafka topic to consume it on the other side by the Cast data product microservice written in Java. This option transforms the data into a read-optimized shape. The Cast data product microservice saves events into PostgreSQL to expose them later through the REST API.

NOTE *Apache Kafka* is an open source distributed event-streaming platform. A *Kafka topic* is like a category to group and organize events or messages. In the previous case, we can see that all events about the Cast data product will land on the team events topic. *Kafka Connect* is a mechanism for connecting a Kafka topic with events from a different technology. In the previous example, we would extract events from the database table and publish them on Kafka.

Kleppmann's pattern is great for building data products in general, but remember that if you are exposing the schema of your database in events, it is not much different

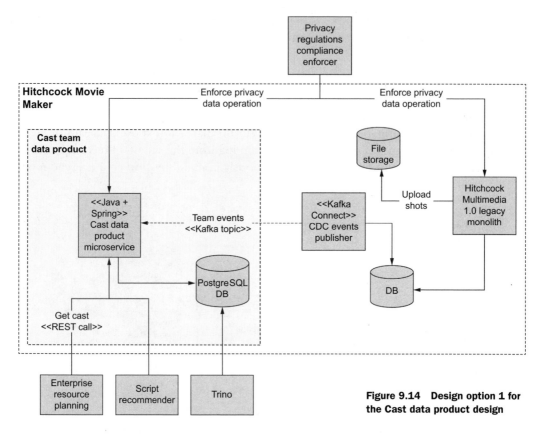

Figure 9.14   Design option 1 for the Cast data product design

from the integration of two systems via the database, but done asynchronously. It is good to transform content into different event schemas that will decouple consumers from the publisher database. It is essential to leave system boundaries even more if a different team owns the consumer.

But let's jump back to architectural drivers of the Cast data product. The team also takes into consideration quality attributes. Security and privacy are ensured on the level of the data product REST API. Compliance with privacy regulations is accomplished by using the privacy regulation compliance enforcer, designed using the enforcer pattern/trait.

> **DEFINITION**   The e*nforcer pattern, or trait,* is a category or trait of a bounded context. It ensures that other contexts carry out specific operations. In our example, we use components like that to ensure that private user data is deleted when needed.

We also care about data analyst needs. You can use Trino to have SQL access to our Cast database.

DEFINITION   *Trino* (https://trino.io/) is a distributed SQL query engine for Big Data. It allows you to query multiple data sources such as SQL databases, MongoDB, Kafka, and S3.

Another option designed by the team can be seen in figure 9.15. We use an Airflow workflow to extract data from the monolith database, transform it, and move it into the Cast Team data product database.

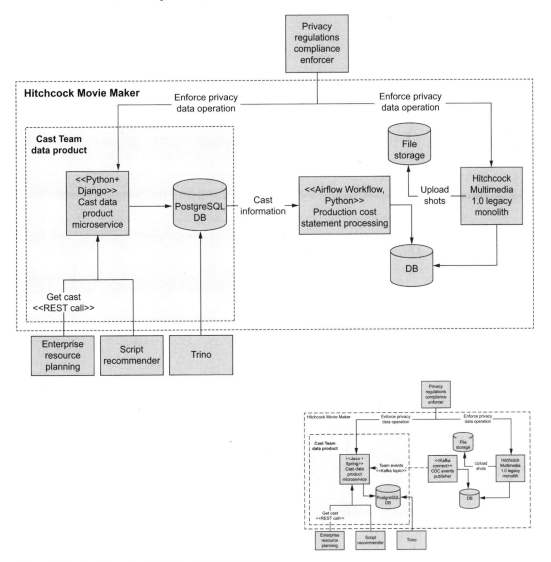

Figure 9.15   Design option 2 for the Cast data product

To learn something new, we won't repeat the pro-con-fix analysis, and propose the tradeoff analysis instead.

KEY POINT   Tradeoffs are needed everywhere. The Oxford English Dictionary defines *tradeoff* as to "exchange something of value, especially as part of a compromise." It is a fundamental concept in architecture design. Whenever we choose architecture options, one is rarely utterly superior to another. Usually, we exchange some quality attributes or values in favor of others. As an architect, you need to be aware that you lose something to gain something else with every decision.

Let's think about what we are exchanging in these two designs. A simple example of a tradeoff in our case is an exchange of loose coupling (event contract in option 1) for rapid development and platform reuse (Airflow workflow in option 2). When you establish what you are exchanging, the next step is to think about what we and our product owners value more. You should look for hints in functional and nonfunctional requirements. If it's not there and you cannot answer this question, you should explicitly ask your stakeholders.

We already resolved one of the data products that has its source in the Hitchcock Movie Maker system, so now let's look at another data product with the same source.

SCRIPTS DATA PRODUCT

Here's a summary of architectural drivers for the Scripts data product:

- The script recommender will consume Scripts data product through a REST API. The script Recommender does not require any extraordinary transformation of scripts.
- We discovered the following quality attribute:
  - *Security*—Scripts are essential for Messflix. This is why they should be protected.
- The script recommender is not a real-time application. It will consume data no more than once a day. Scalability, availability, and performance are not problems.

As you can see, we don't have too many architectural drivers, so this is a hint that the solution should follow the KISS principle.

DEFINITION   *KISS* is an acronym for *keep it simple, stupid*. This design principle has its roots in the US Navy. It means that systems work best when they are simple. We think this is an excellent overarching principle; whenever we doubt which design should be chosen, we follow this principle and choose the most straightforward solution.

After the design session, the team comes up with three possible solutions, depicted in figures 9.16, 9.17, and 9.18.

As you've probably noticed, with each design, we are adding complexity. The first design (figure 9.16) is simply an extension of the current script microservice with a new module that plays the role of a facade through which the script recommender will access the data.

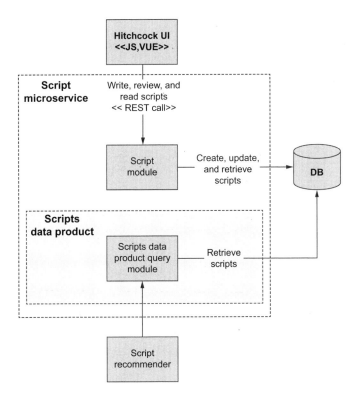

Figure 9.16 Design option 1 for the Scripts data product

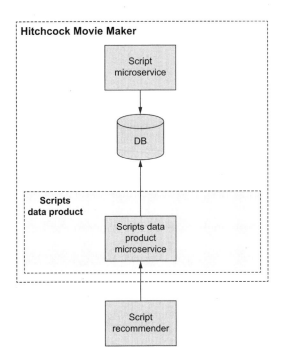

Figure 9.17 Design option 2 for the Scripts data product

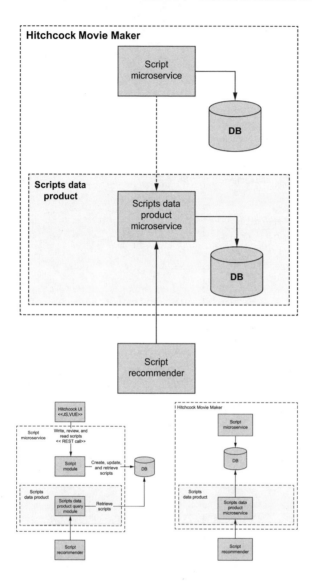

**Figure 9.18   Design option 3
for the Scripts data product**

The design is a straightforward but comes with drawbacks. It extends the responsibility of the script microservice, and as a consequence, it changes it into something like a mini modularized monolith. This solution is also tightly coupled to the original microservice, which makes moving responsibility for the data product in the future almost impossible (or at least not beneficial).

With options 2 (figure 9.17) and 3 (figure 9.18), we are gradually increasing complexity while decreasing coupling. In option 2, instead of being a module in the script service, the data product is now an independent microservice. In option 3, we are moving one step forward and giving the data product microservice its own database.

Options 2 and 3 are similar to the CQRS pattern (for more details, see "CQRS" by Martin Fowler, https://martinfowler.com/bliki/CQRS.html).

> **NOTE** When applying the CQRS pattern to a service, we distinguish two conceptual models of our data: a command model optimized for updates and a query model optimized for reads. This pattern is mainly used in microservice architecture. By applying this pattern, multiple microservices can serve as different command models. But when there is a need to expose data in an aggregated way, we create a new service that consumes events from command services and makes an aggregated view. Using events and async communication is not a mandatory part of this pattern, so you can implement it using the same database for the command and query model, but with the model exposed through an API that is different.

In option 2, we are reusing the same database. To optimize query performance, we could use a database materialized view. Because we're using the same database, this solution is tightly coupled, but we gain the independently deployable Scripts data product service, which increases the complexity of the infrastructure.

In option 3, we have loosely coupled services that follow a "database per service pattern." In this design, we trade off simplicity for loose coupling.

After analyzing all options as a team, we decide to follow the KISS principle in this specific case and choose option 1.

9.3.4 Exposing data for stream processing and batch processing

In the following example, we will move away from Hitchcock Movie Maker and jump into a fancier and more advanced part of Messflix: its streaming platform. We want to detect fraud based on data coming from the streaming platform. In figure 9.19, you can see planned data products.

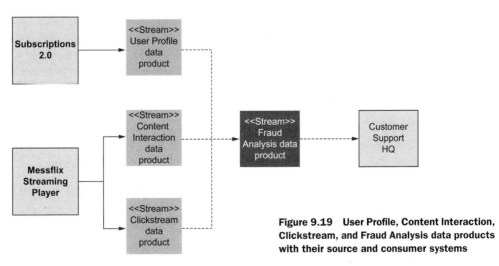

Figure 9.19 User Profile, Content Interaction, Clickstream, and Fraud Analysis data products with their source and consumer systems

We have three Messflix systems here. Subscriptions 2.0 is a system responsible for handling subscribers; it also keeps their private data. Messflix Streaming Player is a platform that serves all the content to the end users. Customer Support HQ is a system responsible for resolving tickets and requests from users or possible frauds.

In this case, the Fraud Analysis data product design will have a powerful influence on the design of the other three source-aligned data products. Just as we did with the previous example, we will jump right to the summary of architectural drivers:

- The data product will be consumed by the Customer Support HQ system by using events.
- Data scientists want to consume all three sources by using SQL statements.
- We discover the following quality attributes:
  - *Response-time*—Fraud incidents are close to real-time concerns. We want to catch criminals red-handed!
  - *Scalability*—We are dealing with data coming from the streaming player. This kind of data has uneven traffic with multiple peaks that are different in size (weekend, evening, newly released super productions, etc.). All of these bring us to the conclusion that scalability will be an essential aspect here.
- Data scientists will perform their analysis a few times a week.

Looking from a high-level perspective, solutions are not very different and, in fact, not very interesting as an example to learn from. Therefore, we will zoom in a bit to see how the use of data products will influence underlying stream solutions and data lake–based batch-processing solutions. But first, let's look at the two possible options illustrated in figure 9.20.

On the container level (C4 model), solutions are not much different. With stream processing, we use stream ports from source data products, and our Fraud Prediction container is doing predictions using a stream-processing mechanism. With batch processing, we are using files and a batch-processing mechanism.

We will not perform a tradeoff analysis for these two options, but your main driver would be response time, and the measure of success for this driver would guide the decision. If a nearer real-time response time is needed than stream processing, or if a longer cadence is possible, think about using the batch-processing mechanism.

But what is more interesting for us in terms of a data mesh is to find answers to the following questions:

1 How do we expose streams as a data product?
2 How should data products take advantage of a data lake solution?

Let's start with event streams.

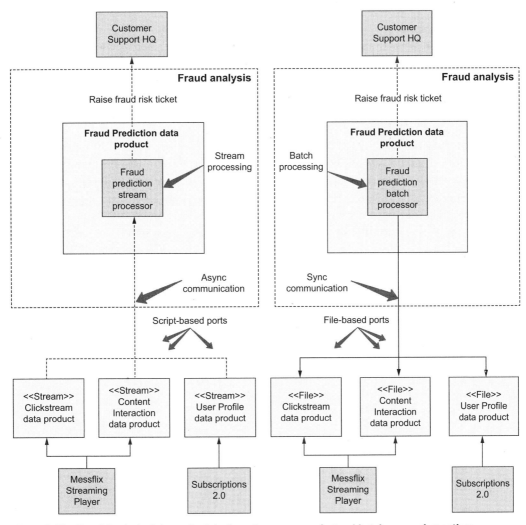

Figure 9.20   Fraud Analysis data product design: stream-processing and batch-processing options

EVENT STREAM AS A DATA PRODUCT PORT

In the first design, we need to feed a stream-processing engine with three streams of events from three different systems. We will describe two ways to expose these events:

- Extract events from files by using an engine like Airflow.
- Use the outbox pattern.

The outbox pattern

The *outbox pattern* (http://mng.bz/06DN), also known as the transactional outbox pattern, is used whenever we want to change the state of the database and publish events or messages consistently. This pattern takes advantage of a native database mechanism: the transaction.

> **(continued)**
> The idea is to save a new state in a database table, and at the same time save events in a table that we call the *outbox table*. If we save events and the new state in the transaction, we can be sure that the system will be in a consistent state. After the transaction is over, another component, which we could call the message relay, will read the outbox table and publish these messages to a message broker.

Another possible way of exposing events was already shown in figure 9.14, in the Cast data product description. It is the use of the turning database inside-out pattern. The only difference in our case would be that the event publisher is a vital part of the data product, and it would be mandatory to transform an event into a new schema that would be our external contract.

Let's see what the other two variants look like (figure 9.21).

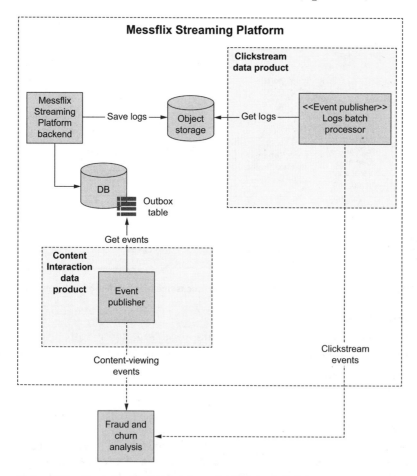

Figure 9.21   The outbox pattern and event publishing in batches

The first idea is applicable whenever we need to transform files into events. When you look at the Clickstream data product in figure 9.21, you can see that it retrieves log files from object storage, extracts and cuts them into smaller events, and publishes them for later consumption on a persistent event log, like a Kafka topic.

Another example is using the outbox pattern. In a nutshell, whenever the Messflix Streaming Platform saves its new state, it is also in the same transaction saving related events into a database table called the *outbox table*. Events are later extracted from the table by an event publisher (such as Kafka Connect or any other similar tool). The event publisher, in this case, will be our Content Interaction data product.

OK, we are able to publish events from our source data products, but what if we want to process data in a batch that requires files?

DATA LAKE AND DATA PRODUCTS

With batch processing, we can expose our data in the form of files to make calculations efficient. But what if we are already using some kind of data lake?

This is the right time to make an important point: a data mesh implementation does not exclude the possibility of using a data lake! In fact, both work together pretty well. What changes is the ownership of the data and data pipelines, and ownership of data lake technology: the platform.

> **KEY POINT** A data mesh implementation does not exclude the possibility of using a data lake; these concepts can be complementary.

When we apply the data mesh way of thinking to a data lake, we see that data product teams will own their areas/folders/buckets/namespaces within the same data lake persistence layer where they store data related to their data product. They will also own data pipelines that transform this data, such as those for cleansing operations. Data lake as a platform is owned not by data product teams but by a platform team. Figure 9.22 shows an example of this setup.

In this chapter, we looked at the architecture of a data product from multiple angles. We haven't touched all of the configurations and possible patterns that can be used, but we've given you the tools needed to make this kind of decision on your own.

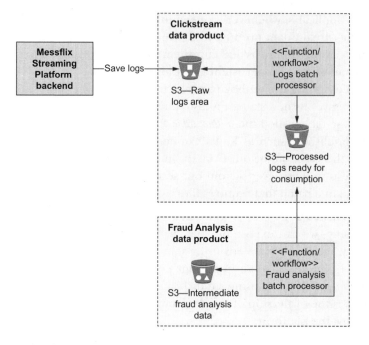

Figure 9.22   Using a data lake with the data mesh way of thinking

Summary

- Architecture is a structure of related building blocks, but it is also a process of designing and making conscious decisions using architectural drivers.
- The C4 model is a formal notation used to document architecture. It was designed to be used at every detail level, including the class level, component/module level, container/service level, and system level. You can use it to visualize from different perspectives such as deployment.
- To design the architecture of a data product, you need to first capture and understand its architectural drivers.
- Architectural drivers are functional requirements, quality attributes, constraints, and principles.
- Some architectural drivers come from the governance body, some from source or consuming systems, and others from functional requirements and descriptions of the data product.
- Designing the data product should be a collaborative and inclusive exercise.
- To choose from design options, you can use a pro-con-fix or tradeoff analysis exercise.
- Never forget about architectural drivers during the design; you should go back to them regularly.
- To deal with file-based data products, you can take advantage of the platform that should include tools like Airflow.

- Turning a database inside out is an easy way to expose data from systems of record.
- The CQRS pattern is an example of how read models can be created. The most favorable way is by creating a new service with a separate database synchronized using event-based communication.
- You can use the outbox pattern to expose events from your system of record.
- A data mesh implementation does not exclude the possibility of using a data lake; these concepts can be complementary.

appendix A

MVP environment selection sheet

System	Users	Development team(s)	MVP pros	MVP cons

appendix B

Metadata description template

Key	Value
Unique identifier	
Data product name	
Project URL	
Terms of use	
Keywords/tags	
Data product owner	
Data product owner contact	
Responsible technical team	
Technical support contact person	
Business unit	
Data product business description	
Security management	
Conceptual model	
Data model	
Users of data product	
Status	
Storage type	

appendix C

Messflix's metadata management policy

Topic	Content
Policy name	Metadata policy
Implementation date	dd.mm.yyyy
Last review on	dd.mm.yyyy
Next review due on	dd.mm.yyyy
Policy owner	John Doe
Point of contact	metadata@messflix.com
Scope	This policy covers all the data that Messflix holds, either as a data controller or a data processor. The policy is valid from data acquisition, and it extends through the life cycle, up to and including data archiving and data disposal. This policy applies to all Messflix employees, including fixed-term, temporary, or permanent contracts, staff on secondment, students, and contractors.
Background	Metadata provides information about other data, including a description of the data. This includes information that provides context to the data (for example, its source) or the coverage of the data (for example, publication date, description, and search keywords). Messflix needs to hold and manage a comprehensive set of specific metadata relating to its collected data. It is required to understand the data, fully extract its value, and employ appropriate security measures to protect the data.

Messflix's metadata management policy *(continued)*

Topic	Content
Policy statement	Metadata provides information about other data and is essential in aiding understanding of the data and ensuring that appropriate security measures are employed to protect the data. Metadata will be defined and centrally maintained for all data held by Messflix, from acquisition to archiving and disposal.
	All data acquired and collected by Messflix from external and internal sources must be accompanied by metadata. The Messflix Metadata Model defines the minimum set of metadata that must accompany all data acquired by Messflix. To provide a framework for managing metadata, metadata ontologies have been defined, and all metadata will be categorized according to these ontologies.
	The Central Metadata Register holds some metadata for Messflix's information assets, including the data product owner, responsible for metadata for the asset. The data product owner will periodically review the quality of the metadata they own and initiate corrective action to address any problems found with the accuracy and quality of the metadata.
Policy detail	**1** Metadata will be defined and centrally maintained for all data held by Messflix from acquisition to archiving and disposal: – New data created by Messflix must be accompanied by metadata. – Data acquired and collected by Messflix from external and internal sources must be accompanied by metadata; the metadata must contain at least a minimum set of metadata elements that are shared across Messflix. – Data held in Messflix-managed data archives must be accompanied by metadata. – Metadata will be retained for data that has been deleted (disposed of), including the date of deletion. – Metadata will be retained for the appropriate period specified by the retention policy. **2** The metadata will be categorized according to the defined Metadata ontologies, and the recorded metadata attributes will align with Messflix's Metadata Data Model. **3** Information about data product owners will be recorded in the Central Metadata Register: – The data product owner will periodically review the quality of the metadata they own and will initiate corrective action to address any problems found with the accuracy and quality of the metadata. – The data product owner will assign a retention period for the metadata according to the retention policy. **4** Metadata will comprise a consistent set of minimum metadata elements as defined by Messflix's Metadata Data Model: – The minimum set of metadata will include descriptive, structural, and administrative metadata. – The data product owner will ensure that their assets are described by at least the set of minimum metadata elements and will ensure that they are recorded in the appropriate data catalog.

Messflix's metadata management policy *(continued)*

Topic	Content
Roles and responsibilities	**Data product owner** The data product owner will be responsible for the following: • Confirming the details of the metadata that they own are correct and of high completeness and are managed following the metadata retention period they have defined • Initiating corrective action to address any problems found with the availability, accuracy, and completeness of the metadata • Liaising with data experts and metadata experts in the data controller organization (Messflix or external data controller) to ensure that the metadata attached to a dataset meets the analytical and governance requirements and complies with all relevant standards **Compliance specialist** The compliance specialist on the data governance committee is responsible for the following: • Informing data product owners of any changes to this policy and related data principles, data standards, and guidance • Ensuring that a communication plan is implemented to notify interested parties (for example, those involved in acquiring, creating, or amending data and metadata) of their responsibilities and the processes that should be followed to ensure that metadata is managed throughout the life cycle. **Data curators** Data curators will be responsible for the following: • Whoever acquires or creates new data must ensure that the corresponding metadata is collected or defined; the metadata must comply with data standards, particularly with the data standards that specify the minimum set of metadata that needs to be provided. • Whoever amends existing data must ensure that the corresponding metadata is amended or kept up-to-date and that the data product owner is informed of the changes. • Whenever new data is acquired or created, a data product owner must be assigned.

appendix D

To ensure a platform's maintainability and usefulness, we should consider the way it will be started as well as the processes of removing obsolete elements. Good practice is to start small and build up, and to remove elements in a controlled fashion, not disrupting operations of platform users. This appendix presents the concepts of the thinnest viable platform (which, as its name suggests, is a method for starting small) and steps for unobtrusive removal of deprecated interfaces.

D.1 Notes on thinnest viable platforms

The Team Topologies approach includes the concept of a *thinnest viable platform* (TVP). We like that idea and believe that, in general, when developing an internal platform, you should always create the platform as the most stripped-down version you can imagine.

The TVP will almost always turn out to be a simple wiki page with an explanation of the few standardized technologies and processes in use. For a data mesh TVP, the wiki page could even include the metadata for the products. After all, you will be starting out with one or two data products, and these will surely fit onto one page.

This exercise will hopefully help you start with a simple and lean platform. Once you write the wiki page, look at it and list the next iterations and see where the most value lies.

> **NOTE** If you're interested in non-data-mesh data TVPs, take a look at the TVP Examples GitHub site at http://mng.bz/69Qe.

D.2 Note on phasing out interfaces

If you keep on modifying the platform kernel but never delete any parts, or do some heavier reorganization, the platform itself will become heavy and too slow to adapt to change, too complex to handle.

Besides being very smart about the up-front split of platform capabilities, is there anything you can do to deal with this situation? Yes! Your team can choose to phase out some parts of the interface. To phase out any platform elements, your team should take the following steps:

1 Create the nonbreaking change.
2 Incentivize users to adopt the new interface functionality.
3 Track adoption of the old interface functionality, both on the production and on the consumption side.
4 Keep the parallel approach running for a long grace period.
5 Once the tracking shows that the old functionality is not needed anymore, set a deadline for deprecation, communicate it to the producers and consumers, and switch out the old functionality.

The basic idea behind this step-by-step process is that the new functionality should be much better than the old one. If both data producers and consumers truly have a much better life with the new functionality, they should stop using the old one at that point.

index